The Making of French
Absolutism

The Making of French Absolutism

David Parker

Senior Lecturer in Modern History, University of Leeds

1983.

Edward Arnold

© David Parker 1983

First published in Great Britain 1983
by Edward Arnold (Publishers) Ltd
41 Bedford Square
London WC1 3DQ

Edward Arnold (Australia) Pty Ltd
80 Waverly Road
Caulfield East 3145
PO Box 234
Melbourne

British Library Cataloguing in Publication Data

Parker, David
    The making of French absolutism.
    1. Despotism   2. France—Politics and
    government—16th century   3. France—Politics
    and government—17th century
    I. Title
    321.6'0944   JC381

ISBN 0-7131-6382-8

Typeset in Linotron 202 Baskerville 10/11 pt. by
Graphicraft Typesetters Limited, Hong Kong
Printed and Bound by Richard Clay (The Chaucer Press) Limited,
Bungay, Suffolk.

To My Students Past and Present

Contents

HUGH CAPET (987–996)
|
ROBERT II (996–1031)
|
HENRY I (1031–1060)
|
PHILIP I (1060–1108)
|
LOUIS VI (1108–1137)
|
LOUIS VII (1137–1180)
|
PHILIP II AUGUSTUS (1180–1223)
|
LOUIS VIII (1223–1226)
|
LOUIS IX (1226–1270)
(Saint Louis)

PHILIP III (1270–1285)
(The Bold)

PHILIP IV (1285–1314)
(The Fair)

Charles
(comte de Valois)
|
PHILIP VI (1328–1350)
(comte de Valois)
|
JOHN II (1350–1364)
|
CHARLES V (1364–1380)
|
CHARLES VI (1380–1422)
|
CHARLES VII (1422–1461)
|
LOUIS XI (1461–1483)
|
CHARLES VIII (1483–1498)

LOUIS X (1314–1316)

JOHN I (1316)
(died aged
4 days)

Isabel m.
Edward II
of England
|
Edward III
of England

PHILIP V (1316–1322)
(comte de Poitier)
no son

CHARLES IV (1322–1328)
(comte de la Marche)
no son

Henry V m. Catherine
of
England
|
Henry VI of England

The Genealogy of the French Monarchs to 1774

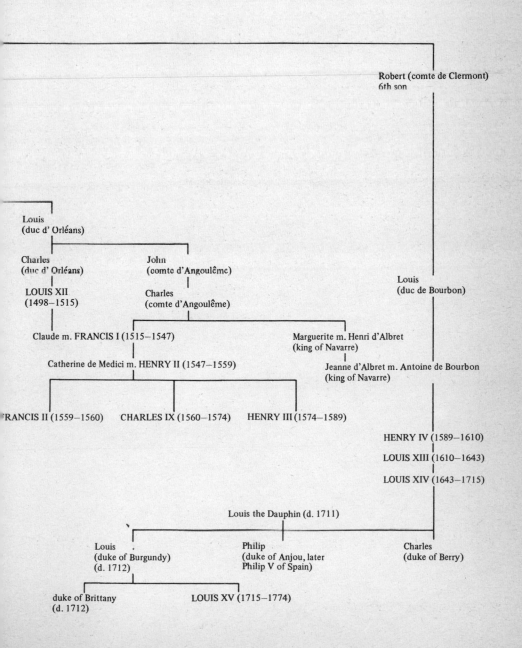

Robert (comte de Clermont)
6th son

Louis
(duc d' Orléans)

Charles
(duc d' Orléans)

John
(comte d'Angoulême)

LOUIS XII
(1498—1515)

Charles
(comte d'Angoulême)

Louis
(duc de Bourbon)

Claude m. FRANCIS I (1515—1547)

Marguerite m. Henri d'Albret
(king of Navarre)

Catherine de Medici m. HENRY II (1547—1559)

Jeanne d'Albret m. Antoine de Bourbon
(king of Navarre)

FRANCIS II (1559—1560)   CHARLES IX (1560—1574)   HENRY III (1574—1589)

HENRY IV (1589—1610)

LOUIS XIII (1610—1643)

LOUIS XIV (1643—1715)

Louis the Dauphin (d. 1711)

Louis
(duke of Burgundy)
(d. 1712)

Philip
(duke of Anjou, later
Philip V of Spain)

Charles
(duke of Berry)

duke of Brittany
(d. 1712)

LOUIS XV (1715—1774)

GERMAN
EMPIRE

Cologne

Mainz

Trier

Verdun

Meuse

Moselle

Rhine

Bruges

COUNTY
OF FLANDERS

DUCHY OF
LOWER
LORRAINE

DUCHY OF
UPPER
LORRAINE

Rouen

DUCHY OF
NORMANDY

Reims

Chalons

Paris

COUNTY
OF CHAMPAGNE

Seine

DUCHY
OF
BRITTANY

COUNTY
OF MAINE

Chartres

Rennes

Orléans

Nantes

COUNTY
OF
ANJOU

Tours

CO
OF
BLOIS

Loire

DUCHY
OF
BURGUNDY

Dijon

Besançon

COUNTY OF
BURGUNDY

CO
OF
TOURAINE

Cher

Poitiers

COUNTY
OF POITOU

COUNTY OF
BOURBON

DUCHY OF GUYENNE
(AQUITAINE)

Clermont

COUNTY OF
AUVERGNE

Lyon

KINGDOM OF BURGUNDY
(ARELAT)

Bordeaux

Dordogne

Garonne

Lot

COUNTY
OF RODEZ

Rhone

Avignon

PROVENCE

DUCHY OF
GASCONY

Albi

Toulouse

MARGRAVATE
OF GOTHIA

Aix

NAVARRE

ARAGON

COUNTY OF
TOULOUSE

COUNTY OF
BARCELONA

Barcelona

0   50   100   150 Miles

0   100   200 Km

Key

Domain of the crown

Eccelsiastical possessions

Boundaries of the kingdom

I CAPETIAN FRANCE (11th–12th CENTURIES)

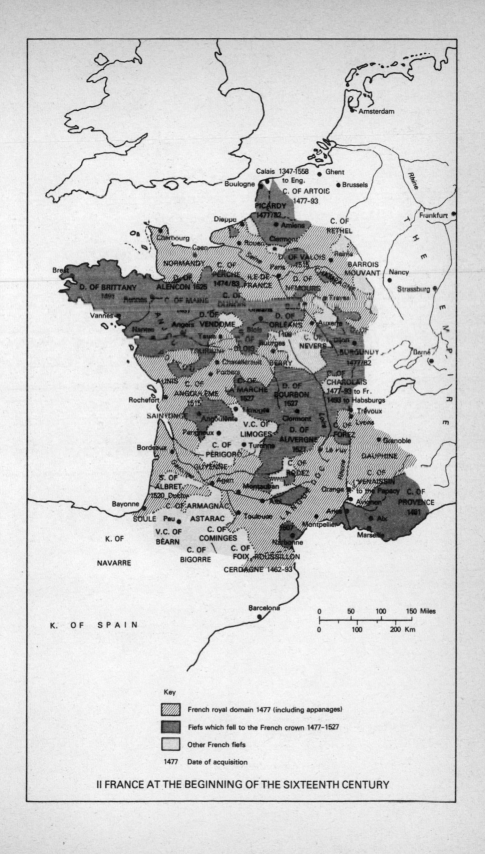

Amsterdam

Calais 1347-1558
to Eng.
Boulogne
C. OF ARTOIS
1477-93
Ghent
Brussels

Frankfurt

Dieppe
Amiens
C. OF
RETHEL

PICARDY
1477/82

Cherbourg
Caen
Rouen
Clermont

D. OF VALOIS
-1515
BARROIS
MOUVANT
Nancy

Brest
NORMANDY
C. OF
PERCHE
ILE DE
FRANCE
Paris
D. OF
NEMOURS
Reims
Strassburg

D. OF
ALENCON 1625
1474/83
Troyes

Vannes
C. OF MAINE
D. OF
DUNOIS

Angers
D. OF
VENDOME
Orleans
Blois
Auxerre
Dijon

Nantes
TOURAINE
BLOIS
-1100
C. OF
NEVERS
D. OF
BURGUNDY
1477/82
Berne

Chatellerault
BERRY
Bourges

AUNIS
C. OF
ANGOULEME
1515
C. OF
LA MARCHE
1527
Poitiers
D. OF
BOURBON
1627
C. OF
CHAROLAIS
1477-93 to Fr.
1493 to Habsburgs

Rochefort
Limoges
Trevoux

SAINTONGE
V.C. OF
LIMOGES
Angouleme
Clermont
D. OF
AUVERGNE
1627
C. OF
FOREZ
Lyons

Perigueux
Turenne
Le Puy
Grenoble

Bordeaux
C. OF
PERIGORD
GUYENNE
DAUPHINE

S. OF
ALBRET
1520 Duchy
Agen
C. OF
RODEZ
C. OF
VENAISSIN
to the Papacy
C. OF
PROVENCE
1481

Bayonne
C. OF ARMAGNAC
Montauban
Orange
Avignon

SOULE Pau
ASTARAC
Toulouse
Arles
Aix

K. OF
V.C. OF
BEARN
C. OF
COMINGES
1607
Montpellier
Marseille

NAVARRE
C. OF
BIGORRE
C. OF
FOIX
C. OF
ROUSSILLON
Narbonne

CERDAGNE 1462-93

Barcelona

0   50   100   150 Miles
0   100   200 Km

K. OF SPAIN

Key

French royal domain 1477 (including appanages)

Fiefs which fell to the French crown 1477-1527

Other French fiefs

1477   Date of acquisition

II FRANCE AT THE BEGINNING OF THE SIXTEENTH CENTURY

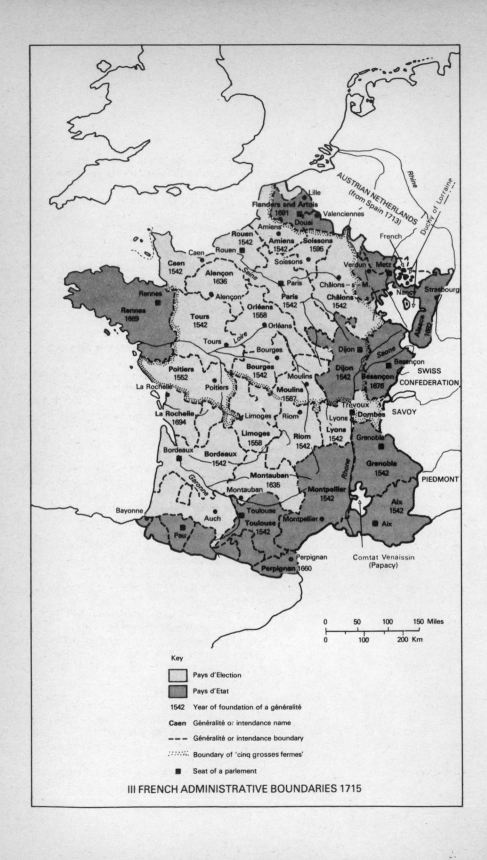

AUSTRIAN NETHERLANDS
(from Spain 1713)

Rhine

Duchy of Lorraine

French

Lille
Flanders and Artois
1691
Douai
Valenciennes
Amiens

Rouen
1542
Amiens
1542
Soissons
1595
Verdun
Metz
Strasbourg

Caen
Rouen
Soissons
Châlons-s-M.
Nancy
Alsace
1682

Caen
1542
Alençon
1636
Seine
Paris
Paris
1542
Châlons
1542

Rennes
Alençon
Châlons
Besançon

Rennes
1689
Orléans
1558
Orléans
Dijon
Saône
Besançon
1676
SWISS

Tours
1542
Loire
Bourges
Dijon
1542
Besançon
CONFEDERATION

Tours
Bourges
1542
Moulins
Trévoux
SAVOY

Poitiers
1552
Moulins
1587
Lyons
Dombes

La Rochelle
Poitiers
Riom
Lyons
Grenoble

La Rochelle
1694
Limoges
Riom
1542
Lyons
1542
Grenoble

Bordeaux
Limoges
1558
Grenoble
1542
PIEDMONT

Bordeaux
Bordeaux
1542
Montauban
1635
Rhône
Aix
1542

Bayonne
Montauban
Montpellier
1542
Aix

Auch
Toulouse
Montpellier

Pau
Toulouse
1542

Perpignan
Comtat Venaissin
(Papacy)

Perpignan 1660

0   50   100   150 Miles
0   100   200 Km

Key

Pays d'Election

Pays d'Etat

1542   Year of foundation of a généralité

Caen   Généralité or intendance name

- - -   Généralité or intendance boundary

....   Boundary of 'cinq grosses fermes'

■   Seat of a parlement

III FRENCH ADMINISTRATIVE BOUNDARIES 1715

Glossary

appel comme d'abus	A complaint to the *parlement* against an ecclesiastic accused of exceeding his powers
avocat	barrister
avocat général	two of these, with the *procureur général* represented the king in *parlement*
bailliage	middle-level jurisdiction with a court empowered to deal with certain civil and criminal cases and others on appeal; the principal official by the seventeenth century was the *lieutenant-général* rather than the bailiff
banalité	feudal obligation requiring a serf to use his seigneur's equipment or material
bureaux des finances	office of the treasurers attached to each *généralité*
cas-royaux	cases in which the king's person or his rights were involved
chambre des comptes	sovereign court dealing with cases arising from the accounts of the treasurers and their agents
chambres mi-parties	bi-partisan courts established by the Edict of Nantes to deal with Protestant complaints
champart	feudal due paid in kind as a proportion of the harvest
compagnies d'ordonnance	see pp.7-8
confréries	religious associations frequently based on a trade or craft, but also on parishes or dioceses
contrôleur général des finances	see p.120
cour des aides	sovereign court dealing with litigation arising from the levying of the principal taxes
coutilier	halberdier
dévots	zealous Catholics, characterized by their concern for moral reform and opposition to Richelieu's foreign policy
eaux et forêts	administration of the waterways and forests of the royal domain
échevin	member of an *échevinage* or town council
élection	secondary fiscal area within a *généralité*, possessing a lower court that dealt with fiscal litigation and had a role in assessing the *taille*
élus	the officers of an *élection*; they had both fiscal and judicial powers
épargne	the royal treasury (see p.11)
étapes	military staging posts created to provide supplies for the armies; also the name given to the taxes levied for this purpose
évocation	the enforced removal of a lawsuit from the jurisdiction of a court
équivalent	tax paid in certain provinces in lieu of *aides*

formariage	seigneurial due payable by a serf marrying outside the seigneury or with someone of different status
fouage	the medieval hearth tax from which evolved the *taille*; later a *feu* was not a hearth but merely an arbitrary device for determining the distribution of taxes in certain provinces
gage	'salary' or payment made by the crown to the *officiers*
gendarmerie	see pp.7–8
généralité	principal adminstrative area for tax purposes
gens du roi	collective name for the *avocats du roi* and the *procureur du roi*, otherwise known as the *parquet*
imposition foraine	see p.19
lettres de jussion	orders to *parlement* demanding immediate and unqualified registration of legislation
lit de justice	session of *parlement* when the king was present
maîtres des requêtes	holders of venal legal office whose prime function was to service the councils of state
octrois	indirect taxes levied by municipalities
parties casuelles	treasury for the receipt of extraordinary revenue, essentially proceeds from sale of office
parlement	sovereign law court, see pp.6–7
paulette	annual levy or tax, also known as the *droit annuel* which ensured the hereditability of an office
prévôts	royal judge attatched to a *prévôté*; sometimes a military or naval judge
prévôté	inferior court
procureur général	the king's attorney, who represented him in *parlement* with the *avocats du roi*
recettes	secondary administrative units in Guyenne originally boasting representative assemblies
régale	the king's right to the income from vacant benefices
rentes	government bonds or annuities, paid in return for loans or capital investment. The *rentes sur l'hotel de ville* were underwritten by the municipality of Paris
semestre	the device of creating a second chamber of magistrates in a *parlement* to alternate with existing ones every six months
sénéchaussée	similar to the *bailliage*, normally in the south of France
sub-délégués	subordinates of the intendants
surintendant des finances	the minister of finance prior to Colbert's reforms
taille personnelle	direct tax from which nobles and other privileged persons were exempt
taille réelle	direct tax levied in the south of France and from which noble land was exempt

Acknowledgements

Together with the students to whom this book is dedicated, I owe more than anything to the many colleagues who share the same historical interests. It is impossible to mention them all and it would be invidious to select a few. Although the format of the book precludes detailed references, I trust that the bibliography will suffice to express my gratitude to those on whom I have relied for material and ideas. To my family I apologize for the many inconveniences which flowed from the increasingly urgent need to complete this book. A particular debt is owed to my wife, Margaret, who read the entire script more than once and whose comments have been invaluable. Thanks are also due to my typist, Mrs Joan Stones, for her indefatigable efforts to decipher my meanings and cope with numerous alterations. To the Royal Historical Society I express appreciation of their willingness to allow me to use some of the material from my *La Rochelle and the French Monarchy. Order and Conflict in Seventeenth-Century France* (London, 1980).

David Parker
Leeds, November 1982

Introduction

Students in search of an introduction to French absolutism face two related problems. One is the way in which Louis XIV has mesmerized historians, as he did his contemporaries, thus perpetuating the myth of the all powerful king who created a new system of government with the aid of upstart or bourgeois ministers. Underlying this approach is a tendency to confuse absolutism with personal rule. This is strange given the obvious fact that *all* monarchies were a form of personal rule, but it has certainly inhibited reflections on absolutism as a system of government. The second problem is that although there are now many specialized works which serve as correctives to the textbook simplifications, they are frequently long and very detailed; and given the very real and sometimes baffling complexity of the French administrative apparatus, the significance of the material is not always apparent.

The objectives of this study are therefore limited. The first is quite simply to show how the system worked: not by offering a comprehensive description but by identifying its principal features and drawing on the works of specialists to convey the flavour of its operations. More importantly, the material has been arranged to place absolutism in the widest perspective and to analyse the forces which pushed France in an absolutist direction. One of the central themes is that the process was generated by contradictions deep within French society which were never fully mastered; indeed some of them became more acute as time passed and the net result was a form of government which did not fully correspond to the aspirations of those who promoted royal authority most vigorously. Absolutism was always in the making but never made.

In recent years much interesting work has been produced on the general formation of nation states, of which France was certainly one of the earliest and most precocious examples. The function of the state (i.e. state apparatus) has also been discussed from a variety of angles. Depending on one's viewpoint it can be seen as either an agent of modernization or of class rule, or perhaps both. The relationship of the absolutist state to the development of capitalism has been the subject of particular attention. Amongst political theorists there is also renewed interest in the relationship of coercion to consent in the maintenance of political authority. Explicit or extended theoretical consideration of such matters would be outside the scope of this study. Nevertheless the opportunity has been taken to allude to them, and it is hoped that, within the present state of our knowledge, this book will provide not merely the necessary empirical foundation but also the requisite sense of perspective to enable students of French absolutism to approach some of these wider issues.

I

The French Monarchy and the Crisis of the Sixteenth Century

It was generally agreed in the early sixteenth century that royal authority was both absolute and limited: absolute inasmuch as the king was divinely appointed and answerable to no one save God, yet limited in the sense that his prime task was to rule justly in accordance with the precepts of divine and natural justice. An absolute monarch was not a tyrant. According to Claude Seyssel whose influential treatise *La Grande Monarchie de France* appeared in 1519, there were three bridles which restrained and directed the use of monarchical power: religion, justice and *la police*. Thus the king was expected to express in his person and deeds Christian virtues, whilst the proper administration of justice was ensured by the capacity of the *parlement* to check the abuse of royal authority. The notion of *la police* was more complex. It included both the fundamental laws of the realm which forbade the king either to alter the law governing the succession or to alienate the royal domain, and also a wider notion of the obligations imposed on the king as head of the body politic. The universally understood analogy of the realm with the human body carried the implication that the former, like the latter, was an organic whole composed of interdependent elements – or members – each with a specific place and rôle. Seyssel's division of the body politic into the nobility, middle and lower classes was actually quite unusual, but the general thrust of his argument which imposed on the king the prime responsibility for ensuring the harmonious co-operation of the various elements certainly reflected the conventional wisdom. This objective was achieved on the one hand by the use of royal power to prevent the natural tendency of each element to stray beyond the functions assigned to it and on the other by protecting its customary rights or privileges. Indeed for some contemporaries the rule of justice was virtually synonymous with the preservation of customary rights. Even those like Seyssel's contemporary Guillaume Budé who were insistent that the king was above the law and possessed the untrammelled right to override both parlement and custom, nevertheless felt that the king should voluntarily place himself within the framework of law and custom 'in order to give authority to his constitutions and ordinances'. Seyssel himself declared that 'this moderation and restraint of the absolute power of kings is to their great honour and profit.' Voluntary or otherwise, the restrictions on the exercise of royal authority were not perceived as performing a purely negative rôle; on the contrary they enhanced the prestige, and consequently the stability of the monarchy. A royal decree ratified by *parlement* carried more weight than one which was not; and if the *parlement* sometimes resisted the will of the king, far from undermining his authority it was fulfilling the rôle for which it had been established by the crown itself. A king who took care not to ride roughshod over the privileges of the provinces, towns, estates, guilds, universities and other bodies which composed the body politic was not simply fulfilling his obligation to rule justly, he was also ensuring the respect and obedience of his subjects. The pervasive nature of such ideas is amply revealed by the fact that, 60 years later, they were still being employed by Jean Bodin, normally regarded as the key figure in the formulation of absolutist theories of government. 'The just monarchy' he insisted 'hath not any more assured foundation or stay than the Estates of People, Communities, Corporations and Colleges.' He cited with approval the opposition of the *parlement* to the decrees of Louis XI and the activities of the notably independent estates of Languedoc. 'A commonwealth' Bodin concluded 'could no more sustain itself without a Senate than the Body can itself without a soul or a man without reason.'

It can be seen that the simultaneous insistence on both the absolute and limited character of royal authority was not as hopelessly contradictory as it might first appear. Beneath the dualism of monarchical theory there was quite a sophisticated rationale. Yet it is also clear that such views could not fully resolve the tension between the absolutist and constitutional tendencies contained within them. This tension was merely lessened by not defining too closely the boundary between the powers of the crown and the rights of subjects. The categories of natural and divine law were by their very nature vague and left a large grey area, with abundant scope for imprecision, when it came to discussing their practical significance for the day-to-day conduct of kings. It was possible to shift from a less to a more absolutist position within a generally accepted body of thought.

Such ambivalence was not however the result of an unwillingness or inability to think clearly. On the contrary, the dualism of political thought reflected very well the real state of affairs. The tensions embodied within it were but a manifestation of the tensions which actually did exist in the relationship between the monarchy and a multitude of subordinate institutions. In particular the notion that the *parlement* possessed its powers of judicial restraint by virtue of authority bestowed upon it by the crown had a firm foundation in reality. Throughout medieval Europe princes and monarchs had of course devolved some of their authority or granted privileges to those who came under their sway. In this sense the French experience was not unique. However, the peculiarities of French development were such that by the early sixteenth century a particularly powerful monarchy co-existed with particularly well-developed traditions of provincial and corporate autonomy. Here the contradiction between the two was, as Pagès noted 30 years ago, flagrant.

The Foundations of Royal Authority

Superficially the rise of the French monarchy was a remarkable success story. It began in the tenth century in the aftermath of the disintegration of the large but fragile kingdom of the Franks under the impact of Scandinavian,

Magyar and Saracen invaders. Profiting from the weakness of the reigning Carolingian dynasty Hugh Capet, son of the duke of France, contrived to secure his election as king of France in July 987. As king, Capet became the suzerain of those that rendered homage to him, the chief source of justice, and he acquired the aura of divinity symbolized by the already developed tradition of annointing the king at his coronation. His material resources, however, were meagre, consisting of a few wisps of territory in the Ile-de-France and the Orléanais. There was no reason for the feudal magnates who ruled the hotchpotch of territories north of the Loire to fear the power of their new overlord. Yet the installation of Hugh Capet marked the beginning of the transformation of the French ruling house from merely the *primus inter pares* into one of the most powerful monarchies in Europe.

Aided by the good fortune of a long line of male heirs, the Capetians quite quickly obscured the elective origins of their rule, consolidated their authority over the lesser barons of the Ile-de-France and utilized their feudal suzerainity to interfere in the successions of the great duchies of Burgundy, Normandy and the county of Flanders. By the reign of Philippe Auguste (1180–1223) the basis had been laid for the remarkable territorial expansion of the next hundred years during which period, by an astute combination of legal manoeuvring, marriage arrangements, and force, the Capetians tripled the size of their domain. Philippe's principal achievement was the destruction of the Plantagenet's attempt to construct an empire straddling the channel, a possibility opened up by the accession of Henry, duke of Normandy and Aquitaine, count of Anjou, Maine and Touraine, to the English throne in 1154. His successor seized the opportunity provided by the crusade against the Albigensian heretics of the Midi to intervene in the affairs of the powerful and extensive county of Toulouse which led to its incorporation in the royal domain.

In the early fourteenth century the Capetians' luck ran out and the possibility of succession by the female line arose and with it the claim of Edward III of England, grandson to Philippe le Bel through his mother, to the French throne. The principle of male succession was upheld and the throne passed to Philippe's nephew, Philippe de Valois, thus inaugurating the dynasty which was to rule down to 1589. However, the English, aided and abetted by the dukes of Burgundy, who were themselves intent on carving out a kingdom on the north-eastern flanks of France, sought to make good their claim. For a period in the early fifteenth century the allies controlled most of northern France and Aquitaine. With a supreme effort, symbolized by the legendary Jeanne d'Arc, Normandy and Gascony were reconquered in the 1440s and the English driven from France (retaining only Calais) in 1453. The Burgundians continued to make trouble, but the line was extinguished when Duke Charles was killed in battle against the Swiss in 1477 and Burgundy reverted to the crown. The lands of the dukes of Anjou, including the huge territory of Provence were inherited by the king in 1481. Guyenne fell to the crown on the death of the king's brother (1491), whilst marriages into the house of Brittany achieved the same effect although the duchy was not formally annexed until 1532. Louis XII's marriage to Anne of Brittany (1499) also brought the patrimony of Orléans into royal hands, and

Francis I, who inherited the throne in the absence of direct male heirs, brought with him his own duchy of Angoulême. By the end of the fifteenth century the seemingly remorseless process of transforming feudal rivals into dependents and then subsuming their territories in the royal domain reached its climax. However the mechanisms of dynastic aggrandizement were by no means played out. Full of confidence, powerful and rich beyond the dreams of his predecessors, Francis I now prepared to make good a variety of inherited claims to Italian territories, notably the duchy of Milan and the kingdom of Naples.

The invasion of Italy threw sharply into relief the ancient and bitter rivalry between the French crown and the papacy. The pope was not merely a territorial ruler whose acquiescence was required for the furtherance of French military projects in Italy; he was the head of the Universal Church and as such had long claimed some authority over the temporal powers of Europe. Whilst the papacy had been involved in its epic struggle with the Holy Roman Emperors, relations with the Capetian dynasty had remained amicable. Indeed it was Charles, duke of Anjou, who in the 1260s had inflicted the decisive defeats on the imperial forces in Italy, thus precipitating the eviction of the Germans and the collapse of their huge empire. Ironically the French monarchy now emerged as the major obstacle to papal pretensions and relations deteriorated rapidly before exploding in the confrontation between Philippe le Bel and Boniface VIII at the turn of the thirteenth century. Ostensibly provoked by the royal claim to tax the clergy without papal consent, the conflict raised issues of fundamental principle. In 1301 and 1302 papal bulls proclaimed both the spiritual and temporal sovereignty of the popes throughout Christendom. The king appealed to a general council of the Church, whereupon the pope not only excommunicated him but also absolved his subjects from their obedience. Boniface's successors, obliged to take up residence at Avignon because of the unstable situation in Italy, annulled his pronouncements and recognized the king's legitimate authority. However, with the Great Schism (1378–1417), when the Avignon pope was challenged by a Roman one, the controversy was renewed. The French proposed that both popes should resign. When Benedict XIII refused to do so, the king at first withdrew his support and then in 1407, after assembling the clergy, issued two ordiances. These declared royal support for the traditional autonomy of the French Church in making appointments to benefices and forbade the pope from claiming any payment from their incumbents. Reaffirmed in 1418, these principles were partially abandoned by Charles VII during the worst years of the struggle against the Anglo-Burgundian invaders, before receiving their definitive form in 1438. Under the impact of the news that the ecumenical council of the Church at Basle had suspended the pope, Charles summoned an assembly of the French clergy whose deliberations crystallized in the celebrated Pragmatic Sanction of Bourges. This confirmed the authority of general councils over the pope, the principle of election to major benefices, the rights of those who had acquired the right to appoint to lesser benefices, and severely curtailed the payment of annates. From this moment gallican principles became an integral element in the foundations of royal authority. Admittedly the

Pragmatic Sanction acknowledged the independence of the Church from *all* outside interference; but by the late fifteenth century the crown was regularly imposing its own nominees on bishoprics and abbeys and indeed to many lesser benefices as well. Moreover the king had acquired a powerful bargaining position vis-à-vis the papacy which sought nothing more than the revocation of the Pragmatic Sanction. Louis XI (1461–83) modified his stance constantly in the course of his dealings with the pope, even suspending the Sanction entirely at one point in order to gain support for his Italian policies. It was for this very reason that Francis I finally negotiated its permanent revocation in 1515 by the Concordat of Bologna. Conciliar supremacy together with the principle of election to benefices were effectively abandoned, whilst papal annates were restored. In return the king obtained the right of nomination to major benefices subject to approval by the pope, thus confirming the *de facto* royal powers of patronage. Opposition to this carve-up of the liberties of the Church was immense; the University of Paris, the *parlement* and the clergy themselves expressed their discontent. Francis, albeit with some difficulty, overrode them all and enforced the registration of the Concordat by the *parlement*. The fact that the king was momentarily in dispute with the defenders of gallicanism should not however obscure the fact that the royal authority was greatly enhanced by the powerful grip which such ideas had in France. French kings might from time to time abandon these principles as short-term interests required, but they could always be utilized to assert the absolute authority of the king over his subjects and to deny whatever claims the pope might make to interfere in the affairs of the French Church and state. In later years, as France was torn apart by religious strife, the strong gallican traditions were to prove a crucial factor in sustaining the monarchy.

The process of subordinating Church to state was also enhanced by the limitations placed on clerical jurisdiction. Traditionally ecclesiastical courts had judged a variety of cases of a non-spiritual character: property involving the Church, feudal obligations to which the Church was a party and so on. In addition, the Church had complete control over litigation relating to heresy, sorcery, widows and illegitimate children, marriage and disputes between clerics. Gradually the areas of competence were reduced, a process helped by the increasing readiness of the clergy to appeal to the royal courts. By the end of the fourteenth century only matters of faith and those pertaining to the sacraments, excommunication or interdiction remained outside royal jurisdiction. Even questions relating to marriage – a sacrament – and heresy began to come before the *parlement*. With the formulation of the *appel comme d'abus* at the end of the fifteenth century which made it possible to take grievances about clerical judgments before the royal courts, the subordination of ecclesiastical justice was virtually complete.

The assertion of royal rights over powerful lay and ecclesiastical subjects and over ever-extending tracts of territory, depended on the ability of the king to make effective his claim to be the source of all authority. From their predecessors the Capetians had inherited the quality of supreme judges; and this they assiduously exploited in order to extend their authority beyond the confines of the domain into the fiefs of the great vassals. Fairs and religious foundations were brought under royal jurisdiction, seigneurial rights such as that of granting pardons, were restricted, whilst those matters, the *cas-royaux*, in which the king could claim to have a direct interest, were extended in number; originally limited to *lèse-majesté*, forgery of the royal seal and similar matters, the category was widened to embrace 'all instances of private war, of usury, of highway robbery, all matters pertaining to ennoblement or legitimisation, to trade or the peace of the realm'.[1] From the beginning of the thirteenth century the kings introduced legislation clearly intended to apply throughout the realm. Royal jurists found theoretical justification for these developments in the principles of Roman Law which accorded to the ruler not merely the quality of supreme judge but also of supreme law-maker.

Such aspirations would have been impossible without a radical transformation of the judicial apparatus, indeed of the entire administrative apparatus on which the monarchy rested. At the outset this consisted of no more than a few great officials, headed by the chancellor and supported by the *prévôts* who combined the functions of sheriff and overseers of the royal domain, beyond which their jurisdiction did not run. Justice was dispensed by the king in his council. By the end of the twelfth century a new figure, the bailiff, had emerged in the provinces. Empowered to conduct monthly assizes and collect fines, their establishment marked a significant stage in the extension of royal authority, particularly as the *bailliage* courts began to hear appeals from the seigneurial ones. This process was carried further by the somewhat later appearance of the *procureurs* who, in addition to assisting the bailiffs, were authorized to initiate prosecutions on behalf of the crown.

At the centre too changes took place as the amount of business coming before the king's court expanded and became ever more technical. Slowly the important work was taken over by specialists and by the early thirteenth century a permanent commission – the *magistra curiae* – was on hand to advise the king and his councillors. From this there emerged the *parlement* which by the mid thirteenth century assumed a separate existence and identity. It ceased to follow the court and in 1278 its procedures were institutionalized. For a time membership of the *parlement* of Paris continued to fluctuate but its basic structure consisting of three permanent chambers – *grand' chambre*, *requêtes* and *enquêtes* – was established. An elaborate hierarchy developed headed by six presidents, with membership of the *grand' chambre* confined to the most senior magistrates, and the whole institution sustained by a growing number of lesser officers – *avocats*, solicitors and clerks. From early in the fourteenth century the king was represented in the *parlement* by the *procureur général*, who was later joined by two *avocats généraux* designated collectively as the *gens du roi*. Steadily, written procedures encroached on the practice of taking evidence orally and the work of the magistrates multiplied. To cope with this it became necessary to increase the number of magistrates in the *enquêtes* and *requêtes* where most of the preliminary sifting of evidence and applications for justice took place. Indeed the number of such chambers increased so that by the end of the sixteenth century there were five *enquêtes* and two *requêtes*. The *grand' chambre* changed little with a membership of

[1] J.H. Shennan, *The Parlement of Paris* (London, Eyre & Spottiswoode, 1968), p.79.

around 30. In 1515 the *chambre de la tournelle* came into being to deal with criminal litigation.

As the realm expanded and royal authority increased provincial *parlements* were created. The *parlement* of Toulouse spluttered into momentary existence at the beginning of the fourteenth century before acquiring a permanent character in 1444. Those at Grenoble and Bordeaux followed very rapidly with the incorporation of Dauphiné and Aquitaine into the royal patrimony. Dijon was given a *parlement* in 1476, Rouen in 1499, Aix-en-Provence in 1501, whilst the *parlement* of Brittany resided variously at Vannes and Rennes from 1554. Thus by the end of the sixteenth century France possessed eight *parlements* and more were to follow.

In addition to the *parlements* a further sovereign court, the *grand conseil*, detached itself from the royal council by the end of the fifteenth century. Its powers were ill defined and very wide ranging. Acting as both a supreme court of appeal and a court of first instance, it was frequently used by the crown to consider cases in which it had a particular interest or which were politically significant. For instance, litigation relating to the patronage of ecclesiastical benefices as agreed at Bologna came within the purview of this court. Above all it was empowered to investigate complaints against royal officials and to determine disputes between other courts. It could even revoke decisions of the *parlement*.

The growth of the judicial powers of the French kings was underpinned by a parallel growth in their capacity to impose their will by force if necessary. Feudal armies by their very nature were small. At the beginning of the thirteenth century the king had a mere 436 knights at his disposition together with the infantry they raised from the tenantry. In case of dire need the great vassals of the king would also summon their dependants on his behalf. At the battle of Bouvines in 1214 Philippe Auguste's army swollen by the presence of urban militias numbered somewhere between 7,000 and 12,000. In addition to being relatively small, the feudal armies were unreliable because the knights' obligation to serve was limited to 40 days, and the infantry were ill prepared. In 1231 Louis IX found it expedient to pay an army sent to chastise the Count of Brittany and henceforth war became increasingly commercialized. Mercenaries and military entrepreneurs began to play a significant rôle. Unfortunately for the king these brought their own problems for, once paid off, they became a major threat to the law and order they were supposed to preserve. During the interludes of the Hundred Years War, organized bands of mercenary soldiers ravaged huge areas of the countryside posing almost as great a threat to the crown as Anglo-Burgundian forces. The result was Charles VII's decision in 1445 to create the *gendarmerie*, France's first permanent military force. At the outset it consisted of 15 *compagnies d'ordonnance*, each of 100 lances, each lance containing one mounted knight supported by three other mounted combatants, two archers and a *coutilier*. This produced a total of 6,000 combatants, an overall figure which remained fairly stable thereafter despite reductions in the size of the individual companies. In wartime the feudal levy continued to be utilized thus increasing the numbers of cavalry. Attempts to create a permanent core of well-trained infantry proved less successful and the king was largely dependent on volunteers and foreign mercenaries. Nevertheless the number of men at the disposition of the crown had risen steadily. The army was the largest in Europe and by 1557 the total size of the royal forces in wartime reached 50,000. Moreover they had at their disposition the best artillery available. From the midfifteenth century major advances had been made in the production of lighter, more manoeuvrable and efficient cannon. It was these that laid the basis for the victories over the English at Formigny (1450) and Castillon (1453) which finally brought the epic struggle to a close.

The companies of *gendarmerie* were increasingly linked with one of the most powerful and critical of the institutions on which the monarchy depended: the system of governors. Although provincial governors began to appear in the fourteenth century, it was only from 1504 that the 11 major governorships were filled on a permanent basis. Under Francis I they came to be occupied largely by princes of the blood or the high nobility, assisted by lesser noblemen or prelates who acted as lieutenants in the governor's absence. Originally governorships appear to have been created for a variety of reasons, such as the need to fill a vacuum created by the death of the titular head of a province or on its reversion to the crown. The governors clearly exercised general authority over the bailiffs and seneschals. But it was not insignificant that, although Francis appointed one or two governors to internal provinces, the major ones were all on the frontiers. Moreover all save one of the 52 governors appointed between 1515 and 1560 were captains of the companies of *gendarmerie*; indeed for a large part of the time they were more likely to be fighting in Italy than resident in their provinces. In addition to controlling the *gendarmerie* it was the governors who tended to hold the most prestigious commissions in the army with responsibility for the direction and planning of campaigns. Amongst the 52 governors there were seven marshals of France, one constable (Anne de Montmorency) and one *grand-maître de l'artillerie*. With substantial justification it has been observed that the institution of the governors was completely militarized.[2]

The imposition of royal authority was clearly dependent on the capacity to wage war on an ever-increasing scale. Yet war was expensive and became more so as the feudal host gave way to the standing army and contingents of mercenaries. This itself made essential the further extension of royal control over the resources of the realm. Above all it required the creation of bureaucratic mechanisms for channelling disposable wealth into royal coffers. Originally the Capetians had at their disposition only the same types of revenue as other seigneurs – feudal dues, such as the *champart*, and proceeds from seigneurial perquisites, such as the *banalités* and *formariage*. In addition they received some income from tolls and rights over trade and they could collect a *taille*, an arbitrary seigneurial levy not to be confused with the later royal tax. The gradual commutation of military service provided an extra form of income and finally there were the proceeds from the administration of justice, from vacant ecclesiastical benefices plus some petty sums

---

[2] R.R. Harding, *The Anatomy of a Power Elite. The provincial governors of early modern France* (New Haven, Yale University Press, 1978), p.27.

from shipwrecks, treasure trove and the property of subjects dying without heirs. Like other lords the king was expected 'to live off his own' and the domain was supposed to suffice for the expenses of the monarchy. Only in times of emergency was it deemed acceptable to levy additional subsidies.

Down to the late thirteenth century the crown managed fairly well, but Philip IV found it necessary to raise additional subsidies in 1294, 1295, 1299 and 1301 for the war against Edward I. With the onset of the Hundred Years War the *ad hoc* nature of such subsidies became manifestly inadequate and there began the first serious attempts to make taxation more permanent and uniform. In the 1340s a sales tax was instituted in northern France, a hearth tax in Languedoc and the inequitable *gabelle* made its first appearance (see below, p.20). Resistance to these taxes was widespread; moreover a massive subsidy approved by a representative assembly of the three estates (ie clergy, nobility and commoners) in the aftermath of the defeat at Crécy (1346) could not be collected because of the ravages of the plague. Ironically it was the capture of King John by the English in 1356 which prepared the way for further fiscal reform. In return for his release the English demanded a hefty sum; so, utilizing his undoubted right to call on his vassals for assistance, the French king introduced a tax on wine and other products known as the *aides pour la délivrance*. In addition the *gabelle* was reimposed. Unfortunately such was the state of lawlessness, and so preoccupied were many communities in raising funds with which to buy off the soldiers for whom the formal cessation of hostilities was immaterial, it proved impossible to levy the taxes throughout large areas. Without law and order the taxes could not be raised, but the maintenance of disciplined troops itself required that the taxes should be raised. To resolve the dilemma the king summoned representatives of the three estates to Amiens who agreed to the establishment of a *fouage*, or hearth tax, throughout the north for the 'defence of the realm' by means of an army 6,000 strong. This was the first tax levied in a period of peace and the direct ancestor of the *taille*. Gradually the distinction between the taxes raised for the royal ransom and those for the general maintenance of law and order was obscured, the *aides* being levied well beyond their original purpose. Thus out of the distress and difficulties of the mid decades of the fourteenth century there emerged the principal taxes of the *ancien régime*.

In 1380 the forward march of royal taxation was momentarily reversed when Charles V, conscious of his impending death and the economic distress of his subjects, cancelled the *fouage* – an act which led immediately to demands for the withdrawal of the indirect taxes by the towns, something the regency government was obliged to concede. Very rapidly it became clear that the crown could not cope and despite widespread unrest the *aides* and *gabelle* were restored. Languedoc continued to pay the *fouage* at unprecedented levels. Yet, once again, in the opening decades of the fifteenth century France was plunged into deep crisis. The revenue from the *aides* collapsed and after 1418, in the wake of the defeat at Agincourt (1415) with only the central parts of southern France under royal control, they were not collected at all. Charles VI's intermittent insanity did not help, and his son depended in the years that followed on the willingness of local and national assemblies to agree to the levying of *tailles*. In 1428, a year of terrible danger to the Valois dynasty, with the English gathering strength for an assault on the south, a meeting of the Estates at Chinon consented to the reintroduction of the *aides*. Then, after the peace with the Burgundians in 1436, the king was able to consolidate all the previous legislation on the levying of the *tailles* going back to 1355–6 and to specify the amounts to be levied on a wide range of wholesale and retail transactions. As each area of the north and centre was recovered so the *aides* were imposed on them. Languedoc however was allowed to convert the *aides* into an annual lump sum, the *équivalent*, under the control of its provincial Estates. Voted in the first instance for three years, the *aides* became permanent. Likewise the *taille* granted in 1439 for one year was levied thereafter without consultation; indeed Charles VII never summoned the Estates again.

Technically the *taille*, the *gabelles* and the *aides* were still 'extraordinary' taxes levied to meet exceptional circumstances. But by the reign of Francis they were in fact providing roughly 90 per cent of the revenue, whilst the 'ordinary' revenues from the domain were becoming less and less significant. Out of a total income of 4.9 million *livres* in 1515 the *taille* produced 2.4 million, the *aides* about 800,000 and the *gabelle* 284,000. In the years that followed the share of the domain revenues shrank even further until by 1576 it constituted no more than one twenty-fifth.

By the reign of Francis I a complex administrative structure had evolved to cope with the expansion of the royal finances. For the domain there were four treasurers, each of whom was responsible for an area, assisted by a number of receivers and the general receiver or *changeur du trésor*. Parallel to this was a much more complex administration for the extraordinary revenues supervised by four *généraux des finances* each responsible for one *généralité*. They were helped by four receivers-general. The *généralités* were subdivided into *élections*, of which there were about 81, each controlled by an official known as an *élu* who combined administrative functions with legal ones as he had the power to judge disputes which arose from the assessment and levying of taxes. In origin, as the terminology implies, these were not royal officials but representatives of the estates imposed on the crown amidst the difficulties of the mid fourteenth century. When King John recovered the initiative after his release in 1360 and introduced the *aides*, he also succeeded in transforming the *élus* into royal agents, paid by him and under the supervision of the higher officials. By this time the *chambre des comptes*, like the *parlement* a specialized offshoot of the royal council with the powers of a sovereign court, had also made its appearance. From about 1320 it had established a separate identity and acquired supreme control over all the fiscal accounts and records of the fiscal officers. Later in the century it was joined by yet another sovereign court, the *cour des aides*, which grew out of the activities of the higher tax officials who gradually extended their powers. It dealt with litigation arising from tax disputes and controlled the *équivalent* of Languedoc, forced loans and clerical tenths. Subsequently a number of provincial *chambres des comptes* and *cour des aides* were created in the same way as the provincial *parlements*.

The basic framework of the fiscal apparatus was therefore well established by the fifteenth century and lasted down to the reign of Francis I. The next major step was a series of reforms in 1523 and 1524 which introduced two quite new officials, the *trésorier de l'épargne* and the receiver of the *parties casuelles*. The former acquired powers to collect and disburse all the income from taxation and from the domains, whilst the latter was responsible for the remaining revenue which was largely comprised of the proceeds from the sale of offices. Thus the traditional distinction between the extraordinary and the domanial revenues was effectively abolished; henceforth extraordinary revenues referred to sale of office, loans and other fiscal expedients which supplemented the regular income. In the process the power of the existing treasurers and the *généraux des finances*, who had operated as a quasi-autonomous financial committee, was reduced. In 1532 on the grounds that the *changeur du trésor* and the general receivers were not paying money into the *épargne* as requested, they were replaced and an attempt was made to ensure that all the king's revenues would be placed in coffers in the Louvre under the tightest administrative control. However, significant sums for routine expenses continued to be paid out by the *trésorier de l'épargne* before they had ever reached the Louvre. This probably contributed to the decision made in 1542 to subdivide the four *généralités* into 17 new units each with its own treasury office, or *bureaux des finances* as they became known. This was the origin of the seventeenth-century *généralités*; by 1600 there were 21 each with a substantial corps of treasurers, receivers, controllers and lesser officials dealing, for example, with revenues from the *eaux et forêts* or the payment of royal garrisons. A consequence of all these changes was to further enhance the power of the *trésorier de l'épargne* who now stood at the head of a single financial administration and finally to destroy those of the *changeur du trésor* whose function as receiver for the domains was rendered redundant. The *élections* survived as the key subdivisions of the *généralités*.

By the reign of Francis I the foundations had been laid for the rule of one of the most prestigious and powerful European monarchs. The French king was no longer merely *primus inter pares*, dependent essentially on the resources of his personal domain. In the process of achieving dynastic security, and under the impact of the warfare that this entailed, the Capetians and Valois had transformed the monarchy into the embodiment of public authority. 'Emperor in his kingdom' the French king was accountable to no one, not even the pope, an image that was further reinforced by the tendency from about 1530 to portray the king as a new Caesar rather than, in the traditional fashion, as a second David or Solomon. At his disposition he had something like 12,000 officials operating within the framework of a complex legal and judicial apparatus. Moreover the realm which they administered was beginning to assume the appearance of a nation with a recognizable national consciousness. When the Capetians ascended the throne the term France described nothing more than their very limited patrimony. Not until the end of the thirteenth century did the distinction between French-born and foreigners appear in the texts and reference to 'the French nations' continued long after. Nevertheless it is possible from the same time to distinguish between *patria sua*, used in the customary way to describe a region or locality, and *patria communis* which meant the whole nation. From the thirteenth century too the archives ceased to follow the king around and the principal institutions settled in their Parisian homes. Although far from being the permanent residence of king and court, Paris began to acquire the character of an administrative capital. Undoubtedly, despite the difficulty of measuring such things, the long struggle against the English encouraged the growth of a national sentiment and loyalties amongst sections of the population. With the final expulsion of the foreigners the way was open for the extension of the dialect of the north, the *langue d' oil*, to the southern regions of the *langue d'oc*. It was used by the *parlements* of the south and was common amongst most of the upper classes with the exception of Gascony, Provence and some smaller areas.

Authoritarian by nature, Francis I had the means to rule more or less as he wished. The Estates-General never met; even when he was captured at Pavia (1525) the regent turned not to an Estates-General for assistance but to the *parlement*. This institution itself, despite a continuing assertiveness, was often treated peremptorily by the king, who made it clear to the magistrates that it was not for them to question his demands. Cases were taken away from them and referred to the *grand conseil* or even to arbitrary commissions such as that for the treason trial of the duke of Bourbon. Francis I disregarded *parlement*'s complaints about fiscal abuses and above all he determinedly overrode its opposition to the Concordat of Bologna. The attempt to interfere in royal appointments to major benefices resulted in an annulment of its proceedings, the suspension of four members and a humiliating demand to see the records of its deliberations. The nadir of the relationship between king and *parlement* was reached in July 1527 when the royal council issued a decree forbidding it to interfere in affairs of state and to seek annual confirmation of its authority. Francis merely communicated the decree to the representatives of the *parlement* without according them a chance to reply.

On the fiscal front Francis was equally ruthless. He browbeat towns into providing larger and larger sums of money, extending royal control over them with the creation of officials known as *contrôleurs des deniers communs*, and compelling them to submit a declaration of the value of their communal revenues. The Church was also treated harshly. Clerical tenths, originally subject to papal approval, were levied with increasing regularity and, from 1545, four times a year. Such opposition that emerged was overcome by a threat to seize the defaulting clerics' temporalities. Similarly some magistrates of the *parlement* of Bordeaux were imprisoned for resisting a forced loan. In 1544 following a rebellion at Lagny-sur-Marne, he ordered the seigneur de Lorges to sack the town and then forbade the inhabitants from taking legal action to secure compensation.

With the reign of Francis a high point was thus reached in the steady consolidation and concentration of power. In some respects the style and activities of this monarch clearly anticipated those normally associated with the rulers of the next century. But between them there was to come a half century during which royal authority virtually disintegrated in a maelstrom of civil anarchy and religious strife. Notwithstanding the significance of the developments so far described, it is clear, in retrospect, that the crown remained extremely vulnerable. Indeed far from resolving the antagonism between the centralizing and decentralizing forces contained within the body politic, the elevation of the monarchy simply intensified them.

The Restraints on Royal Authority

The preceding account has been intentionally designed to show the growth of monarchical power in the most favourable light. Yet it should be apparent, even from this, that the process was slow, arduous and subject to violent setbacks. Its most obvious feature was the prolonged struggle with the English, first the Plantagenets, who as dukes of Normandy and Acquitaine were the crown's most powerful vassals, and then with the Lancastrians who took up the cudgels in defence of Edward III's claim to the French throne. The territories in English hands having been wrested from them by the 1370s, the whole process had to be repeated in the following century when for a time it seemed that the realm would be totally dismembered by the Anglo-Burgundian forces. Charles VI was compelled to recognize his son-in-law Henry V of England as his rightful heir. Even after their expulsion, the English continued to make trouble; when in 1465 Francis II of Brittany and the king's brother Charles comte de Berry put themselves at the head of the so-called League of the Public Weal, the English made alliances with both. Not until the treaty of Picquigny, 10 years later, and the death of Charles the Bold of Burgundy in 1477 was the territorial base of the French monarchy assured.

It was not only the lands dominated by France's principal enemies which were slow to come within the royal orbit. Brittany, as we have seen, was not finally annexed until 1532. Provence was only bequeathed by its last rulers to the French king in 1481 and even then he ruled over this territory merely as count of Provence. Similarly, although the rulers of Dauphiné had abdicated in favour of the French crown in 1348, it could not be fully integrated into the royal domain; for it was a fief of the Empire and there were evident dangers in the king becoming a vassal of the emperor. Instead Dauphiné became the fief of the heir to the throne (henceforth the Dauphin), providing in the process the means for wayward sons to defy their fathers. In 1456 Charles VII descended with his army on the province to put an end to its quasi-independence, compelling all the dauphinal officers to swear allegiance to him. Not until 1560 however was the Dauphiné formally annexed by the crown. At this stage still outside royal control were the extensive lands of the house of Foix-Navarre which included the independent principalities of Béarn and Navarre, the counties of Foix and Périgord and the viscounties of Bigorre, Nebouzan and Soule. This patrimony was to sustain the prestige and activities of Henri de Navarre during the wars of religion.

The slow process of unifying the realm was made even slower by the practice of bequeathing apanages on the younger sons of the king. This went back to the earliest days of the Capetians but it was Louis VIII (1223–6) who, in order to satisfy his numerous children, created apanages on a large scale. Indeed he gave so much away that he left himself only the old domain and Normandy. Subsequent monarchs were less generous but nevertheless they felt obliged to continue the practice and sometimes alienated territory on a considerable scale. The apanage created for the third son of John the Good (1350–64) included Berry, Auvergne and Poitou – virtually an eighth of the realm. Auvergne slipped from royal control altogether, not being recovered until the confiscation of the lands of the treasonable duke of Bourbon in 1522. The concessions made to the eldest sons which frequently included a considerable share of royal taxes were only partially successful in preventing fratricidal antagonisms from pulling the kingdom apart. Indeed the opposite effect was sometimes produced. The starting point of the attempt by the dukes of Burgundy to carve out a kingdom of their own was the apanage granted in 1363 to the youngest son of John the Good. Moreover the failure to insert any clause stipulating the reversion of the territory to the crown meant that on the death of Charles in 1477 the rightful heir became his son-in-law Maximilian of Austria. In the settlement Franche Comté, together with Flanders – the first great fief brought to heel by the Capetians – passed into Habsburg hands, thus preparing the way for the subsequent encirclement of France and the bitter Franco-Imperial rivalries of the next 200 years.

The slow and piecemeal fashion in which the French realm was brought together was reflected in its lack of institutional homogeneity, most significantly in the failure to develop anything which resembled a national parliament of the English type. There was in France, as in England, a tradition of 'taking wise counsel' by assembling the chief vassals of the crown when appropriate; in addition it was generally, albeit somewhat vaguely, supposed that those who contributed to the necessities of the king should have a voice in the matter. Moreover in 1302, only slightly after the establishment of the English parliament, the French Estates-General took shape bringing together representatives of the clergy and nobility with those of the third estate, who were drawn essentially from the larger towns. Yet its subsequent development was to prove much less vigorous than that of its English counterpart and by the sixteenth century it had been more or less discarded as a useful royal institution. Called with some regularity during the crises of the 1340s and 1350s, the Estates' consent was a significant factor in the establishment of the first permanent taxes. However, after John succeeded in transforming the *élus* into royal agents, the rôle of the Estates diminished steadily and was only really revived by the further difficulties of the 1420s and 30s. For a while the need for consent to taxation appeared as though it might enable the Estates-General to acquire a degree of stability but, once again, as royal authority was restored, it fell into limbo. Summoned in 1468 to enable Louis XI to renege on the concessions made at the time of the League of the Public Weal, and in 1484 on the minority of his son, the Estates did not meet thereafter until the onset of the religious wars.

In part the failure of the Estates-General to develop was a consequence of its potential for obstruction and the nagging fear that it might get out of hand. In 1356 when King John was a prisoner, not only did the deputies 'vote little and complain much'[3] but they were actually involved in the

---

[3] M. Wolfe, *The Fiscal System of Renaissance France* (New Haven, Yale University Press, 1972), p.18.

seizure of Paris by the rebel Etienne Marcel. In 1380 they showed a willingness to take advantage of the weakness of the king to secure the withdrawal of taxes. Moreover, as the royal grip on taxation grew the principle of consent to it was expressed with increasing vigour whenever the opportunity arose. At the Estates-General of 1484 it was coupled with demands for the suppression of the *élus*. Not surprisingly French kings had henceforth little time for this institution.

Yet it would be a mistake to attribute the failure of the Estates simply, or even largely, to their capacity for obstruction. On the contrary – as the early history of the English parliament shows – the consolidation of royal power and the development of national unity would have been well served by the existence of a single representative institution. Unfortunately the Estates-General was not fully representative of all the French regions and partly for this reason was incapable of overriding the all-pervasive forces of provincialism and localism. Indeed not a single meeting of the Estates during the fourteenth and fifteenth centuries was a truly national gathering. The delegates from distant parts were frequently unwilling or unable to attend. Burgundy, Dauphiné, Provence and Roussillon were not represented at all before 1484. Moreover, when the Estates did attempt to play a constructive rôle in supporting royal requests for assistance, they all too easily aroused opposition in the provinces. As often as not taxes approved by the Estates had to be renegotiated with local assemblies and communities. In the 1420s when *aides* were approved, many of the regions of the north transformed them into a *taille*. At the Estates of 1484 the government was obliged to negotiate with the representatives of each province separately, and the following year special meetings of the local Estates were called. In one sense such separatism, particularly when it penetrated the meetings of the Estates-General, undermined its own position *vis-à-vis* the king. A united front was difficult to achieve. But equally the monarch was left to contend with a multiplicity of local interests and the frequent need to negotiate directly with them.

The early history of regional and local assemblies is shrouded in uncertainty. Some like those of Béarn, where the inhabitants of the valleys and communities were protected by charters of liberties which the seigneur swore to uphold, can be traced back to the twelfth century. Assemblies representing all three estates were active in Provence in the thirteenth century. But in general the first flowering of such assemblies came from the mid fourteenth century as rulers strove to achieve security at a time of deepening conflict and distress. The Estates of Languedoc, which rapidly acquired *de facto* control of taxation, originated in the decision of Philip VI in 1345–6 to summon separately the Estates of north and south. In Dauphiné the new French rulers combined the traditionally separate meetings of the three estates in order to seek financial assistance. For similar reasons the Burgundian Estates were assembled in 1357 by their ruler, the future King John, a practice which survived when the duchy was transmitted by him as an apanage to his son. In Guyenne assemblies were fostered by their English overlords who, in 1368, conceded the principle of consent to taxation. Towards the end of the fourteenth century many of the Estates, like the Estates-General, suffered something of an eclipse. For a period in Languedoc taxes were levied without consent by royal officials until the renewed onslaught of the English brought a new lease of life. Consent to taxation was recognized in Languedoc in 1428 and, about the same time, conceded in Provence and Limousin.

In Normandy the English themselves were responsible for reviving the Estates to the point at which they were being summoned annually. When Normandy returned to French rule, after some hesitation, this practice was confirmed and consent to taxation formally acknowledged. Developments were slower in Brittany; the dukes had long summoned meetings of the clergy and nobles but they were not joined by the representatives of the towns until the mid fourteenth century, and only right at the end of the ducal period did the Estates emerge as a clearly identifiable institution.

Some of the Estates developed administrations of their own in the fifteenth century. Those in Béarn elected officials known as *syndics* from 1468 and later appointed secretaries; auditors were empowered to vet the viscount's fiscal administration and the Estates assumed the right to appoint the treasurer of Béarn. A permanent commission was established to deal with affairs between sessions. From 1480 the Estates of Provence also appointed *procureurs du pays* to act in similar fashion. In Languedoc the Estates had an official clerk from mid century, later supplemented by *syndics* and a treasurer. They established their own archives at Montpellier and presided over a sophisticated fiscal administration which rested on the subordinate assemblies of the secular dioceses into which the province was itself divided.

The autonomy of the Languedoc Estates was further bolstered by their success in exploiting royal apprehensions about the loyalty of the province to achieve the withdrawal of the *élus* in 1443. Provinces subsequently secured by the crown also escaped the *élus*. By the end of the century there thus crystallized the broad distinction between the *pays d'états* on the periphery of the realm – Burgundy, Dauphiné, Provence, Languedoc, Guyenne and Normandy – where taxes were negotiated with the Estates and the *pays d' élections* where the crown raised them directly through its own officials. That this distinction was somewhat blurred by the fact that there were regions, notably Normandy and parts of Burgundy, where both assemblies and *élus* operated, serves only to highlight the lack of institutional uniformity. Occasionally the government attempted to impose *élections* on areas without them, but invariably withdrew on payment of a lump sum by the Estates; this happened in Guyenne in 1545.

Sometimes the rather paradoxical consequence of the consolidation of the provincial Estates – a name they acquired only during the fifteenth century – was the reduction or even elimination of the rôle played by assemblies of sub-regions or local communities. This can be seen in Burgundy where the dukes developed central Estates at the expense of the lesser ones scattered throughout the hotch-potch of territories they had amassed. By 1477 local Estates were left only in Auxonne, the Charolais and the Mâconnais, albeit with a real measure of autonomy. In Guyenne by contrast, where the provincial Estates were not much employed, the lesser assemblies, *recettes* and *sénéchaussées*, continued to have a vigorous existence, down to the mid sixteenth century. Moreover they were not the only local assemblies. Bordeaux despite being the home of an *élection* boasted a multiplicity of representative institutions; in addition to meetings of the three estates there were separate assemblies for each as well as for the *filleules*, or daughter towns of Bordeaux, whose representatives swore to protect the privileges of the city. In return the mayor and aldermen of Bordeaux promised to defend the *filleules*. Up river the Estates of Agenais acquired the right to meet when they liked, to elect *syndics* and levy a small tax to pay their expenses. Rouergue, at first part of Languedoc but later absorbed into Guyenne, also possessed vigorous Estates with the authority to vote taxes and distribute them amongst the subordinate *recettes*. An attempt by Francis I to undermine their right to appoint receivers was successfully resisted. Yet more regional Estates developed in the Condomois, Astarac and Bazadais from the reign of Louis XI and in the Lannes where they had been active under English rule. Although no other province displayed the variety of the local assemblies of Guyenne, the remarkable democratic assemblies of the mountainous communities of the east and south are worthy of note. In Dauphiné the *escartons*, at which neither the nobility nor the clergy had a right of attendance, continued to meet until the Revolution of 1789.

This exclusion of the first two estates also brings sharply into focus the fact that the customs and principles which determined the composition procedures of the assemblies varied considerably. In the Agenais and lower Auvergne the first two estates ceased to attend, thus transforming the assemblies into organizations dominated by the major towns. Exceptionally, the Estates of Béarn comprised two houses in the English style – one of barons and prelates, the other of the commons. In Burgundy only nobles with fiefs could attend, in Dauphiné those with judicial prerogatives, whilst in Brittany such restrictions gradually faded away. Where all three orders met voting was normally by order with one vote for each. However in Dauphiné the estates assembled and voted together. In Provence voting was by head but the nobility always seemed able to muster more votes than the other two estates and an attempt by the third estate to limit the representation of the privileged orders failed. Uniquely in Languedoc, sometime during the reign of Louis XI, the third estate did succeed in establishing this principle.

Although the Estates and assemblies regarded themselves as the principal guardians of the liberties and privileges of the communities within their orbit, they were not the only manifestations of provincial autonomy. Many towns also profited from the slow and difficult unification of the realm to acquire and maintain substantial political and financial privileges. When for instance the strategically and economically vital port of Bordeaux returned to French rule in 1451, Charles agreed that amongst other things the inhabitants would not pay any taxes. This accord was soon violated and the Bordelais invited the English to return. Although they were then driven out by the king, Bordeaux remained a very privileged, effectively self-governing city, exempt from all *aides*, *tailles* and other subsidies. Some towns actually received their first charters from the English, such as that bestowed on La Rochelle in 1199 which endowed it with a 100-strong municipal council. When, in 1371, the Rochelais helped expel the English they were rewarded with a further extension of their privileges. This included conferment of hereditary nobility on the mayor and *échevins* and their exemption from taxation. In addition, the municipality was given complete authority over its finances 'and all governors, judges and others' were forbidden to act 'in this sphere'. Bourges, which effectively became the seat of the monarchy during the worst days of the Hundred Years War, had come into royal hands from the viscounts of Bourges, a region of allodial holdings with barely any obligations on the peasantry. Presumably in order to retain the allegiance of the townsfolk, from the time of Louis VI (1108–37) all who came to Bourges were freed and put directly under the protection of the king. They could only be called to account for their misdemeanours by the *tribunal des bourgeois*, there was no taille and women were free to marry without the consent of the king. Loyalty to the king during the Hundred Years War resulted in further privileges such as exemption from the *franc-fief* and the feudal levy. The bourgeois of Toulouse similarly traced their privileges back to their feudal origins in 1233 when, in return for assuming responsibility for the defence of the city, they had acquired from the count of Toulouse not only exemption from the feudal levy but jurisdiction over the town and the adjacent parishes. This authority, confirmed by the crown in 1337 and 1442, was later supplemented by further legal and military privileges including exemption from the *taille*, and the right not to be taken from the town for trial. Marseille likewise had a tradition of autonomy that went back to the thirteenth century. Here the key event was the agreement made in return for recognition of his sovereignty with Charles comte d'Anjou, king of Naples and Sicily in 1257. By this Marseille acquired a special status as belonging to the 'adjacent lands' which were not subject to the administration of the counts of Provence and virtually exempt from taxation. This status was retained after the incorporation of Provence in the realm and the Marseillais recognized the king only as *seigneur de Marseille*.

Acceptance of the importance of the towns, or at least of the need to assure the loyalty of the oligarchies which dominated them, clearly played a part in the policies of both Charles VII and Louis XI. Although they did treat individual towns very harshly, there was no general reversal of their privileged position. Charles freely exempted them from the *taille* and Louis XI even conceded taxes or *octrois* as they were called, to some towns in perpetuity. Le Mans which had no organized municipal government received a charter in 1481 which conferred on it franchises identical to those of La Rochelle. This process continued in the first half of the sixteenth century despite the propensity of Francis I to browbeat municipal representatives. Rennes, Nantes, Clermont and Saumur all received constitutions. Inevitably such constitutions further multiplied the variety of procedures for electing or co-opting the towns' councils, which ranged in size from the large *échevinages* of the Rochelais type to the small consulates of the south. Although the government was able to interfere in municipal elections and maintenance of privileges sometimes had to be paid for by a hefty forced loan, the general nature of the relationship between town and crown was such that even a strong ruler was obliged to mix intimidation with negotiation, manoeuvre and compromise.

A central preoccupation of both Estates and towns, as should now be plain, was the defence of fiscal privilege. It was indeed in the sphere of taxation that the forces of particularism made their most significant impact on the development of the French state. Despite the extension of the fiscal powers of the crown, the need to accommodate the interests of a host of local communities and regions with a great variety of traditions inevitably inhibited the development of a uniform financial apparatus. Not even the *taille* was levied in a common fashion; the obligation to pay in the north was determined by the status of the individual, with exemption for the nobility (*taille personnelle*), whereas in the south it was the status of the land that counted (*taille réelle*), so that nobles had to pay for their non-noble properties (i.e. those that were not subject to the feudal levy). In Dauphiné the two systems coexisted, being *réelle* in the mountain regions but *personnelle* elsewhere. Burgundy paid virtually no *tailles* at all as a result of Louis's recognition of its privileges. In Provence and Brittany the basic tax remained the medieval *fouage* paid in minimal amounts. Although it was possible to impose additional burdens on these provinces, their privileged position meant that the burden of the *taille* fell essentially on the northern and central regions. Many towns did not pay the *taille* either.

Nor was the crown able to impose the *aides* throughout the realm. These were very unpopular taxes and, as noted earlier, many communities insisted on turning them into a hearth tax. A number of regions – including Poitou, Auvergne and Artois – thus paid a direct tax which was under the control of the Estates. Languedoc in particular conducted a long struggle to be treated differently and from 1443 was given the right to pay a lump sum, the *équivalent* in lieu of *aides*. Burgundy, Provence and Brittany paid neither, although Brittany had its own indirect taxes known as the *devoirs*. A major consequence of these developments was that merchants selling in the north and centre of the realm paid higher taxes than those elsewhere. This made it possible for the government to establish export taxes not simply on goods that were destined for other countries, but on those shipped from areas which paid the *aides* to those which did not. Thus originated in the late fourteenth century the *imposition foraine* levied on merchandise as it passed from the older central provinces into Brittany, Burgundy, the *midi* and the newer provinces of the north. The result was France's 'infamous tariff wall running from the south of Lyons in the east along a meandering curve through the south central provinces and ending just north of Bordeaux in the west.'[4] To this was added the *traite d'Anjou* for goods transhipped from Normandy to Brittany. By contrast with export taxes, impositions on imports developed very late. They appear to stem from the decision of Louis XI that all imported silk was to pass by way of Lyon and pay a 5 per cent tax. Gradually this tax was extended to other products entering Lyon and by the reign of Francis the *douane de Lyon* comprised a valuable package of revenues from cloths, gold, silver, alum and spices. Nothing reveals more clearly the lack of a sense of national territorial unity than the encouragement of import duties in a specific region. Also serving to destroy any measure of uniformity were

[4] Wolfe, *Fiscal System*, p.346.

the multitude of internal tolls and tariffs; there were alleged to be 120 royal and seigneurial tolls on the Loire system alone.

The third major tax, the *gabelle*, reflected in a similar fashion the unsteady outward expansion of the realm. Again only in the central and northern areas did the *gabelle* exist in its full form. Here the government exercised a monopoly of the sale of salt and increasingly compelled purchasers to buy minimum amounts, thus controlling the trade and maintaining demand. Such a policy was not so easy in the producing areas which, partly for this reason, were treated more lightly; in the western region stretching from Poitou to Gascony there were no royal storehouses and the *gabelle* consisted of a tax of 20 or 25 per cent. The same regime operated in those parts of Normandy where the salt was culled from the sea. A further band of provinces from Limousin to Dauphiné paid a tax akin to the *imposition foraine*, Burgundy some lesser tariffs, whilst Brittany had no *gabelle* at all. When Francis and Henry II tried to undermine the privileged status of the western provinces they precipitated an immense resistance involving towns and communities from La Rochelle to Bordeaux. Although crushed, the revolt bore fruit in 1553 when these provinces were allowed to purchase total exemption from all salt taxes, an act which enhanced their privileges and deepened the existing contrasts between one region and another.

The impressive fiscal reforms of Francis I notwithstanding, the forces of localism and particularism could not be suppressed or circumvented. Indeed nothing reveals this more pointedly than the king's decision to abandon his attempt to funnel all revenues into a single central treasury and the associated creation of the provincial *bureaux des finances*. This not only confirmed the customary practice of local disbursement of funds but institutionalized it in increasingly powerful corporate bodies. Given the fact that never more than a quarter of the revenues reached the central coffers, the royal ambition of accumulating a reserve of 3 million *livres* was obviously unattainable. Throughout his reign Francis had to resort to very *ad hoc* methods in order to sustain his bellicose policies. When Paris was threatened by the English in 1523 and by imperial forces in 1536, it simply fell upon the citizens to find the wherewithal for their defence. In 1545 they also had to find 120,000 *livres* for the relief of Boulogne and 90,000 the following year.

Not surprisingly the government began to explore possible ways of raising money from the private market in a more systematic fashion. One new method was found in the *rentes sur l'hôtel de ville de Paris* enabling those willing to lend to the crown to do so through the municipality of Paris which stood as a guarantor of the repayments. Used only sparingly by Francis himself, the *rentes* nevertheless mark a significant moment in the escalation of the rôle played by private credit. The king also turned to the great financial and banking centre of Lyon, pressurizing the municipality into becoming a royal fund-raising body and negotiating with merchant bankers either individually or in groups. Out of these activities there emerged in 1555 the general syndicate known as *le grand parti* designed to consolidate the debt and ensure regular repayments. A further method of increasing the flow of cash was by tax farming; long the custom as far as indirect taxes were concerned, it was the responsibility of the *élus* to lease these to the highest bidder. During the reign of Henry II it also became the practice to lease out several farms *en bloc* with groups of purchasers combining to acquire them. It was but one step from this to the allocation of the entire revenue from specified sources to those able to extend large loans to the crown (the *partisans*) or to those who dreamt up new fiscal devices or ways of improving the yield from existing taxes (the *traitants*). Condemned by many as monopolistic, such procedures undoubtedly increased the opportunities open to the local financial officials to enrich themselves at royal expense and to increase thereby their own independence. They also had the effect of blurring the line between the official fiscal apparatus and the expanding network of private financiers, thus contributing to that confusion, so characteristic of the *ancien régime*, between public office and private property.

Nothing contributed more to this, however, than sale of office; an old fiscal device, employed with growing readiness by Francis I, it became rampant under his successor. All the fiscal offices became venal and at every level of both the fiscal and judicial administration new posts were invented for sale. Henry created for instance an equal number of forestry officials in each of the *bailliages* regardless of the amount of forested terrain. Most striking was the introduction of the *présidiaux*, an entirely new layer of appellate courts between the *bailliages* (or *sénéchaussées*) and the *parlements*. Ostensibly established to cope with the increasing pressure on the judicial system, there is little doubt that financial motives played a significant part. Henry also introduced a further novelty with the device of *l'alternatif* which allowed two people to hold a single post alternately. Limited initially to certain categories of financial offices, *l'alternatif* was later extended to others. Not only were offices sold on an ever widening scale but it became commonplace to resign them in favour of a son or nephew, and on payment of a fine, providing it was paid 40 days before the death of the holder, a post could be transmitted to any designated successor.

Not only did these developments conspire to increase the dependence of the crown on financiers, precisely when it was endeavouring to extend its control over the resources of the realm, but they also added a new dimension to the forces of regional and local autonomy. Offices became part of the patrimony of well-to-do families who, entrenched in the provinces as they frequently were, thus acquired both an additional reason for, and the means of , preserving their privileged status.

Perhaps it is the growth of the provincial *parlements* that best reveals the contradictory nature of these processes and the tensions at work within the royal administration; for the very existence of the provincial *parlements* was itself testimony both to the extension of royal justice and to the need for an accommodation with local interests and feeling. The creation of the most important of these *parlements*, that at Toulouse, certainly reflected this need. Worried by the possibility of the inhabitants of the south throwing in their lot with the Burgundians, Charles V created a *parlement* in 1420, subsequently merging it with a *parlement* at Poitiers. However, pressure from the Estates of Languedoc achieved its permanent establishment in Toulouse from 1444. Similarly Bordeaux was granted a *parlement* by Louis X 'at the request of the people of the three estates of our *pays* and Duchy of Guyenne, and especially of our town of Bordeaux and the *pays* of Bordelais'. Many of the provinces had their own judicial traditions which had to be acknowledged or utilized. In Dauphiné this meant transforming the ancient court into a *parlement*; in Normandy the royal courts emerged out of its exchequer, inherited from the medieval dukes, the *parlement* taking final shape in 1499. Francis I even gave the inhabitants of the tiny principality of Dombes a *parlement* when he confiscated it from the duke of Bourbon in 1523, at the same time confirming their other privileges, notably exemption from the taille and the right to mint money. This act was as much a recognition of local interests as it was of their subordination to the will of the crown. It is certainly a mistake to imagine the *parlementaires* as a new class of royal agents pushing aside those who dominated the provinces. On the contrary, many of the traditional nobility found new opportunities in the *parlements* for consolidating their position, though they were often pushed aside by wealthy upstarts.

The local élites who staffed the *parlements* and the intermediate courts became the guardians of the multiplicity of laws and customs governing the various provinces that had been drawn into the royal domain. Apart from canon law, from which much legal procedure was derived, there existed both Roman and customary law. Roman law, based on the principles embodied in the great Imperial law codes, was essentially a southern phenomenon, whereas the north was subject to a wide variety of regional and local customs embracing everything from feudal dues to the use of torture. This broad geographical division is however insufficiently precise. In Provence for instance Roman law had been supplemented by the *ordonnances* of the medieval counts, a flood of royal legislation and a host of decrees by municipal and seigneurial courts. Throughout large areas of the south-west inheritance customs were still in the process of formulation in the sixteenth century. The *parlement* of Bordeaux administered Roman law modified by custom. On the other hand the jurisdiction of the *parlement* of Paris extended to areas like Auvergne which were subject to written law. Virtually every court was obliged to apply several codes and customs. In 1497 a beginning was made on the codification and systematization of customary law with the establishment of a royal commission for this purpose. The results of its efforts survive in the *coutumiers*, truly remarkable collections of the customs of the provinces and *pays* of the realm compiled with painstaking care by the jurists of the early sixteenth century. However, the net result of their endeavours, although a tribute to the enhanced prestige of the monarchy, was to freeze French law in its semi-formed state. The hope entertained by a number of eminent jurists that the next step would be the production of a general law code for the entire realm never materialized.

The uniform extension of royal authority was further constrained by the fact that whilst many new courts were created, none were ever abolished. Indeed the first contact the average inhabitant was likely to have with the law would be not in the royal courts but in one of the 80,000 or so seigneurial courts which continued to flourish. Technically subordinate to the royal courts, they dealt with a wide variety of civil and criminal matters, from payments of rents and dues to infractions of the peace. Those seigneurs who wielded rights of high justice, as opposed to middle or low justice, even had

powers of capital punishment. In addition they also enforced public regulations such as those relating to the wine harvest, theatrical performances,
shops, and even the playing of violins. Appeals from the seigneurial courts
went directly in some areas to the superior royal courts, but in Brittany and
Auvergne for instance it was necessary to go through several seigneurial
jurisdictions before reaching them. The lowest echelon of royal courts
consisted of the *prévôtés* or their equivalents (*vicomtés* in Normandy, *vigueries* or
baillies in Provence and Languedoc, *châtellenies* in the Ile-de-France). Responsible to the bailiffs or sénéschals, the officers of these lowly courts
nevertheless dealt with a range of civil and criminal matters, some of which
the superior courts were obliged to refer to them in the first instance. Above
them stood the *bailliages* and *sénéchaussées* – some hundred in number by the
end of the sixteenth century – exercising comprehensive powers of justice
including an exclusive right to deal with matters designated as *cas royaux*.
Most military matters from the feudal levy to fortifications, those relating to
the nobility and their prerogatives, ecclesiastical affairs, acts of violence,
malversation, and treason, together with the crimes of nobles, ecclesiastics
and officers came within the orbit of these courts. Cases went on appeal from
them to the newly created *présidiaux* which had the power to issue sovereign
judgments in civil cases involving sums of up to 250 *livres*. They also dealt
with criminal cases on appeal from the *prévôtés*. The *parlements* were of course
the supreme courts of appeal and there were matters such as the *régale* over
which they alone had competence. In addition they exercised a day-to-day
authority over virtually everything of concern to the communities within
their jurisdiction: troop movements, religious communities, supplying of
markets, public works, roads and canals, and much more besides came
within their sway.

Nor should it be forgotten that as well as the officers of justice there were
many others who exercised legal functions. These included the officers of the
salt warehouses, of the royal waterways and forests, the admiralty courts and
ecclesiastical courts, customs officials, those of the royal mints and, from
1569, the *tribunaux consulaires* established in many towns to deal with
commercial litigation. More importantly, the principal financial officials,
notably the *élus* and treasurers, had powers of arbitration in matters within
their purview. The *chambres des comptes* and *cours des aides* were of course
sovereign courts, a status also attained by the *cour des monnaies* in 1552.

It is not surprising that in a town like Amiens, which possessed neither
admiralty nor *parlement*, there were something like 15 bodies sharing in the
administration of justice. It would be more accurate to say 'competing'
rather than 'sharing' for the prime consequence of the proliferation of courts
and the expansion of the judiciary was to intensify the rivalries between one
body and the next. Between the *parlements* and the financial courts there was
obviously immense scope for conflict; nor did the *parlements* take kindly to the
présidiaux which took away valuable cases and diminished their authority.
The *élus* similarly resented the arrival of the treasurers who rapidly began to
assert their own sovereign status and corporate identity. This conflict was
rendered more complex by the fact that whereas the *élus* were responsible to
the *cours des aides*, the treasurers fell within the jurisdiction of the *chambre des*

comptes. All in all the combined effects of regional variation, venality of office and a growing corporate rivalry, acted as a powerful brake on the capacity of the crown to assert its will.

In addition to their legal functions, the *parlements*, notably that of Paris, acquired the means to intervene in political affairs. During the fourteenth century the practice of registering royal edicts became regularized and was followed somewhat later by the procedure for remonstrating against those deemed unacceptable. The *parlements* also began to make effective use of *arrêts de règlement*, edicts which could set policy in those many areas not clearly covered by royal ordinances or custom. Nothing revealed more sharply the growing political capacity of the *parlement* of Paris than its refusal to register the Concordat of Bologna which it regarded as an unacceptable infringement of gallican liberties. When it did finally succumb to the enormous pressure exerted by Francis I the *parlement* made clear that the edict was registered under duress. Although the *parlementaires* were ultimately unable to defy the will of the king, it was also true that for his part he felt unable to dispense with registration. 'The whole episode' it has been observed, 'strengthened the court's political role and deepened the impression that royal legislation enforced against *parlementaire* advice or without recourse to customary processes was of doubtful validity'.[5] This was certainly the opinion of theorists like Seyssel.

It should not however be supposed that the restraints on the exercise of royal authority were wholly of an institutional and legal kind. Indeed it should be apparent, even from the preceding general survey of the political superstructure, that what was also at issue was the relationship between the monarchy and the privileged classes. Defence of provincial or urban liberties could be virtually synonymous with defence of the privileges of those who controlled the Estates and municipalities. Most obviously, the nobility through their possession of the land, their economic and legal domination of the peasantry and their capacity to use force, were a major obstacle to the extension of royal power. The great magnates, despite the burgeoning sense of national identity, had almost no sense of loyalty to either king or country. During the Hundred Years War significant and influential French houses had no qualms about putting their resources and their clients at the disposition of the English. In the early stages Godefroy d'Harcourt and Philippe de Navarre actually gave homage to Edward III. After the murder of Charles VI's brother at the instigation of his Burgundian cousin in 1407, the conflict degenerated into a murderous rivalry between branches of the royal family and their supporters which made it as much a civil war as a national one. Indeed even after the expulsion of the English, their aid was sought by those anxious to further their family interests. The League of the Public Weal brought together in rebellion with the king's brother the ducal houses of Burgundy, Brittany and Bourbon. When yet another Bourbon rebelled in 1523 he received support not only from Henry VIII but also from the Emperor Charles V.

This last episode was a classic illustration of the persistence of feudal

[5] Shennan, *Parlement of Paris*, p.197.

values and mechanisms in the relationship between king and magnates. Charles, duke of Bourbon, was the king's most powerful vassal. As constable of France and governor of Languedoc, he wielded enormous military and political authority and his territorial possessions comprised three duchies, seven counties, two viscounties and seven lordships. Within them he could raise troops, levy taxes, dispense justice and summon the Estates. The ducal administration included a high court of justice. In the early Italian campaigns Charles served the king well. Relations only deteriorated when Francis, on the death of the duke's wife, seized part of her territories to which he asserted a claim. Matters were not improved by fears that Charles intended to marry one of the emperor's sisters and it is possible that he unwisely declined to marry the queen-mother.[6] Whatever the precise truth in this case, land and lineage remained the mainsprings of noble activity. Relationships between the king and his magnates were personal ones, continuing to depend on a reciprocal recognition of patrimonial interest and honour, and were barely modified by notions of either sovereignty or nationality.

Even if nobles did not go so far as to break their allegiance, they retained an attachment to fighting which was not always in the crown's interest. During the Hundred Years War the roaming bands of mercenary soldiers were as much a threat to the populace as the enemy. After the Treaty of Arras in 1435 they laid waste to huge areas from the Ile-de-France to Languedoc, from Guyenne to Burgundy and even beyond. It should not be imagined that these noble leaders were merely small-time bandits. Although not quite in the ducal class, they included men of the highest distinction, former companions of Joan of Arc, who were capable of negotiating with the crown whilst murdering and pillaging. They established their own courts and treasuries. The crown responded as best it could. A number of high-ranking nobles were indicted for treason during the fifteenth century and some were executed. With the establishment of the *gendarmerie* it became treasonable for anyone to raise their own army without royal permission. The crown also claimed the sole right to collect taxes, the *cour des aides* declaring in 1412 that 'it is unlawful for any seigneur whoever he may be to take any tax whatsoever'. Nothing could have been plainer, but as the subsequent repetition of such legislation indicates, its implementation was a protracted and troublesome business.

Moreover the political loyalty of the upper classes required concessions. The most significant of these for the long-term future of France was the principle of tax exemption. Down to the end of the fourteenth century the nobility and clergy had by and large contributed to royal taxes; whatever concessions had been made were *ad hoc* and limited. It was not until the turbulent reign of Charles VI that the formal distinction between the privileged orders and the rest crystallized. In 1404 the king imposed a tax on the entire kingdom but exempted the nobles in arms, the clergy who were to pay an alternative tax, and paupers. Subsequently members of *parlement*, the *chambre des comptes* and the other royal officials were added to the list. Two

[6] R.J. Knecht, *Francis I* (Cambridge, CUP, 1982), pp.146 ff.

years later the nobles of Languedoc who did not engage in trade were exempted from the *tailles* and sales taxes. From this moment exemptions multiplied and the regime acquired the regressive tax structure which was to become one of its most characteristic features and a permanent impediment to the effective mobilization of the kingdom's wealth.

Yet even this fundamental concession extracted from the monarchy at a time of weakness did not satisfy the nobility. Their insistence on special treatment, perhaps intensified by the economic contraction of the late fourteenth century and the success of sections of the peasantry in winning concessions from them, grew ever more shrill. The great princes received partial satisfaction through the apanages, which they frequently ruled as mini-kingdoms with substantial judicial and economic powers. Where necessary this was supplemented by royal pensions and gifts. It has been estimated that up to half the revenues of the dukes of Burgundy at the beginning of the fifteenth century and half of those of the dukes of Bourbon at the end, came from royal sources. Nor was it only a handful of dukes that benefited; in 1423 the entire 13,000 *livres* owed in taxation by the county of la Marche together with sums due from *seigneuries* in Languedoc were conceded to the count. Louis XI surrendered the escheated holdings of the count of Armagnac to 24 people, virtually all nobles in royal service. In 1484 there were some 900 people—not all nobles—on the pension list and by 1523 the cost for 720 pensions came to 800,000 *livres*, approximately equivalent to the entire proceeds from the *aides*.

More than anything else, however, it is the system of governorships which best illustrates the subtly changing relationship between crown and nobility. For it was at one and the same time both an instrument for the extension of royal authority and a superb mechanism for the preservation of noble interests. The governorships, as their most recent scholar has stressed, were not a bureaucratic form of administration but a patrimonial one, bestowing on the holders immense powers of patronage. In the first place the governors had at their disposition all the places within the companies of *gendarmes* of which they were the captains, and were thus able to make or break the careers of those in search of fame and fortune. Not surprisingly the large majority of the troops in any company were inhabitants of the governorship of the commander, whilst the senior positions were invariably occupied by relatives. The *gendarmerie* was 'the Renaissance monarchy's compromise with the indigenous patron–client networks in the provinces'.[7]

Governors were also able to promote people to offices in their own frequently large households and to use their authority to appoint to royal offices within their jurisdiction. Many also participated in the selection of mayors and town councillors. Above all they acted as brokers at court, seeking offices, sinecures and pensions for their clients. This was encouraged by the crown. An increasingly important function of the four chancellery secretaries was to process the recommendations of the governors for the favour of the crown; requests and concessions were systematically recorded. Charles IX, when reprimanding a secretary for laxity in this respect,

[7] Harding, *Anatomy of a Power Elite*, p.25.

explained that 'without governorship nominations he had no way of filling vacancies, archbishoprics and offices of justice and finance and governments and captaincies with men of knowledge, sincerity, loyalty and value'.[8] The expansion of royal institutions notwithstanding, effective government depended on the ability of the crown to manipulate the personal and patrimonial ties which bound people together.

All too easily the system could, of course, work in the other direction. It is not without reason that provincial Estates and towns themselves began to lavish pensions and gifts on their governors. On becoming governor of Languedoc the duc de Montmorency received 12,000 *livres* and a lesser sum annually thereafter. When he fell from royal favour in 1541, Francis got rid of him by first abolishing and then re-establishing all the governors save he. Estates were forbidden henceforth to make payments to the governors. Suffice to say, the practice continued and governors to a greater or lesser degree continued to protect the interests of their provinces. Indeed, there was always a danger that the system would not merely go into reverse but break down completely. For the paradox of the Renaissance monarchy was that as its own power had grown, the various other loci of authority – provincial Estates, sovereign courts, *bureaux des finances*, municipalities – had themselves become institutionalized; at the same time the traditional feudal clans were absorbed by the clienteles around the governors. France became a realm of powerful corporate bodies, of privileged orders and venal office-holders, whilst the crown itself lacked a truly centralized administration, uniform laws or uniform taxes. In this situation the need to control patronage was actually greater than ever. The obverse of patronage was faction, and should patronage fail, faction would destroy the precarious equilibrium between the power of the monarchy and the multitude of restraints upon its full exercise.

The Crisis of the Sixteenth Century

Even a strong ruler like Francis I could not abolish faction. Indeed he directly contributed to the rivalries that beset the court and government by the favouritism displayed towards his youngest son, Charles d'Orléans, to the disadvantage of Henry, despite the fact that the latter had become heir to the throne on the death of the dauphin in 1536. Around the two surviving sons there developed strong factions, with Charles finding much support from his father's mistress, the duchesse d'Estampes, and her clientele whose careers and fortunes she assiduously promoted. Henry was backed by Anne de Montmorency to whom he was indebted for negotiating his release from Imperial custody in 1531 after four years as a hostage on his father's behalf. Montmorency's military prowess subsequently brought him the office of constable of France and for a period he dominated the political scene; but with the failure of his policy of *rapprochement* with the Empire, he lost both his position at court and his governorship of Languedoc.

Henry's loyalty however endured and his accession to the throne in 1547 brought with it the anticipated palace revolution. Old favourites and

[8] Harding, *Anatomy of a Power Elite*, p.32

advisers were swept aside. The duchesse d'Estampes was sued by her husband and even imprisoned for a time, whilst Montmorency returned in triumph. He was restored to his governorship of Languedoc, his brother to that of Paris and the Ile-de-France; four years later Montmorency was elevated from the ranks of the barons to become a duke and peer of the realm. Equally significant, however, was the arrival in the royal council of two sons of the duc de Guise, also nephews of the cardinal of Lorraine. One was François, comte d'Aumale, and the other Charles, archibishop of Rheims. Within a few months François had become a duke, whilst Charles acquired a cardinal's hat and virtually complete control of ecclesiastical patronage. For the moment nevertheless, they were obliged to share power with Montmorency. Only on the death of the king were the Guises able to carry their ambitions further. During the short reign of the sickly Francis II (July 1559–December 1560), who but 16 months earlier had wed their neice, Mary queen of Scots, they totally dominated the young king and secured a monopoly of patronage. Whilst the house of Lorraine and its dependents were paid their arrears of pensions or obtained new loans, their rivals were deprived of all royal largesse. Montmorency lost not only his place at court but also the county of Beaumont which he had been given in 1527. Not surprisingly there was a rush of people anxious to become Guise clients. It was said of François that in addition to the loyalty of 500 nobles, he had the support of 26 companies of *gendarmerie* summoned to the Orléanais in October 1560, ostensibly for the king's protection.

The intense antipathy of those excluded by the Guise monopoly of patronage was exacerbated by the acute financial distress of the monarchy, which made it necessary both to curtail pensions and, after 50 years of draining conflict, to come to terms with the equally exhausted Habsburgs. Either of these actions would have been sufficient to generate noble discontent, but together, at a time when inflation was eroding their revenues, they proved disastrous. But the crown had little choice. By the end of Francis's reign the debt to the Lyon bankers alone was over 2.4 million *livres* and in the years that followed the situation deteriorated rapidly. Henry II compounded the financial problems consequent upon the refusal to abandon the futile claims in Italy by dispensing millions of *livres* each year in gifts and pensions. Nearly all the *aides* and *gabelles* were alienated as well as some of the *tailles*. In 1547 for instance, he bestowed on his mistress all the revenues from the sale of office for a year, and in 1554 the duc de Guise obtained all the income from the internal tariff, the *traite d'Anjou*. To meet these soaring expenses it was necessary in 1557 to raise over 9.5 million from the *grand parti* of Lyon. Unfortunately in August the French army was defeated at St Quentin, precipating a wave of anxiety amongst the bankers, which steadied by the news of peace, then worsened on the death of the king during a tournament held to celebrate it. With the royal debt to the Lyonais at 11.7 million *livres*, interest payments ground to a halt and it became impossible to raise new loans. No less than an undeclared bankruptcy, these events precipitated the break-up of the consortium, permanently depriving the crown of any means for organizing a consolidated national debt.

This clearly was not the moment to have to cope with the demands of the nobility flocking back from the war. Deprived of their spoils, they returned to find that the prodigality associated with Henry was a thing of the past. Montmorency was not the only victim of the decision to recover royal domain alienated for non-military reasons. By December 1560 the Guises claimed that they had already reduced court and household expenditure by more than 2 million *livres*. Such a worthy achievement was however unlikely to impress those outside their clientele.

Hatred of the Guises for political and material reasons now fused with the mounting Protestant resistance to their policy of religious repression. Not surprisingly some of the major princely houses who had suffered from Guise pretensions quickly became associated with the Huguenot cause, bringing to it the prestige of their names and not inconsiderable resources. Although Montmorency himself remained attached to his Catholic faith, a number of his sons did not, whilst his celebrated nephews, Gaspard de Coligny – admiral of France — François d'Andelot — colonel general of the infantry — and the Cardinal Châtillon brought a considerable following of their own with them into the Protestant movement. Above all it was the early attachment of the Bourbon princes, Antoine, king of Navarre, and Louis, prince de Condé, that transformed the reform movement into a political force with all the benefits of powerful clientage systems. Around the great names there gathered those impelled by a variety of causes – hard times, greed, military ambition, religious conviction – frequently too confused to disentangle. The rising tensions finally erupted in the abortive Huguenot coup of March 1560 intended to capture the court and destroy the Guises. Although mostly the work of 'petty seigneurs of ancient lineage',[9] Condé was probably involved and was shortly arrested, to be saved from execution by the unexpected death of Francis II – an event which ushered in the regency of Catherine de Medici who quickly asserted her independence of the Guises in both political and religious affairs. Her determination to search for theological compromise and her decision, reflected in the edict of January 1562, to tolerate an organized Protestant Church, furnished the duc de Guise with a reason, or pretext, for leaving the court. He had indeed already formed the triumvirate for the defence of Catholicism with his former foe, Montmorency, and St André, a marshal of France. With the massacre of Protestants at Vassy in March 1562 by Guise and his followers, the descent into the maelstrom had begun.

It can readily be seen that the crisis which overtook France in the 1560s was precipitated by an essentially traditional nexus of factors. With the collapse of Valois dynastic ambitions abroad, itself a consequence of the excessive fiscal burdens required to sustain them, the latent antagonisms exploded into an open factional struggle for a share of the crumbling royal cake. This was then compounded by a long period of minority rule which allowed those at the centre of affairs to indulge in an old-fashioned and vicious feud for control of the government. Nor did the situation improve with the demise of some of the principal contestants in the first bout of fighting. True, the death of Antoine de Bourbon did allow Catherine to give his post of lieutenant general

[9] J.H.M. Salmon, *Society in Crisis. France in the sixteenth century* (London, Benn, 1975), p.125.

of the kingdom to Condé, but the assassination of the duc de Guise poisoned the atmosphere for years to come, particularly as Coligny was implicated. On his return from the council of Trent the Cardinal Lorraine took up the cudgels, refusing to accept a decree of the council absolving Coligny from responsibility. The traditional family enmity towards the Montmorencys was also renewed, partly because François de Montmorency, governor of Paris, prevented Lorraine from entering the city with an armed escort. Tensions mounted with the news of a Spanish force making its way along the eastern frontier, and fears that the court was in collusion with the Spanish contributed directly to a Protestant attempt to ambush the king in September 1567. Catherine's efforts to mediate failed partly because she fell ill and partly because of Condé's determination to retain links with the prince of Orange. For a while Guise regained the ascendancy, exerting notable influence over the heir apparent, the duc d'Anjou. After the death of Condé in battle and the return of peace in 1570 Catherine resumed her search for a *modus vivendi* by bringing Coligny back to court and reviving an old proposal to marry Henri de Navarre to her daughter Marguerite. But this time it was Coligny who proved unco-operative over the Netherlands connection, his insistent advocacy of an anti-Spanish military campaign in the Low Countries rendering all agreement impossible. Once again pent-up resentment and frustration led to violent solutions; an attempt on Coligny's life followed, which in turn sparked off the horrendous massacre of Protestants on St Bartholomew's night of 1572.

At court the already manifest antagonism between Anjou and his younger brother Alençon took a murderous turn when Alençon tried to do away with the heir-apparent during the siege of La Rochelle in 1572. Shortly, Anjou departed to become king of Poland, so Alençon transferred his malevolence to King Charles himself, becoming the focal point of yet another attempted coup in which Navarre and François de Montmorency were also involved. Catherine was obliged to arrest a number of them but somehow she survived, even after the death of Charles in May 1574, until Anjou returned in September as Henry III. Alençon continued, however, to make trouble at court, gathering around him an obnoxious crew of swordsmen, before finally escaping to place himself at the head of a powerful combination of malcontents and Huguenots. A key figure in this alliance was Damville, brother of François de Montmorency, and governor of the highly independent province of Languedoc. When Navarre also fled the court, the government was obliged to negotiate. The terms of the treaty, confirmed in the Edict of Beaulieu (May 1576), make abundantly clear what was at stake as far as the grandees were concerned. Henry I de Condé was restored to the governorship of Picardy, Navarre secured Guyenne, Damville retained Languedoc, whilst Montmorency recovered his various offices. The unscrupulous Alençon was bought off with apanages in Anjou (of which he took the title), Touraine and Berry.

Almost inevitably this settlement, which also gave the Huguenots extensive freedom of worship and the right to hold royal office, was unacceptable to the Guise faction, leadership of which had been assumed by the young Duke Henry after the death of the cardinal two years earlier. He now placed himself at the head of the emergent League for the Defence of Catholicism.

The king's first reaction was to try to capture the movement himself by instructing provincial governors to support the local associations and to endeavour to modify the militant, indeed radical, oaths sworn by their adherents. This tactic was moderately successful inasmuch as a number of malcontents were detached from their former allies, and Anjou himself accepted a command in the royal army sent against his former allies. Peace came in the autumn of 1578 but as soon as the various clans came together at court the old tensions erupted. The royal household became a hotbed of intrigue and prey to violent skirmishing involving the bully boys of both Anjou and Guise as well as the king's favourites. Eventually some of the latter met their death at the hands of the Guise retainers and Henri de Guise withdrew from court, thus initiating another bout of inconclusive warfare. Anjou departed for the Netherlands where he accepted the sovereignty of the rebels, involving himself in yet more unsuccessful adventures until his rather squalid life came to an end in 1584.

With this event the confusion of the factional conflicts resolved itself into a straightforward issue, for now Henri de Navarre, in the absence of any more royal sons, became heir to the throne. Immediately the forces of the Catholic League came together in a determined effort to bar his way to the throne and to preserve the religious purity of the realm. Once again Henry III tried to capture the leadership of the movement, refusing to reconcile himself with Navarre unless he abjured his faith. In July 1585 the government accepted the demands of the League revoking all treaties of pacification and concessions made to the Protestants. Guise obtained the governorship of Verdun, Toul and Chalons. This served only to whet his ambitions and usher in a further period of Guise domination, culminating in his entry into Paris, despite royal orders to the contrary, in the spring of 1588. Here he was sustained by the revolutionary movement known as the Sixteen which seized control of the municipality. The king, hoist by his own petard, fled the capital, only to capitulate once again. Guise was made lieutenant general of the kingdom and the Cardinal de Bourbon was acknowledged as heir-presumptive to the throne. Finally Henry III resolved to act in virtually the only way that was now possible. On 23 December Guise was summoned to the royal quarters where he was killed by the guards. His brother Cardinal de Guise was arrested and then murdered. It was a remarkable repetition of the events of 1563 and, as then, far from resolving matters, the assassinations heralded an intensification of conflict. Leadership of the League passed to the duc de Mayenne and royal control of large areas of the realm slipped away. The king was at last compelled to turn to Henri de Navarre for help. However, the alliance was never put to the test for in July 1589 Henry III was struck down by a fanatical Jacobin monk. Navarre now became Henry IV of France, at least in name. The League for its part was determined to prolong resistance and to elect its own Catholic king. Fortunately for Navarre the Leaguer princes could not agree on whom to select from possible claimants, and when Henry announced his decision to abjure in July 1593, the ground was cut from beneath them. 'Paris was worth a mass' it seemed; a statement which reveals much – not about the king's personality but about the very nature of the civil wars.

Factional conflict for control of the realm was compounded by the willingness of the participants to turn abroad for assistance. Indeed the few qualms they showed in doing so reveal the extent to which the loyalties of the French nobility were still determined, as they had been in the Hundred Years War, by concepts of individual honour, personal obligation and notions of lineage, rather than any sense of national consciousness. Although national interests were beginning to take shape and give rise, particularly in north-west Europe, to the phenomenon of inter-state relations, 'international affairs' were still to a remarkable degree an expression of rivalries which knew no national boundaries. At the beginning of the civil wars Condé and Coligny thought it perfectly natural to negotiate an alliance with Queen Elizabeth of England; towards the end, the duc de Guise was happy, along with others no doubt, to accept a pension from the Spanish king. Throughout the entirety of the fighting, foreign troops were on French soil in support of the various contestants. After the death of Henry III, as the struggle crystallized into a contest for the succession, the Spanish occupied large areas of north-eastern France and even had a garrison in Paris for a time. Particularly close ties developed between the Huguenot leaders and the Dutch rebels, in some cases reinforced by family ties – Coligny and his Montmorency cousins were all related to Horn, the Dutch nobleman executed by the Spanish. As we have seen, it was the fear of being drawn by Coligny into war in the Netherlands that helped to precipitate the chain of events leading to the massacre of St Bartholomew. Similarly illustrative of the part played by personal ties was the execution of Mary queen of Scots by Elizabeth in 1587, an event which in France served only to arouse Catholic passions and bolster the Guise cause.

It would of course be a mistake to assume that all the conflicts that beset provincial France during the civil wars simply revolved around the divisions amongst the princes and grandees. There were many who were not attached to any of the major households who had their own vendettas to pursue, or were occupied entirely with local issues. Nevertheless it was the collapse of efficient government engendered by the inability of the crown to control the magnates which released the constraints on a multitude of competing interests. Tavannes complained that 'he received different dispatches – those from Guise said kill them all, those from the Queen to save them all'.[10] Into the vacuum created by such lack of direction stepped those anxious to assert their own authority, to establish a personal power base or clientage system. One of the most remarkable features of the situation was the proliferation of subordinate 'governors'; some of these were actually commissioned by the crown to maintain order and combat sedition, but frequently they were mere captains of towns or garrisons who then usurped the title and functions of governor, or they were simply appointed by the princes and religious parties. By 1572 there were 24 governors in the diocese of Castres alone. Such were the protests that in 1576 Henry III suppressed all the governors created since 1562 but the order was not implemented. Left to their own devices, governors, legitimate or otherwise, rapidly developed their own organizations or put themselves at the head of the local religious associations. From

---

[10] Harding, *Anatomy of a Power Elite*, p.54.

1561 in Provence there existed a secret party led by the governor of Aix which attacked Calvinist assemblies. At Toulouse a 'league for the defence of the Catholic religion' was initiated by the *parlement*, the cardinals of Toulouse and Albi, the dukes of Joyeuse and Monluc together with several municipal governors. This league developed its own administration with provisions for raising an army within 30 days as well as the necessary taxes. The Calvinists established a similar regime in eastern and central Languedoc, obtaining 400,000 *livres* from the local Estates who put themselves at the service of the royal lieutenant. A permanent council was established for executive control. By the end of the first religious wars there were similar associations bound together by oaths under governors all over the south.

These however were merely the forerunners of the much better known Protestant Federation of the 1570s and the Catholic League of the 80s. Galvanized by the massacre of St Bartholomew, the Huguenots of the *midi* set about establishing assemblies in each town or region. These elected administrative councils of 24 which, in turn, sent representatives to a central assembly. They then appointed an executive council of 24, a legislative body of one hundred, and a supreme court. No member of the hundred was to assume military command, for which there was a separate hierarchy. Subsequently, the assembly appointed Condé as commander-in-chief and protector of the reformed churches and bestowed on him a civil council. The Catholic League differed in that it consisted of a number of autonomous associations each under the authority of provincial councils. Twenty-two are known to have existed in the provincial towns. In general these were dominated by nobles, urban notables, superior royal officers and upper ranks of the clergy. With the odd exception they were certainly much less democratic than the highly popular organization of the Sixteen which, resting on a combination of lesser judicial officers and priests, conducted the Parisian coup of 1585.

Such democratic characteristics that did manifest themselves were undoubtedly a source of irritation to the upper classes, who sought to use these organizations for their own power and profit. For them the collapse of central government offered a splendid opportunity to make good the loss of royal patronage. Crucial for this purpose was control of the towns or the support of the urban notables. Huguenot municipal magistrates diverted parts of the royal funds to Condé, whilst Catholic municipalities like Toulouse seized tax powers. In the 1570s the Protestant Federation simply commandeered the *bureaux des finances* and levied the traditional royal taxes. In addition it imposed *traites* on the territories that it controlled. When Henri de Navarre succeeded Condé as protector of the churches he was granted subsidies by the Huguenot assembly but subsequently raised taxes on his own authority. Similarly during the years of the League the provinces north of the Loire were largely in Guise hands and with them the royal revenues. Those collected at Dijon, Troyes, Rennes and Rouen were denied to the king, who was reduced to creating rival bureaux in the odd pockets that remained loyal. When Mayenne became leader of the League he took over the financial machinery in Champagne and usurped the authority of the crown *vis-à-vis* the Estates of Burgundy. Negotiating with them on his own behalf, he increased the *aides* and *traites*, sold offices, alienated the revenues from the royal domains, minted money, received the tithe and forced the province to sustain his court and household. Nor were the leaders of the great religious parties the only ones to operate in this way. In the county of Nevers the rulers revived their own *bureaux des finances, chambre des comptes* and even an administration for the *eaux et forêts*. The nobles of Guyenne seized tax powers, whilst municipal magistrates, as at Bordeaux from 1578, appropriated revenues for their own expenses. Despite repeated prohibitions on the appropriation of its funds and attempts to limit the powers of the governors, the government was frequently obliged to sanction the activities of both nobles and municipalities. Even in the interludes of peace the king had little alternative but to authorize the maintenance of troops by the nobles in order to prevent continued disturbances and pillaging. When the Edict of Nantes finally brought the years of strife to an end, it included a clause, similar to those contained in the earlier treaties, absolving all who had seized royal funds from responsibility, thus legitimizing their actions and their ill-gotten gains.

Not surprisingly the general fragmentation of authority also led to a resurgence of activity by a number of representative institutions. Sometimes this was directly stimulated by the factional struggle, as, for instance, in Lower Auvergne where the provincial governor, a Guise client, wished to levy the *taille*. Henri de Navarre also bolstered provincial estates in order to consolidate his support and is said to have provided 'an admirable model for a constitutional King' in his hereditary lands.[11] Generally however, it was the combination of the need to take measures for local self-defence and the equally desperate need for the crown to replenish its coffers that gave renewed life to provincial Estates and local assemblies. In Upper Auvergne the towns and provostships met regularly for their own defence, whilst in the Agenais the third estate met with such regularity that it acquired a virtually separate identity. The provincial Estates of Guyenne met at least 46 times between 1561 and 1581 to vote taxes that were then collected by the assemblies of the *recettes* and *sénéchaussées*. In Provence it proved impossible to summon the Estates with sufficient speed and there developed from 1578 an additional if smaller representative body known as the assembly of the communities; this included representatives of 19 towns, the consuls and archbishop of Aix and two representatives of both the clergy and nobility.

Some Estates conducted a prolonged resistance to the ever insistent royal demands for aid. Those in Normandy demanded that it be reduced to the levels of Louis XII's reign, and in 1579 refused to grant any funds without a settlement of their grievances; these amounted to a comprehensive demand for reform of both Church and state, including an investigation of financial abuses, the suppression of the treasurers, the *bureaux des finances* and the *élections*. When Henry III gave his consent they impertinently demanded it in writing. Similarly in Brittany the Estates put up a consistent resistance to tax demands, refusing outright in 1573 to grant 90,000 *livres* for the war against

[11] J.R. Major, *Representative Government in Early Modern France* (New Haven, Yale University Press, 1980), p.253.

the Huguenots. Five years later the Estates of Burgundy, instead of agreeing to a request for aid, asked that the king be held accountable for his debts to the province and declined to pay until they had been liquidated.

Although many municipalities found themselves firmly wedded to one or other of the dominant factions, this helped them also to ignore royal legislation of which they disapproved. The edict of 1581 ordering the establishment of closed guilds on the Parisian model for every craft could only be implemented in those towns where royal officials were in control. There were also some important urban centres which threw off not only government control but that of the grandees as well. La Rochelle, although the home of the council of Jeanne d'Albret in the years after the massacre of St Bartholomew, profited from the turmoil to establish its status as a quasi-independent commune. It obtained almost total exemption from royal taxes, freedom of governor and garrison and recognized no authority save that of the mayor under the king. At the same time it was granted a special status in the Huguenot organization which was allowed to impinge on its autonomy no more than the crown. Underpinning this political independence was an economic prosperity fostered by the burgeoning Atlantic trade and the profits from the lucrative wine and salt trades. The great Mediterranean port of Marseille likewise sustained an impressive array of privileges and for a time in the 1590s was ruled by a sort of popular Catholic dictatorship which acknowledged no authority but its own. If other urban centres could not match the combination of political independence and prosperity displayed by La Rochelle and Marseille, they none the less exploited the weakness of the crown to good effect, obtaining confirmations of ancient charters and fiscal privileges.

In addition to the obstruction of the grandees, provincial assemblies and municipalities, the crown once again, after an interlude of over 50 years, had to contend with that of the Estates-General. Compelled to summon this body in the worst moments of crisis, the net effect was to confirm the useless nature of the Estates as an instrument of effective government. The meeting of 1558, called in the aftermath of the French defeat at St Quentin, was marked by a distinct reluctance to consider the request for 6 million *livres*, of which a third was sought from the clergy and the remainder from the closed towns. Only the loss of Calais shook the deputies out of their lethargy, but the loan still had to be negotiated with individual towns. In 1560, in contrast to the practice under Charles VII and Louis XI, the deputies assembled and deliberated by order instead of together. Although this deprived them of the initiative in their dealings with government, it also made it much more difficult for the crown to make progress. In order to do so the chancellor was obliged to permit the Estates to appoint a committee to oversee the collection of taxes; at the same time he promised substantial economic reforms including measures for the recovery of the royal domain and alienated taxes, as well as for the repayment of royal debts. In the event, his concessions yielded nothing from either the second or third estates, but the clergy, meeting at Poissy the following year, did agree to provide a total of 22.6 million *livres* over a 16-year period. No further central assemblies were summoned until 1576 when, once again, the crown was compelled to give way before the widespread pressure for a presentation of grievances. These Estates also came at a moment when Henry III was endeavouring to outflank the Catholic League by supporting it, and there was a strong League presence amongst the deputies of all three orders. However, although the king agreed to resume the war against the Huguenots if the necessary finance was offered, the third estate was by no means agreed on such a crusade. Some of the extreme Leaguers left in disgust and the king was quite unable to persuade the deputies to support any of the proposals for raising additional revenue or for reforming the tax system. Indeed the third estate demanded outright cancellation of all *gabelles*, a reduction of tax farmers' profits, a diminution in the number of royal officers, fewer pensions and an investigation into the wealth of the tax officials. For some of their demands they received support from the nobility who, for instance, joined with them in seeking abolition of the *élus*. Yet, even on this, the measure of agreement was limited, for whilst the nobles recommended that the functions of the *élections* be taken over by the *bailliages*, the third estate suggested that they be transferred to the towns. Similarly the third estate's anxiety about the scale of pensions distanced them from the nobility, whose own preoccupation was to limit the acquisition of noble status by commoners.

Given the obstructionism and division that characterized the Estates of 1576, it was not surprising that when next the government turned to questions of fiscal reform it should choose an alternative method. In late 1583 it summoned as assembly of notables consisting of 66 nominated experts from the royal council and the sovereign courts, together with a number of prelates and magnates. This did succeed in producing a series of proposals for commonsense reforms; had the situation allowed, something might have been achieved with regard to corruption, excess bureaucracy, venality, the royal debts and the recovery of the royal domain. But the eruption of the activities of the League and the domination of the duc de Guise forced the king in 1588 to bow before his demands for a further Estates-General. Despite the overwhelmingly Leaguer character of this gathering, the deputies were as hostile as ever towards the royal requests for funds to prosecute the war, insisting instead that the *partisans* and *traitants* should be squeezed. They also demanded the calling of provincial Estates. By the time the assassination of the Guise brothers brought the unsatisfactory proceedings to an effective end, the demise of the Estates-General as an integral part of the machinery of government was almost a foregone conclusion.

Had the deputies of 1576 been more amenable to royal requests, it is conceivable that they might have secured for the Estates a continuing rôle. Although they raised the question of consent to taxation more clearly and more stridently than ever, the Estates failed to see that it was necessary to give, as well as to obstruct, if a permanent influence was to be achieved. From their point of view it was perhaps foolish to turn down the king's proposition that they appoint a representative to confer with his officials about the fiscal crisis. For one scholar at least the Estates-General of 1576 was possibly 'the last chance for the nation to turn down a road other than the one leading to divine right monarchy'.[12] The merit of such a judgment

---

[12] Wolfe, *Fiscal System*, p.165.

appears to be confirmed by the fact that the clergy in return for their concessions at Poissy, which they subsequently renewed, were able to bargain with the king and secure a place in the constitutional arrangements of the *ancien régime*. They managed to preserve the fiction that the financial promises constituted a 'free gift' and, despite the enormous sums extracted from them in forced loans, through sale of Church property, taxes on benefices and sales of ecclesiastical offices, retained full administrative control over the entire process. By 1586 the clergy acquired the right to meet every 10 years to renew or adjust the contract with the king and to hold smaller assemblies every two years for the verification of accounts (later amended to five-year intervals). Such assemblies offered both a useful mechanism for putting pressure on the government and a means of obtaining confirmation of exemption from royal taxes as far as the personal wealth and activities of the clergy were concerned. In other words, in return for surrendering a share of its massive wealth, the Church succeeded in maintaining the privileged status of its members.

With the fading of the Estates-General the principal forum of political activity became the *parlement* of Paris. This, as we have seen, was not a representative body but a judicial corporation increasingly confident in its own capacity to act in an independent manner. Despite the peril to the country, the *parlementaires* were remarkably resistant at critical moments to the policies of the royal council. Right from the beginning of the wars they objected, for instance, to the attempt to distinguish between rebellion and heresy and constantly opposed policies aimed at finding a religious compromise. In addition, they compounded the crown's fiscal problems by refusing to register financial edicts. In 1578 Henry III sent 22 such edicts to the *parlement*, two of which it registered and the remainder it rejected on the grounds that they were oppressive. In some instances only by resorting to *lits de justice* and descending on the *parlement* in person was the king able to have his way. All this gave the idea of consent to taxation a further boost, and in 1586 the first president of the *parlement* went as far as to claim that the right to register financial edicts was a fundamental law of the realm. Above all the *parlementaires* conducted a determined resistance to proposals for reform which would have eroded their position as owners of office. Thus the Edict of Orléans (1561) which called for the suppression of offices created since Louis XII, the banning of judicial pluralism and the prohibition of relatives sitting on the same bench, ran into immense difficulties. Its registration was so long delayed that Chancellor Michel de l'Hôpital felt compelled to warn the magistrates that they were instituted to render justice, not meddle in the legislative process. Nevertheless, when the edict was finally registered it contained revisions insisted on by the *parlement*. Throughout the years that followed, its defence of vested interest was a significant impediment to fundamental reform. Moreover, unlike the Estates-General, the *parlement* had established a place for itself in the constitutional structures of the regime; its support which gave legitimacy to the actions of the crown became more, not less essential as the crisis deepened.

However the responsibility for the failure of reform should not entirely be laid at the door of the government's critics and opponents; for the crown itself could not afford to press too vigorously for a reduction in venality or the profits of the tax farmers and financiers. At the beginning of the wars royal debts were an estimated 43 million *livres*; the assembly of notables calculated that in 1583 they had risen to a prodigious 114 million. Although crown revenues had also soared from 13 million *livres* in 1576 to reach 23.5 million, excluding the proceeds from sale of office and extraordinary levies on towns, the deficit was clearly unmanageable. There were repeated crises of liquidity. With the collapse of the Lyon consortium, venality of office and the operations of *traitants* and *partisans* became indispensible, their institutionalization unavoidable.

Even if the contemporary estimate that by 1588 the revenue from the *parties casuelles* constituted a third of the total was exaggerated, there was no doubting its significant rôle. Despite the repeated proclamations of the government that it would abolish or reduce venality, and despite the widespread support such a policy would have enjoyed, it became none the less an evil necessity. The system of the *alternatif* (see above, p.21), more or less cancelled by Francis II, was not only restored by Charles IX but extended to cover an increasing number of officials. Hundreds of offices with useless functions were created and sold; thus in 1583 all persons who sold fish in the towns were obliged to take an oath and purchase their office. All the smaller salt distribution bureaux were upgraded to have a full complement of eight officials. Towns, *bailliages*, parishes, *élections* were blanketed at various moments with new alternative or additional officials and in every institution and community the numbers rose. At the beginning of the century for instance the population of Dijon included 600–700 officers; by its end there were 1,200. Moreover despite occasional vacillations in official policy, the vast majority of offices became both inheritable and, subject to the 40-day clause, transferable. From all of this no one benefited more than the financiers who bought up offices and the associated tax farms and revenues.

Conversely no one suffered more than the productive sectors of the population on whom fell the burden of an ever-growing but parasitic bureaucracy. In effect what began to take shape was a gigantic mechanism for extracting the wealth of the country, the adverse consequences of which were compounded by the ebbing away of the economic prosperity of the early decades of the sixteenth century. Even before the onset of fighting there were clear signs of strain within the economy as the countryside struggled to furnish the rapidly expanding population, much of it urban, with grain. Mounting inflation, partly caused by the pressure on agricultural produce, partly by the influx of Spanish silver, was already widening the gulf between rich and poor. Whilst those with something to sell grew rich, the ranks of the indigent were vastly swollen. Indeed much of the urban expansion was not due to prosperity but to the influx of the poor from the countryside where meagre plots of land no longer sufficed to sustain the occupants. Many nobles with fixed revenues were also badly hit by inflation.

Open warfare intensified all these strains both by virtue of the fiscal burdens it generated and by the devastating consequences in those areas – and there were many – directly affected by the fighting. From the 1570s the rise in population – continuous from the mid fifteenth century – came to an end and was even reversed in some regions. By the 1580s evidence of a dramatic collapse of payments of the tithe, feudal dues and rents, sometimes falling to a mere half of their customary levels, can be culled from regions as far apart as the Ile-de-France and Languedoc, Burgundy and the Charentais. Either production itself had collapsed or the tenants were simply unable to meet all the burdens imposed on them. The numbers of substantial peasant holdings tended to diminish, a process exacerbated in some regions by the success of the nobility in transforming their tenants into share-croppers. Mostly however it was the urban office-holders who benefited, buying up the lands of impoverished nobles and peasants alike, and then consolidating their position by money-lending and speculating in grain or other produce.

The diminished vitality of the rural economy was inevitably reflected in both the trading and manufacturing sectors of the economy, for these depended on it both for the provision of goods for exchange and as a market for manufactured articles. In eastern France the slackening of commercial activity was also intensified by the general shift of activity to the Atlantic; by 1580 the tax farms on the north–south trade axis at Chalons and Arles were yielding no more than a third of the revenue of the 1540s. Textile manufac-turing was also in dire straits. In some towns within the orbit of Paris – Meaux, Melun, St Denis, Senlis – production ceased entirely. In Lyon the disappearance of perhaps three quarters of the banking houses was com-pounded by a grave situation in the silk industry. There were however some notable exceptions to this bleak picture as most of the western ports continued to enrich themselves through overseas trade and Marseille sustained itself through ventures in both the Levant and Atlantic. Yet such exceptions only confirm that one of the major consequences of the general disruption of activity was to reinforce the fragmented nature of the French economy. Thus whilst the merchants of Marseille dominated the Levantine trade, their influence within France hardly extended beyond Provence; detectable at Arles, Pézenas and Cannes, it faded out at Lyon and was barely discernible at Toulouse. In the west the great commercial centre of La Rochelle was similarly isolated, cut off from the interior by marshes and essentially dependent on the salt, wine and other produce which came down the small rivers of the region. Even more striking as an indicator of the lack of integration of the French economy is the fact that of 4,000 letters of exchange dealt with in Lyon between 1570 and 1574 only 10 were from French merchants. Economic activity in each of these centres was more dependent on affairs beyond the realm than on any links between them, revealing very clearly the unintegrated character of the domestic economy. Indeed there was no such thing as the French economy; rather there existed a number of regional economies – that of the eastern provinces drawn into the orbit of Germany and the Rhine, that of the northern and western provinces increasingly dominated by the Dutch and that of the *midi* under the pull of the Mediterranean. The lack of commercial integration was reinforced by significant variations in agricultural practices and systems of exploitation. Whilst the north, the great cereal-growing region of France, was a land of open fields and three-fold crop rotation, of a semi-proletarianized peasantry, concentrated hamlets and nuclear families, the western provinces by contrast were characterized by hedgerows and small fields, two-fold crop rotation, scattered dwellings and many multiple or extended households providing for their own needs. Even within a region there could be marked contrasts as in Upper Normandy between the *pays* de Caux and the *pays* de Bray. The former was a zone of open fields and mixed farming sustaining a prosperous peasantry and petty nobility, the latter a poorer one with large stretches of grazing land, supplemented by rural textile production around Dieppe and Rouen.

Given continued economic growth and peace no doubt the regional and local imbalances could have provided the basis for a lively national market notwithstanding the difficulties of long-distance communication. As it was, the combination of fiscal pressures and the violent disruption of economic exchange prolonged the existence of regional and local economies whose essential function was to feed and cloth their own populations. Particularly in the large urban centres a prime concern of the authorities was to enforce regulations ensuring that supplies of essential foodstuffs were available in the market-place. In this, as in other ways, the difficulties of the late sixteenth century reinforced the preoccupation of the urban oligarchies with the defence of their particular privileges and interests. They certainly regarded each other as rivals rather than as members of a class bound by common economic interests, an attitude which mirrored the actual state of affairs.

In this context, sale of office and tax farming were perfectly explicable attempts to overcome the difficulties of tapping the wealth of provincial France. Yet such devices were manifestly counter-productive, largely serving to exacerbate social tensions and generate unrest. In the first place, sale of office was an affront to the values and interests of the traditional nobility who, resentful of the emergent office-holding nobility, the *noblesse de robe*, never ceased to complain that virtue and blood were no longer rewarded. It was also extremely vexatious to the lesser men of the legal world – the *procureurs* and lawyers – who found the route to high office barred, whilst peasants and artisans united in their hatred for the proliferating fiscal agents. Moreover the competition for precious resources inflamed all the existing antagonisms, not just between the royal agents and the local communities but also between one faction and another, between nobles and peasants, one corporate body and the next.

French society began to disintegrate. The nobility developed new codes of honour which allowed them to slaughter each other in senseless bouts of duelling. Deaths mounted higher than in any other country, including Italy from whence the custom had been imported, and the rules were frequently forsaken for ambushes and underhand attacks. In between fighting each other the nobles turned to humbler prey. Lawless bands of nobles, reminiscent of those of the Hundred Years War, roamed the countryside. As previously, these were sometimes companies of the official forces. Damville's brother apparently led a troop which specialized in rape, ransom and horse theft. Lesser men imitated their betters. A certain captain Merle terrorized the hill towns of the Gévaudan and Auvergne for 10 years. Royal regulations which made it illegal to take a horse out of garrison during off-duty periods or for groups of more than 10 to assemble at such times were to no avail. The *gendarmerie* as a method of absorbing and controlling upper-class violence was clearly a failure. Unfortunately mercenary troops to which the crown increasingly turned could create equal devastation, particularly if they were not paid promptly.

Finally the populace erupted. In 1578–80 bitterness at excessive taxation, resentment of the soldiery and class antagonism exploded in a wave of uprisings which swept the eastern provinces. In Provence 600 Leaguer nobles were massacred as they slept; in Dauphiné peasant and artisan unrest culminated in the uprising at Romans – now famous through Le Roy Ladurie's study of it[13] – where the municipal authorities were overthrown. A central demand was that the privileged should pay a fair share of taxes. Brutally suppressed, these movements were none the less merely a prelude to the enormous revolts which gathered momentum in Brittany, Normandy, Périgord and the Limousin between 1589 and 1595. In Normandy something like 16,000 people were involved and in Périgord perhaps 40,000 were assembled at one time. Whilst the Norman uprisings seem to have been essentially directed at the soldiery and against the *taille*, the Breton revolts took a much more anti-noble turn, marked most dramatically by the massacre of 60 nobles at a wedding party. Deeply religious, the Breton peasantry however lost something of their effectiveness by their willingness to support the League whose noble leaders rarely lost an opportunity to turn on their turbulent followers. Similar interplay of religious and social conflicts led directly to the abandonment of the Normandy peasants by their noble leaders, thus providing the opportunity in 1589 for the royal forces to wipe out 3,000 of them. In contrast, the uprising of the Croquants, which from 1593 (with the exception of Limousin) involved the entirety of the western provinces from Quercy to Poitou, was characterized by the absence of religious differences. These were put aside in the pursuit of a united resistance to the oppressors of the common people; each parish produced a company with its own officers which 'in battle order with drum beating and flag unfurled'[14] then marched to join up in huge mass assemblies. From the proclamations issued, it is clear that the main objects of their wrath were the soldiers, the *taille*, the vexations of their seigneurs, the tax officials and the urban notables. They demanded formal representation of the *plat pays* through the election of a syndic, reduction of the *taille* and that the nobility should pay taxes on their non-noble properties. Although the Estates of Périgord (in 1595) refused to entertain these demands, the Croquants were never suppressed and all arrears of taxes were cancelled.

The one element of the civil wars which has not yet been discussed as a factor in its own right is the religious one. This has been deliberately left aside in order to emphasize not only the extent to which the strife is explicable in non-religious terms, but also its profoundly traditional nature; the crisis of the sixteenth century clearly had its roots in processes which stretched back into the distant past and many of its fundamental features were little different from those which had characterized the Hundred Years

[13] E. Le Roy Ladurie, *Carnival* (London, Scolar Press, 1979).
[14] *Chroniques de Jean Tarde*, ed. G. de Gerard (Paris, 1887); cited by Salmon, *Society in Crisis*, p.285.

War. Yet, as is apparent, even from the earlier analysis, religion cannot really be separated out in this manner. Genuine revulsion against simony, nepotism and pluralism within the Church reinforced resentment of those who monopolized ecclesiastical patronage; religious egalitarianism and dislike of the rich and powerful – most clearly displayed by the supporters of the Paris Sixteen – went hand in hand. To every factional rivalry religious antagonisms brought a new dimension. In Provence, Guyenne and Champagne the families of the provincial governors split over questions of faith. Representative institutions were likewise torn apart. For six years there existed two provincial Estates and two assemblies of the communities in Provence. Urban rivalries were inevitably intensified; thus in the Périgord, Bergerac became Protestant, whilst Périgueux and Sarlat remained Catholic. Further south militantly Catholic Toulouse was but a day's ride from the great Huguenot stronghold of Montauban.

For the crown such religious disunity was not merely an additional problem compounding all others, but a frontal assault on the essentially religious nature of monarchy itself, a direct challenge to divinely bestowed authority; an authority granted to kings precisely so that, through just and virtuous rule, they might maintain the integrity and good order of the body politic, which would in turn reflect and sustain the harmony of God's universe. Religious dissent thus constituted an intolerable threat to the natural political and social order. Not that at first French Protestantism was perceived in this fashion, for during the early decades of the sixteenth century it was often difficult to distinguish between those labelled 'Lutheran' and those better described as Christian Humanists. Certainly there was an absence of clearly defined confessions of faith. Only in October 1534 with the celebrated 'affair of the placards' when attacks on the Catholic doctrine of the mass were posted up in public places in Paris, did the issues crystallize sufficiently to reveal the radical nature of Protestant beliefs. The response of the authorities was immediate; hundreds of heretics were deprived of their property or imprisoned, whilst not a few died at the stake. If in the years that followed, Francis, perhaps inhibited by some inner qualms as well as the need to reassure his Protestant allies, did not follow a consistently repressive policy, the general stance of the government was nevertheless clear. It equated heresy with sedition. This view led logically to the *parlement* being granted its wish to have supreme control over such matters, the traditional prerogatives of the ecclesiastical courts notwithstanding. Francis also gave official backing to the articles drawn up by the Sorbonne enunciating the basic tenets of Catholic dogma, worship and organization as well as to its index of proscribed books. During the last years of his reign prosecutions by the *parlement* rose steadily. Its commissioners were despatched into the countryside with full powers of investigation and punishment, thus preparing the way for the work of the *chambre ardente*, a special chamber of the *parlement* created in 1547 to deal solely with cases of heresy. Some of the provincial *parlements* lent a willing hand; at Toulouse there were 200 prosecutions between 1540 and 1549 and 18 death sentences.

Yet not only did the French Reformation continue to gather momentum, but many of those who fled to Geneva returned to France from the mid 1550s as trained and disciplined evangelists for the Calvinist faith. The 'Lutheran' congregations began to give way before the highly organized Calvinist churches which took root in the main towns. With the collapse of royal authority in 1560 these were then reinforced by a massive flood of noble adhesions to the cause, many no doubt repelled by the Guise brothers' savage defence of Catholic orthodoxy. The Huguenot party was now sufficiently strong to leave Catherine de Medici with little alternative but to search for some sort of religious compromise. Yet this required (amongst other impossibilities) that the *parlement* also moderate its stance, which it steadfastly refused to do. Its response to the Edict of Pacification of January 1562 was to dispatch a deputation to court with remonstrances reminding the king that it was impossible for two religions to co-exist within a state, for such a policy would result in the ruin of the state itself. On the contrary, the correct policy was to suppress all forms of Protestant proselytizing. Only after a three-month delay and under intense pressure did the magistrates finally agree to register the edict and then with serious reservations designed to reflect their belief that it was merely a temporary expedient. Registration of the subsequent peace treaties favourable to the Huguenots – Amboise (1563), Longjumeau (1568), St Germain (1570), La Rochelle (1573) – were all 'carried without the usual ceremony and before the Grand Chambre alone.'[15] One or two of the provincial *parlements* took their resistance even further. The *parlement* of Aix instead of registering the Edict of Amboise reproduced an earlier decision declaring Catholicism the only lawful faith. So determined were the magistrates, the crown was obliged to suspend the most recalcitrant.

The strength of their position lay in the fact that their insistence on the incompatibility of religious diversity with the interests of the state merely articulated the conventional wisdom shared by the overwhelming majority of Frenchmen, including those ultramontane Catholics who otherwise resented the interference of the *parlements* in ecclesiastical matters.[16] Moreover this viewpoint appeared to receive its justification in the increasing tendency amongst Huguenot writers and leaders to emphasize the limitations on royal authority even to the point of legitimizing resistance. Up to a point Protestant apologists were doing no more than reflect the general resurgence of constitutional ideas discernible in the late 1560s, and at first their justifications for resistance amounted to little more than an amplification of the checks on royal power envisaged so many years before by Seyssel. Condé's manifesto of 1567 appealed to the ancient constitution of France, which he said 'was a monarchy limited from its origin by the authority of the nobility and the communities of the provinces and the great towns of the kingdom'. However in the aftermath of the massacre of St Bartholomew, a straightforward claim to be the true defenders of the traditional constitution was an inadequate basis on which to promote mass resistance or indeed the

[15] Shennan, *Parlement of Paris*, p.212.
[16] Ultramontane was the word used to describe representatives or supporters of the papacy north of the Alps. From the early eighteenth century it has been used to describe those most zealous for papal authority.

establishment of an autonomous Huguenot organization. In a spate of tracts and pamphlets Protestant writers now wove together a variety of strands of thought in a powerful justification of armed struggle. Firstly Seyssellian notions of *la police* were consolidated by historical investigations of the French constitution. The most famous work of this type was Hotman's *Francogallia* (1573) which sought to demonstrate the elective origins and character of the monarchy and to accord a supreme rôle to the Estates-General. In order to enhance the appeal of his work Hotman carefully supplemented traditional notions of the contractual relationship between king and subjects by incorporating suggestions from Calvin's writings to the effect that representative institutions possessed a restraining power. Other theorists developed these arguments by utilizing the idea drawn from the early German reformers that 'inferior magistrates' were themselves ordained by God and thus acquired not merely the right but the duty to resist tyrannical kings. There was also an increasing tendency to suggest that the 'inferior magistrate' drew his power from the people who merely delegated their authority to him. Some pushed this line of reasoning even further, arguing that political authority was only established by the consent of the people whose natural existence was one of liberty; this was sacrificed on condition that rulers maintained their obligation to ensure the welfare of the subjects. All these currents of thought finally culminated in that truly magnificent synthesis, Du Plessis Mornay's *Vindiciae Contra Tyrannos* of 1579. The central argument of this work, into which all others were neatly slotted, is that royal authority rests on two contracts: one made between the king and the representatives of the people, and the other between both of these on the one hand and God on the other. The magistrates (and here Mornay gave the crucial rôle, albeit not an exclusive one, to the *parlement*) thus have a responsibility both to God and people to uphold the rule of law. Failure to fulfil their obligations, even if that required the use of force against unjust and ungodly kings, renders the magistrates guilty of the same crime or sin.

It should not be thought that such views were the exclusive property of the Huguenots. Indeed some of them were partly derived from earlier Catholic thinkers, whilst the militant supporters of the League exploited with equal ease the sort of constitutional ideas propounded by Hotman. The League of 1576 declared its intention of restoring the 'rights, pre-eminences, franchises and ancient privileges as they were in the time of Clovis', whilst the Leaguer Estates-General of 1588 exalted the claims of that body with an unequivocal assertion of its right to consent to taxation. Moreover, in order to justify their attempt to deny the succession to Henri de Navarre and to replace him with their own candidate, the League was obliged to espouse theories of elective monarchy. Not only that, but Catholic theologians were vigorous in resurrecting arguments stretching back to the ancient world about the lawfulness of killing tyrants. Much less restrained than the Huguenots, who remained extremely cautious about extending rights of resistance beyond the magistrates, Catholic writers moved steadily towards a position which allowed any individual to strike down a tyrant. Such a view was further buttressed by a renewal of papal claims to depose secular rulers. In 1586 the Jesuit Bellarmine produced the first volume of his exceedingly inflammatory

Controversiae in which he argued that the pope possessed an indirect authority over kings. Three years later Sixtus V not only excommunicated Henry III but declared his subjects absolved from their natural allegiance; three months after that the king was assassinated by the Dominican monk Jacques Clément.

2

The Drive to Absolutism

Henry IV is one of the most celebrated of French Kings with a secure reputation as a maker of war, love and epigrammatic witticisms. The contrast between such a versatile ruler and his inadequate predecessor could not have been more marked. This fact underlined by the return of peace and a measure of prosperity as France entered the seventeenth century has unfortunately encouraged a tendency to overlook or underestimate the continuing fragility of royal authority.

When Henry succeeded to the throne the Catholic League was in control of Paris, most of the major towns of the north, and large parts of eastern France. Despite the acute factional rivalries and social tensions that afflicted the League, and the inability of the Estates-General convoked by Mayenne in 1593 to agree on a rival candidate for the throne, its resistance was not effectively broken until Henry abjured his faith in July of that year. During the course of 1594 nearly all the Leaguer towns were recovered and most of the great magnates settled with the king. But there were those, bolstered by support from Spain against whom war was declared in early 1595, who were determined to prolong the struggle. In Brittany the duc de Mercoeur fought on until early 1598. For their part the Protestant grandees, alarmed by Henry's conversion, also made life difficult for him. In 1597 the dukes of Bouillon and La Tremouille not only refused to bring their forces to the relief of Amiens when it was taken by the Spanish, but also began to seize royal revenues. Allegedly over 1,200 nobles from the Limousin and the Auvergne had committed themselves in support, whilst in response the Catholics of Auvergne and the neighbouring regions began to form their own association. However with the almost simultaneous declaration of peace with Spain and promulgation of the Edict of Nantes (April and May 1598) the realm entered its most peaceful decade for half a century. Not that the magnates abandoned their old ways; even the execution of the duc de Biron for treason in 1602 failed to deter others from intriguing against Henry, sometimes with a degree of success. The cast-off royal mistress Henriette d'Entragues pressurized the king into legitimizing her son, although her accomplice the comte d'Auvergne, himself the son of Charles IX by Marie Touchet, ended up in prison. The troublesome Bouillon threatened to use his strategically placed principality of Sedan and his family connections with the German Protestant princes to lend support to a Huguenot uprising. In the event the plot fizzled out and Bouillon submitted to the king in 1606, securing however a pardon and confirmation of all his offices. Three years later the prince de Condé, fearing that the king had designs on his wife, fled to the Spanish Netherlands, an event which precipitated the mobilization of the army.

Henry's major problem was to find the wherewithal both to buy off those whose loyalty could be bought and to sustain the forces necessary for the restoration of law and order.[1] Sully later estimated that it cost 42 million *livres* to buy off the leaders of the League, an inflated figure which recent scholarship indicates should be scaled down to 24 million. Nevertheless this imposed an enormous strain on royal resources. In the crucial year of 1594 gifts to individuals reached 5 million, whilst the secret expenses of the crown were recorded as 13 million, a figure not reached again until 1626. The governor of Orléans received 250,000 *livres* for opening his gates, whilst Villars Brancas who delivered Rouen allegedly obtained 715,000 *livres* in addition to the post of admiral of France. The son of Henri de Guise settled for the governorship of Provence. The comte d'Auvergne received an annual pension of 100,000 *livres* and in 1598 the king issued instructions that he was to be paid before the Swiss mercenaries in order to prevent him from fomenting trouble. This itself was a risky policy. In 1590 a fortnight had been lost after the royal victory at Ivry whilst demands for arrears of pay were dealt with; at one moment in 1595 the Swiss refused to cross the Marne. The king survived only by increasing the burdens on the population to the limits of endurance and by defaulting both on debts to his foreign allies and to the holders of *rentes*, who by 1595 were nine years in arrears. Nor was Henry given much assistance by his officers and magistrates. On the contrary, the *Chambre des Comptes* issued a scathing denunciation of the scale of pensions and gifts, attacked the maladministration of the royal debts and together with the *parlement* strenuously resisted the sale of further offices. Some of the provincial Estates proved equally obdurate. Asked for a contribution of 396,000 *livres* in 1596 those of Rouergue could muster only 180,000. Quercy furnished only a quarter of the 400,000 requested. By the summer of 1596 the financial administration was in a state of collapse. Henry was obliged to cease campaigning and agreed to summon an assembly of notables to discuss financial reform. This met at Rouen between November and the following January. Its principal proposals were for a 5 per cent sales tax and the division of the royal revenues into two funds, one for war and the royal household, the other for the repayment of the contracted debts. In addition it was agreed that there should be an investigation into the malversation of the financiers. However in face of widespread resistance the sales tax eventually had to be abandoned, funds continued to be diverted for military purposes so that those appointed to administer the repayment of the debts found they had nothing to administer, whilst the investigation of the financiers was suspended in return for a payment of 378,000 *livres*; in effect this was nothing more than yet another forced loan and was itself raised by financiers.

Only the peace of 1598 restored some freedom of manouevre to the crown and in the years that followed, under the determined direction of Sully who was virtually given a free hand by the king, the royal finances acquired a remarkable stability. By 1610 perhaps as much as 15 million *livres* had been accumulated in the royal coffers. Yet it was only possible to achieve this by

[1] For a highly illuminating analysis of the relationship between politics and finance in Henry IV's reign see R.J. Bonney, *The King's Debts* (Oxford, Clarendon Press, 1981), ch.1.

operating an undeclared bankruptcy. Sully continued to default on debts to
the English government, the Swiss mercenaries, the princes of Germany and
other lesser creditors. Payments of the arrears in *rentes* were abandoned and
by 1605 stood at 15 years in some instances. Essentially the surplus on the
current account was achieved by reducing expenditure and maximizing
revenues rather than by thorough-going reform. Returning prosperity produced additional revenue from indirect taxes, the administration of which
was improved; most notably the *aides* were consolidated into a single farm.
Regular income from sale of office was ensured by the institution of the
celebrated *paulette* or *droit annuel*, a tax of one sixtieth the value of an office
which allowed its holder to dispose of it without any restriction. By the end of
the reign the *parties casuelles* were accounting for 12 per cent of the ordinary
revenues. The financiers were also squeezed; in 1601 Sully forced them to
disgorge 600,000 *livres*; six years later he was asking for 1.2 million, although
it is not clear how much he actually obtained. The most striking fact about
Sully's term of office was the significant rise in the proportion of revenue
which came from extraordinary sources; between 1605 and 1609 they
accounted for over a third of all income. Far from undermining the position
of the financiers this had, of course, the opposite effect. Royal dependence on
them was once again made plain in the early months of 1610 when, as the
campaigning on the Rhine got under way, it became apparent that Sully's 15
million reserves could not last long. Between January and July alone he was
obliged to find 3.5 million over and above his estimated expenditure.

Henry's political and financial problems were compounded by the outright
refusal of significant sections of the population to accept him as the legitimate
king. This was despite the fact that in 1593 even the Leaguer *parlement* of
Paris, irritated by Spanish pretensions to the throne, finally came down in
favour of the strict application of the laws of succession, and despite Henry's
decision to abjure. Indeed, whilst these developments certainly played a rôle
in winning over moderate Catholics to the royal cause, there were many
whose ultramontane convictions remained unshakeable or were even har-
dened by the patently insincere conversion of the king. The granting of the
Edict of Nantes only served to reinforce Catholic hostility; the *parlement* of
Rouen refused to register it for nine years. In the eyes of many the king
remained a heretical usurper of the throne, incapable of discharging the duty
imposed on him by his coronation oath of maintaining the faith and thus the
integrity of the body politic. Theories of tyrannicide continued to be widely
disseminated alongside views which asserted the power of the pope to
absolve subjects from their natural allegiances. One of the most influential
tracts was the Jesuit Mariana's *De Rege et Regis Institutione* published in 1599
which defended the right of individuals to kill tyrants. Thus the astonishing
fact about the assassination of Henry in May 1610 by the disturbed Ravaillac
was not that it happened, but that the king had survived so long. It was
indeed the twentieth attempt on his life, and in every one can be detected the
influence of ideas of regicide and tyrannicide. Pierre Barrière who intended
to kill the king in August 1593 apparently consulted a Capucin, a Carmelite,
a Jacobin and a Jesuit before deciding on his mission. The law student
Jacques Chastel, the next to make the attempt, had been educated by the

Jesuits and, according to his own testimony, much influenced by the views of a Benedictine monk, which had so deepened his sense of his own sinfulness and fear of God's retribution that he had resolved to atone by an act of manifest public utility. Because of alleged Jesuit complicity in this affair they were then banned from France, a measure which however proved too much for the *parlementaires* of Bordeaux and Toulouse who refused to implement it. There were of course Jesuits who, far from subscribing to the views of Mariana, were profoundly royalist and this no doubt assisted those who pressurized the king into permitting their return in 1603. However the fact that Ravaillac himself left the Feuillants to join the Jesuits merely served to strengthen the widely held view that they were morally culpable for the attacks on the king and, finally, for his death.

Henry's assassination inaugurated yet another regency, presided over by yet another Medici; it also brought with it the prospect of a return to the anarchy of the sixteenth century. The enforced retirement of Sully, the only Protestant amongst the great officers of the crown, and the increasingly *dévot* complexion of the government disturbed the Huguenots who began to take measures for their self-defence. Unrest amongst the great nobility also began to mount. Between 1610 and 1614 the government was obliged to spend at least 10 million *livres* in order to retain their allegiance: 4 million to Henri II prince de Condé, 1.7 million to Mayenne, 1.3 million to Conti and 1.2 million to Nevers. All of which proved insufficient in the end to stop Condé raising the standard of revolt and demanding an Estates-General. This duly gathered towards the end of October 1614. Although both the elections to the Estates and its proceedings were successfully manipulated by the queen-mother, she was unable to prevent the deputies from producing extensive proposals for financial reform, including a demand for the reduction of venal offices and the abolition of the *paulette*. Much to the anger and consternation of the *parlement* the government promised to implement this demand. For his part Condé was equally dissatisfied with the outcome of the Estates and within a few months was once again in open revolt. This time he managed to secure an alliance with the Huguenots, now thoroughly agitated by the failure to implement the Edict of Nantes, the lack of consideration given to their grievances and the menacing tones of the clergy who were making it clear that they regarded the edict as merely a temporary concession. A number of other magnates including Bouillon and Sully also lent their support to Condé; renewal of civil war seemed imminent. Averted by the reconciliation of Condé with the queen-mother, his growing influence at court finally compelled her to arrest him in September 1616. A number of magnates left for the provinces, whilst the Huguenots, alarmed when the powerful and wayward duc d'Epernon flooded the hinterland of La Rochelle with troops, began to defend themselves. For several months the realm teetered on the brink of open conflict. Had it come it would have placed the government in dire straits. The rebellions had already cost 31 million *livres*, expenditure was running at record levels of 34 million per annum, whilst the revenues for 1618–20 had already been anticipated to the turn of 2 million.

Then suddenly in April 1617 in one of the most significant of all palace coups the Louis XIII ordered the removal of the court favourite Concini

and sweeping his mother aside brought the regency to an abrupt end. Although many years of trial and difficulty lay ahead for the young monarch, it can be seen in retrospect that his assumption of personal power was one of the most significant turning points in the ascent from the abyss of the civil wars. Contrary to all reasonable expectations the fortunes of the monarchy were about to take a decisive turn for the better; for beneath the stormy waves, threatening at any moment to overwhelm the fragile ship of state, powerful currents were at work which, in the end, would serve it well.

The Restoration of Religious Unity

It is conventionally argued that the assassination of Henry IV, with all the odium that this brought to the Jesuits, provoked a royalist and gallican backlash which was ultimately to the crown's advantage. There is indeed merit in this view. Foremost amongst those to spring to the defence of gallican traditions was the *parlement* of Paris which seized the opportunity to roundly condemn a number of ultramontane tracts. That there was widespread support for its position became clear at the Estates-General of 1614, when the third estate elected to head its *cahier* of grievances with a most explicit defence of royal autonomy. The king was beseeched to recognize as a fundamental law the principle that French kings held their power of God alone and that there was no temporal or spiritual power which could deprive them of their sovereignty nor 'absolve their subjects from the fidelity and obedience they owe'. Undoubtedly the murder of Henry IV reinforced the conviction that it was necessary to defend the divinely bestowed authority of the king against all those who challenged it. Gallican sentiment became a crucial element in absolutist ideology and could be utilized by the government as needed. In 1625 two Jesuit tracts, the *Mysteria Politica* and the *Admonitio ad Regem*, appeared attacking the irreligious nature of France's anti-Spanish foreign policy and upholding the Habsburgs as the true defenders of international Catholicism. Without difficulty Richelieu who had come to power during 1624 obtained from the Parisian authorities a decree condemning the works as seditious and full of 'propositions contrary to the authority of Kings established by God'; denunciations were also forthcoming from *parlement*, the Sorbonne and less fiercely from the Assembly of Clergy. A further illuminating episode occurred 10 years later when the Assembly of Clergy agreed to support a royal request that the marriage of the king's brother Gaston d'Orléans with Marguerite de Navarre be annulled, despite the fact that marriage was a holy sacrament subject to papal jurisdiction. The government argued that the marriage had been accomplished without royal consent and, because Louis had no heir, threatened to disturb the laws of succession; the assembly decided that the marriage was indeed contrary to the customs of the realm which themselves had been sanctioned by the Church.

Despite the obliging response of the clergy in this instance, it would however be misleading to suggest that it typified their general stance or constituted more than a partial reflection of public attitudes to the question of Church–State relations. Gallican independence was in fact severely constrained by the widespread influence of ultramontane ideas. In any event it should be firmly placed in the context of the French counter-reformation which, far from being a purely national movement, drew on the whole range of Catholic tradition available in Europe. Moreover it is highly arguable that militant Catholicism played a more significant rôle in the restoration of royal authority than did gallicanism. In view of the subversive activities of the Catholic League and the equally insidious writings of Jesuit theologians, this may seem a perverse observation. Both Henry III and Henry IV were the victims of paranoid religious sectarianism. None the less it was the power of the Catholic renewal which also blocked the spread of Protestantism and recharged the ideological batteries of divine-right monarchy; in compelling the crown to revert to its traditional religious rôle the League also provided the means whereby a degree of conformity and reverence for authority could be instilled into a restless community.

If the military strength and influence of the Protestant magnates bolstered by the impregnability of some major towns enabled the Huguenot organization to survive the long years of war and, at the end, to extract the Edict of Nantes from the king, this should not obscure the extent to which Protestantism had retreated. In many key centres this was the direct consequence of the inability of the Huguenots to consolidate the military coups which brought them to power. In Rouen, the most significant Protestant enclave north of the Loire, the recovery of the city by the Guise in 1562 cost many notables their properties, if not their lives. Great courage was henceforth required to make open profession of the Reformed faith. A similar story can be told for Toulouse where the abortive Protestant coup of 1562 was followed by repeated waves of blood-letting and persecution. After the massacres of 1572 the Huguenot congregations in many areas never recovered. In Rouen it proved impossible to resume services on a permanent basis until 1579 and in that year there were only 70 baptisms, one tenth of the number recorded in 1565. From a community of 16,500 the Huguenots had been reduced to 3,000 or even less. Most importantly 1572 appears to have been the high-water mark for Parisian Protestantism as many notables and merchants succumbed to the pressure and intimidation of their opponents. Only in the great Huguenot strongholds, notably Montauban and La Rochelle, or in those areas where the local authorities declined to persecute the Protestant congregations, did they remain stable or continue to grow. The disposition of military force and the ability to use mass violence, combined with lesser forms of harassment, clearly played a key rôle in determining the religious geography of France. From 1584 the threat of a Protestant succession to the throne served only to inject new life into the Catholic associations and confirm the fate of French Protestantism as an essentially provincial phenomenon confined to the remoter provinces of the south and west. By the end of the 1580s the Catholic League had secured the bulk of northern France and its councils dominated the major cities. Even in the south it recorded major successes, notably at Toulouse and Lyon; Marseille developed its own form of Catholic dictatorship, whilst at Bordeaux, as at Toulouse, the repressive policies of the *parlement* limited Huguenot effectiveness despite its strength in the surrounding regions.

From the moment of Henry IV's accession to the throne it was obvious that major concessions were essential if he was to preserve it. Even to secure the co-operation of the Catholic commanders of the royal army bequeathed to him by his predecessor, the new king was obliged to agree to protect the Catholic faith, to summon a national council within six months for his religious instruction, to limit concessions to the Protestants and to place towns won from the League in Catholic hands. Only with a signed agreement to this effect did the commanders recognize Henry as king by fundamental law. The impossibility of his position was further revealed by the fact that Henry felt constrained to retain the services of François d'O, the *surintendant des finances*, despite his refusal to sign the agreement. The *surintendant* was indispensable both for his financial connections and because his dismissal would have alienated much Catholic support. Henry's abjuration, although skilfully delayed to maximize its political benefits, was only a matter of time.

This event is all too often treated as though it were essentially a political compromise, neatly executed by a king who cleverly gathered about him a coalition of moderate – or *politique* – opinion which left the hard-liners isolated. True the abjuration was brilliantly timed to exploit the divisions within the League, but this view obscures the fact that the price of detaching moderate opinion was to capitulate on the central issue. Moreover such an approach also devalues the significance of the royal abjuration, which cannot be reduced to an act of political expediency. For Henry personally it may possibly have been no more than that; but for the realm in general it constituted a renewal of the deepest traditions of the French monarchy, an acceptance of the principle that there could be but one religion of which the king was the foremost defender. Indeed the essential condition of papal assent to Henry's abjuration was that he should establish a single religion in France in conformity with the traditional obligations expressed in the coronation oath. There was no possibility of the immediate implementation of such a proposition even if the king had so wished, but the pressures which had compelled his conversion were deep-seated and persistent. When insisting that the *parlement* of Paris register the Edict of Nantes Henry felt obliged to reassure the magistrates that he knew well that his realm 'could only be saved by the conservation of the Catholic religion.' Similarly he told the clergy that 'I know that Religion and Justice are the mainstays and foundations of this realm which maintains itself through Justice and piety'. Nor should these declarations be dismissed as mere words. In 1603, as we have seen, the Jesuits were permitted to return to France despite widespread suspicion of them. More ominous as a foretaste of things to come for the Huguenots was the re-establishment of the Catholic bishoprics of Lescar and Oloron in Béarn, still part of Henry's personal patrimony and Protestant for 50 years.

Of course Henry was obliged to concede the Edict of Nantes to his former *co-religionnaires*. Moreover although political assemblies were specifically outlawed by the edict he was also constrained to yield before the *de facto* use of them by the Huguenots. Nor did he interfere in the virtually autonomous government of their principal towns, merely dispatching Sully to La Rochelle when its Catholic minority complained of maltreatment. Yet the significant point about the king's attempt to compromise was that it failed to fulfil the expectations of those who had sought his abjuration. To many of them the insincerity of his position was manifest and their continual denial of his religious integrity contributed directly to the atmosphere which made his assassination possible.

Despite the gallican reaction which Henry's death provoked, there can be little doubt that it did in part achieve the objectives of those who most desired it and open up the way for an eventual onslaught on the Huguenots, in which naturally both gallicans and ultramontane Catholics could unite. With Sully soon squeezed out of office, the government under the auspices of Marie de Medici and dominated by Villeroy and Jeannin, both former agents of Mayenne, soon revealed where its sympathies lay. Attempts to manipulate the Huguenot assembly at Saumur in 1611, followed by a conspiracy to deprive the Huguenot leader Henri de Rohan of his governorship of St Jean d'Angély and a foolish intervention in the affairs of La Rochelle, quickly aroused Huguenot anxieties. These were further heightened by the apparent inability or unwillingness of the regent to resist the apologists of papal supremacy. In late 1614 the clergy, with the aid of the papal nuncio, obtained the suspension of a decree of *parlement* ordering that yet another Jesuit tract justifying tyrannicide be burnt. This was in fact merely a prelude to their success in pressurizing the government to suspend all discussion of the first article of the third estate with its unequivocal enunciation of gallican principles. As if this were not enough, the first estate also demanded the reception of the decrees of the Council of Trent in France; when this was denied they proceeded a few months later at their next assembly to make a unilateral acceptance of them which the government neither approved nor condemned. At the Estates the clergy also issued an unambiguous request for the prohibition of the 'exercise of the reformed religion', whilst Cardinal du Perron declared that the edicts of toleration were only a provisional concession. The first objective of the Church was the restoration of Catholicism in Béarn, for which it now began to mount an intense campaign.

Already in a high state of nervousness, and exasperated by the failure to deal with their complaints about the increasingly widespread denial of their civil and religious rights, the Huguenots decided, after some months of agonizing, to throw in their lot with the rebellious Condé. Although this opportunist prince almost immediately abandoned his allies, the persistence of the Huguenot assembly gathered within the safety of the walls of La Rochelle was such that it extracted some major concessions from the crown. By the Treaty of Loudun (May 1616) the government agreed that the 'gallican Church should be conserved in its rights and liberties' and that the acceptance of the Tridentine decrees by the clergy 'was without consequence'. It was also agreed that commissioners would be despatched to investigate Huguenot complaints. Unfortunately, as far as Béarn was concerned, the government made it absolutely clear that its ultimate intention was to reunite the principality – never contemplated by Henry IV – with France. For the moment, however, it did not have the resources to overcome the resistance that might be expected and the tensions at court were acute, as the arrest of Condé in September 1616 revealed.

When news of the unexpected death of Concini and the assumption of personal power by Louis arrived in Huguenot circles they breathed a collective sign of relief. Although once again an assembly had gathered at La Rochelle and was locked in bitter disagreement with the government over the continuing disregard for its grievances, the deputies resolved to disperse and send representatives to profess their loyalty to the king. Sadly, they had badly misjudged the situation. Not only did Louis refuse to admit them, but one of his first major acts was to issue a decree declaring complete freedom of worship in Béarn and the restoration of the Catholic Church to all its former rights and possessions. It was in fact another three years before he was able to enforce his will but when the opportunity arose it was seized with alacrity and a determination that brooked no opposition. Louis's mother had never ceased to make trouble and in 1620 he was obliged to descend on Normandy to suppress an incipient rebellion. Then he turned southwards with his army to confront Marie at the Ponts de Cé, where she offered only feeble resistance. But much to Protestant consternation Louis did not stop there; by the middle of September his army was at Bordeaux and a month later it occupied the principality of Béarn. The Estates were returned to the control of the bishops, the sovereign courts were welded into one *parlement* and the local militias were suppressed.

Thus began perhaps the most decisive decade in the restoration of royal authority. Two further and equally determined campaigns ensured that by the end of 1622 the military strength of the Huguenots was almost broken. Abandoned by every leader of rank except the duc de Rohan, the Protestants also lost about half their strongholds despite the failure of the royal troops to take either Montauban or Montpellier and the wise decision not to risk an all out attack on the bastions of La Rochelle. It was from there that for two years the Protestant assembly directed the resistance, adopting for the purpose a new constitution for the defence of the churches, by which the realm was divided into eight departments, each with its military, financial and judicial machinery under the supreme authority of the assembly itself. Provoked into this act although the Huguenots undoubtedly were, such a measure nevertheless constituted a direct affront to royal authority and Louis was resolved to rid himself of 'these illicit assemblies ... much better employed in popular and republican states than to maintain the obedience which is naturally due to us.' By the autumn of 1622 the Protestants were no longer strong enough to resist the royal will and at the Peace of Montpellier political assemblies were banned. Quite clearly the next objective was the reduction of La Rochelle – a formidable project hampered by rising complications on the international front, lack of resources and Rochelais naval strength which far outshone that of the crown. Nevertheless the progressive isolation of the town continued, taking a major step forward in September 1625 when a fleet largely composed of vessels lent by the English and the Dutch engaged the Rochelais navy, inflicting irreparable damage and securing control of the vital offshore islands of Ré and Oléron. After Richelieu managed to secure a breathing space in the escalating conflict with Spain by the Treaty of Monçon (March 1626), practically the entire military and financial resources of the crown were turned on this Protestant citadel and 'fount of heresy'. The

English government belatedly realizing that it was perhaps not in its own best interests to see La Rochelle fall, and subject to Puritan pressure, finally dispatched the celebrated relief expedition under the duke of Buckingham. This suffered both from his incompetence and the acute divisions amongst the Rochelais, many of whom were reluctant, even at this stage, to join with a foreign power. By the time they did so in September 1627 an army over 15,000 strong was camped beyond their walls. In early November the English were dislodged from the island of Ré and left for home, leaving Richelieu to set about the creation of his famous dyke and miles of trenches, which one long year later brought the remnants of the starving population to their knees. As a military and political force capable of defying the crown the Huguenots were finished. In the south Rohan struggled on for a few months but to no avail.

After 1630 the restrictions imposed on the Huguenots became tighter than ever. Reduced to holding infrequent national and provincial synods, carefully watched over by royal agents, they were unable to resist measures designed to undermine the activity of their churches and break communications between them. The battle to ensure the proper application of the Edict of Nantes was not only lost but it was soon apparent that the authorities intended to interpret it in the strictest possible way. In effect this frequently meant a reinterpretation. Thus in 1634 the intendant of Languedoc informed the chancellor that it was already the practice there to prohibit services by non-residing pastors. The following year a ruling was obtained from the royal council which made the patronage of a bishop superior to that of a *seigneur*, thus undermining the freedom of worship accorded by the edict to *seigneurs* who possessed rights of high justice. From the late 1650s this privilege was not allowed to any *seigneur* who acquired rights of high justice unless specifically referred to in the letters patent. Similarly, reformed worship was excluded from episcopal towns. At the same time the civil rights of the Huguenots were systematically eroded; they were eased out of public office, found their artisans excluded from *gilds*, prevented from entering into mixed marriages and even, in one area, denied the use of church bells. Most significantly measures were taken to restore partial or even complete control of strongly Protestant municipalities to the Catholics. At La Rochelle this was achieved by the complete destruction of its municipal autonomy, elsewhere by stipulations that the councils were to admit a certain number of Catholics or simply by direct intervention. In 1652 the consuls of Montpellier – all Catholic by this time – were maintained in office by order of the government. To make matters worse the Huguenots were no longer able to direct their grievances to the king but were obliged to address themselves to the *chambres mi-parties*. Despite their bipartisan composition these courts had never provided an entirely satisfactory means of redress, but now they were simply manipulated to ensure Catholic domination of their proceedings. Even this was insufficient to satisfy the clergy who sustained a constant campaign for their complete abolition.

It is perhaps surprising that the Edict of Nantes was retained at all. True the government had repeatedly assured the Huguenots that it was conducting a war against rebels and not heretics and it repeatedly renewed the provisions of the Edict of Nantes to prove it; yet there can be little doubt that this was a tactic designed to divide the opposition rather than a statement of principle. In the aftermath of the victory over the Huguenots, Richelieu was able to state without dissimulation that 'diversity of religion in a state was dangerous' and he urged the king not to lose 'the opportunity of buying off and exterminating heresy'. He did however nurture the hope for years that this could be achieved in a more or less peaceful fashion culminating in a spectacular confession of error by the Huguenots. Such a notion was perhaps less absurd than might be thought for some prominent Protestants were indeed attracted by the idea of a reunification of the faiths. But the major reason for stealth rather than an immediate withdrawal of toleration lay in the need to reassure France's many Protestant allies in the long struggle against Spain. The government was also prey to a continuing, probably misconceived, fear of renewed open resistance. In the last phases of the Fronde (see below, pp.97 ff.), with yet another dissident prince de Condé endeavouring to raise the south-western provinces in revolt, the government actually removed all the limitations imposed on the Huguenots since 1629. A storm of protest from the clergy ensued, and four years later the government not only reversed its stance but yielded to demands for even more restrictive measures. By the time of Louis XIV's majority the Edict of Nantes was in many respects a dead letter. After all, as the clergy pointedly informed the new king, it was only a privilege granted to members of the reformed Church and not a general declaration of toleration.

Quite apart from the political constraints on its dealings with the Huguenots, the French government remained very wary of succumbing to the constant pressure of militant Catholics whose own loyalty was suspect because of their opposition to the war against Spain and their exaltation of papal authority. Even the weak and sympathetic government of Marie de Medici did not accede to the clergy's wish that the decrees of the Council of Trent should be received in France. None the less it remains true that the restoration of monarchical authority and prestige owed much to the renewal of the ties between Church and state and the willingness of Louis XIII to place himself at the head of an anti-Protestant crusade. Despite the assurances given to the Huguenots, the king was quite prepared, when urging the clergy to part with some of their wealth, to affirm that he was indeed engaged in a religious war. 'Once La Rochelle is taken' he told them 'the monster of heresy will be defeated'. And in return for the massive subsidies earmarked for the siege of La Rochelle by the assemblies of 1621, 1625 and 1628, the clergy made it quite clear what they expected. The bishop of Rennes addressing Louis on behalf of his colleagues reminded him that 'kings are sent from heaven to avenge earthly offences against the Divine Majesty, to punish those who transgress his laws and to maintain the splendour of the Church by justice, by strength and with the arms which God, of whom they are the living image, has given them for this purpose'. On hearing that Buckingham had been repulsed from the island of Ré the pope congratulated its heroic defender and expressed confidence that 'under a king so devoted to the faith ungodliness will be banished for ever.' Louis did his best to oblige. As the wars against the Huguenots reached their climax, agents were infiltrated into the Protestant camp to send back a stream of advice about how to win them back to the Catholic faith. One argued that it was necessary to 'display the beautiful order of the Catholic hierarchy as it was in the first four or five centuries after the ascension of Jesus Christ'. Where persuasion failed a little bribery, intrigue and intimidation did not come amiss. Royal agents penetrated deep into the Protestant south with pensions and military posts for distribution. Louis XIII personally intervened to obtain the defection of great Huguenot magnates. When the duc de Lesdiguières, governor of the Dauphiné, finally abandoned his *co-religionnaires* after months of uncertainty and insistent pressure from the court, it was with the king's assurance that his freedom of conscience would be respected. Yet the duke understood well what was required. On 1 July 1622 'in the great church of Grenoble in the most spectacular manner possible with extraordinary joy' he adopted the Catholic faith. Similar pressure was brought to bear on the duc de La Tremouille who finally abjured with great acclaim in the army encamped around the walls of La Rochelle, evoking the comment from the pope that Richelieu knew how to win souls as well as towns.

The crusading atmosphere that characterized the last wars against the Huguenots gave royal propagandists and obsequious pamphleteers every opportunity to elevate the king to the level of a demi-God. Three elements received constant emphasis: his divinity, his invincibility and his justice. Replying to a manifesto produced by Rohan's brother Soubise in 1625, the government journal *Mercure Français* insisted that kings 'should be looked at as one looks at the sun', with eyes averted; 'because they are the lieutenants of God.... we are obliged to treat them as we do God.' Military victory reinforced the image. 'God caused him to be born amidst the misfortunes of France' declared one admirer of Louis 'so that he might restore her to her former splendour.' Every success of the king was exploited to show divine approval, whereas even minor incidents such as the collapse of a roadway in La Rochelle, were transformed into 'miracles of God performed in the midst of his enemies.' Victory was however tempered with mercy. 'Amidst the spate of bloodletting and pillage and nauseating excesses his judgment, his prudence and his justice were always there to be admired.' When he finally entered La Rochelle, armed and mounted as befitted a royal conqueror, he also came as God's lieutenant to whom the administration of divine justice had been entrusted. He distributed bread to the starving remnants of the population and pardoned all but a handful.

Whilst this dramatic moment would not have been possible without unprecedented concentration of military power, it is equally true that the way was prepared by a resurgence of Catholic spirituality. Louis XIII's personal piety and commitment to the faith, so markedly different from his father's attitudes, were only the public expression of a movement for reform and renewal which pervaded all sections of French society. To locate the roots of this it is necessary to return to the days of the Catholic League. Frequently treated simply as the last phase of a struggle for political control, the period of the League's domination is increasingly viewed as critical for the impulse which it gave to the subsequent movement for reform. The clearest manifestation of this was the development of popular and very open forms of devotion. During the 1580s Paris and the other great centres of the League witnessed an astonishing variety of elaborate ceremonials and processions, often of a highly penitential character, involving, for instance, shoeless and white-clad children. One of the most popular devotions was that of the perpetual adoration; in Rouen this involved displaying the sacrament on an altar decorated with relics over which a guard was mounted for a week at a time, whilst special prayers and sermons were said. Nor was it the only indication of a resurgence of Catholic religiosity in this vitally important centre.[2] After two decades of relative inertia under a largely ineffectual archdiocesan council marked by the establishment of only one new religious order and the visits of some Jesuit preachers, a new buoyancy became apparent. Above all the opposition to the permanent establishment of the Jesuits was broken; within a decade of its foundation in 1593 the Jesuit college claimed 1,800 students. New *confréries*, most notably the Penitents whose puritan rigour is suggested by their name, brought with them their torchlit processions and their insistence on the virtue of regular communion. Rouen also witnessed the first attempt, albeit abortive, to establish a branch of the Spanish Carmelites in France, an objective pursued by a certain Quintanadoines, a member of a well-established Rouenais merchant family of Spanish origin, who in common with so many others was greatly inspired by the mystical experience and reforming endeavour of St Teresa of Avila (d.1582) and St John of the Cross (d.1591). That these developments had more than a superficial impact seems clear from the evidence now available of a significant increase of pious offerings in Rouen during the 1580s, especially as this included offerings made to the Holy Virgin; for the cult of the Holy Virgin was one of the most controversial of Catholic devotions and destined to assume a significant place in counter-reformation France. In 1638 Louis XIII was to enlist the support of the Holy Virgin by putting the realm under her protection to ensure the birth of a son to his pregnant wife.

Although some of the *confréries* associated with the Catholic League were subsequently suppressed by a suspicious establishment, the intense spirituality of the 1580s spilled over into the following decades when the movement for reform reached unprecedented heights. Sometimes the continuities were obvious. Mme Acarie for instance, a lady of robe[3] and League background, influenced by Quintanadoines's translation of a life of St Teresa, was largely responsible for the permanent establishment of the Carmelites in 1604. Associated with her was Cardinal Bérulle who was in turn to exercise influence over many of the next generation of reformers, notably Duvergier du Hauranne, the future abbé de St Cyran and protector of Port Royal. In a more general sense the penitential mood of the 1580s, reflecting as it did the widespread sense of foreboding and distress, lent its flavour to much of what followed. Retreat from the world, self-denial and mystical communion with

---

[2] This material is drawn from P. Benedict, *Rouen During the Wars of Religion* (Cambridge, CUP, 1981), ch.8.

[3] The nobles of the robe were those who had acquired their status through holding royal office. Some offices bestowed personal nobility on the holder immediately. From the beginning of the seventeenth century it was accepted that hereditary nobility could be acquired after three generations of service to the crown in an office-holding capacity.

God became significant features of French religious life, manifest not only in the austere rules of the Carmelites but also in the penitential practices of the Capucins and the contemplative character of the Visitandines established by St François de Sales in 1610. Such developments were sustained by manuals of devotion and theological works emphasizing the need for direct communion with God, the overriding power of his love and man's utter dependence on him. Two of the most notable works were Sales's *Traité de l'Armour de Jésus* written in 1616 and Bérulle's *Grandeur de Jésus* of 1623. The ground was thus well prepared for the reception of the more intellectual Augustinianism normally associated with the French publication in 1640 of Bishop Jansen's controversial work. Jansenism although in many ways a distinct movement from its precursors, shared their puritan ethics and sense of man's inadequacy.

Yet enormously significant as these tendencies were, it is impossible to confine the French counter-reformation within them. Alongside the austere and contemplative orders there sprang up those devoted to charitable, missionary and teaching endeavours. The Capucins preached as well as prayed, whilst the Visitandines were transformed into a teaching order. Bérulle is perhaps more famous for his foundation of the Oratory intended for the improvement and education of the clergy than anything else. In 1633 François de Sales founded the eminently practical and outward going *Filles de la Charité*. Moreover these were but the most outstanding moments in a surging tide of reform. To them should be added the work of a host of wealthy men and women who plunged themselves into reforming activity. The overall results were spectacular. By 1643 the Jesuits had 100 establishments the length and breadth of the realm, a remarkable achievement albeit outshone by the Capucins' 285. On the death of Bérulle in 1629 the Oratory had 44 houses, whilst the Visitandines reahed 86. Sixty monastic houses were founded in Paris alone between 1600 and 1640.

It is against this background that must be set the clergy's unilateral decision to approve the Tridentine decrees. Although these could not be accepted formally in France without risk to the principles of gallican independence, they contained much that corresponded exactly to the prevailing direction of French Catholicism. The insistence on the residence and training of the clergy, the observance of the sacraments – notably the necessity for regular communion and confession – the reaffirmation of the indispensible rôle of the priesthood, the belief in the intercession of the saints and the concept of purgatory, were all quite compatible with the spirit of reform. Moreover such principles were also very much in the interest of the monarchy. Parochial conformity enforced by a well-trained and disciplined clergy, themselves watched over by a committed episcopacy, was perhaps an unattainable ideal, but it was not an ideal that the crown could afford to reject.

Warfare and the Control of Violence

If religious ideology was instrumental in propelling France in an absolutist direction, it is also apparent that this ideology was moulded by very earthly considerations. Looked at in political terms the campaigns of the 1620s can be seen as perhaps the most crucial phase in the enormously protracted but progressive extension of royal authority. Success brought with it enhanced control over the distant provinces of Languedoc and Guyenne as well as Béarn; strategic strongholds like La Rochelle and Montpellier could now be exploited in the crown's interest, whilst a host of lesser places lost their capacity to resist. Above all the onslaught on the Huguenots facilitated the incorporation of the magnates in the royal service. By 1622 most of the great Huguenot magnates had abandoned the cause, usually in return for royal favour and office. Troublemakers like Condé and Epernon turned their energies against the Huguenots rather than the king; Condé recovered the influence he desired at court, becoming an implacable foe of the Protestants, whilst Epernon acquired the governorship of Guyenne. As the king extended his military and financial control he was able to reward the nobility with offices, military commands and the property of those who foolishly prolonged their resistance. Moreover the age-old problem of how to satisfy the nobility once the period of fighting came to an end was also resolved because immediately the Huguenots had been crushed the offensive against Spain began. Even former rebels – like the duc de Rohan – found an outlet for their military talents and aspirations.

Although in some ways the bitter and prolonged Franco-Spanish struggle was a conflict between emergent nation states, it nevertheless retained the dynastic character of earlier wars. The Habsburgs and Bourbons were of course related to each other by the marriage of Louis XIII and Anne of Austria, and when peace was finally restored in 1659 an essential element in that settlement was the marriage contract between Louis XIV and Maria Teresa, second daughter of Philip IV. A further, much discussed, aspect of the Peace of the Pyrenees was the pardon for the Grand Condé, son of Henri II, who after his rebellion in the Fronde had entered the service of the Spanish crown. That rebellion itself flowed from the failure to recompense him for his undoubtedly magnificent contribution to the royal cause. Not only was Condé the victor of the great battles of Rocroi (1643) and Lens (1648) but he also commanded the forces which regained Paris for the regent in the early months of the Fronde. Mazarin and Anne, fearful of his influence, repaid him by not only refusing the offices he sought for himself and his clients, but also by interfering in a family marriage project.

It is thus readily apparent that the tensions generated by the interaction between noble interest, dynastic rivalries and warfare were fundamentally the same as ever. In the activities of Condé, who moved from service in one royal house to another, can be seen a still powerful echo of the inseparability of civil and 'international' rivalries which had characterized the conflicts of the fifteenth and sixteenth centuries. An ability to wage war remained necessary not only to ensure the crown's position within and beyond the frontiers of the realm, but also as a mechanism for channelling and satisfying the aspirations of the magnates. In this sense, as Victor Kiernan has observed, war for the monarchy was 'not a political option but an organic necessity'.

Moreover the disciplining of the population to accept royal authority and with it the direct and indirect consequences of large-scale warfare was itself a horribly violent process. The campaigns against the Huguenots were in themselves a massive exercise in coercion, involving a violent reduction in traditional privileges and the imposition of new burdens even on those areas not immediately involved. Guyenne in addition to being compelled to find the wherewithal for the purchase of vessels from the Dutch for use against La Rochelle and for 500 suits of clothing and shoes for the besieging forces, also found that it had to raise 100,000 *livres* to repair the damage caused by the stay of the Régiment de la Valette in Bergerac. There followed two decades in which the military and fiscal demands placed on the countryside rose to scarcely imaginable heights. In the frontier provinces the sacrifice of human and economic resources was at its most obvious and when the local communities endeavoured to lessen their misery by trading or communicating with the enemy, the punishment could be ferocious. Corbie deemed in 1636 to have surrendered too easily, found its governor condemned to death; it was deprived of all its privileges and the Benedictine monks, whose behaviour was particularly suspect, were thrown into prison whilst their property was sequestered. It was not however just the frontier provinces that suffered. In January 1646 the Régiment de la Reine spent a night in two parishes of the duchy of Thouars. Eighty-four inhabitants subsequently complained of losses totalling 2,647 *livres*, the equivalent of a year's revenue from a substantial noble estate or the purchase cost of perhaps three dozen ploughs and horses. Naturally the long suffering populace took its revenge where it could. In Abiat in the Périgord in 1640 three or four hundred armed rioters attacked a company of cavalry that was seeking billets in the town; the captain was killed, many soldiers wounded, the horses stolen and the baggage pillaged. Such incidents merely served to intensify the coercion; in this instance a *commissaire* was dispatched with sovereign powers to carry out the necessary prosecutions and from his judgment there was no appeal. Royal agents usually had at their disposition a small troop of musketeers to facilitate the raising of the *taille* from recalcitrant communities but these became insufficient. Special brigades were set up for the purpose at Poitiers in 1638, Bordeaux and Caen in 1641, at Limoges the following year and in several other centres in 1643 and 1644. In many of the frontier areas tax rebellion became so endemic that troops were constantly diverted to help. When Normandy erupted in 1639, with large parts of the province slipping from government control for four months, an army of 4,000 foot-soldiers and 1,200 cavalry was dispatched to re-establish the tax offices, punish the rebels and obtain payment of the winter quarter.

What begins to emerge from these developments is the fact that, despite the age-old character of the problems facing the monarchy, they became so magnified in the seventeenth century as to create a qualitatively new situation. Richelieu estimated the peacetime military requirements in 1626 to be 18,000–20,000 infantry and 2,000 cavalry, roughly twice the size of Henry IV's army. Whereas in the sixteenth century the number of wartime combatants had, at most, just reached 50,000, by 1625 the government was paying an estimated 60,000 soldiers. During the next decade the figure leapt upwards to a truly astonishing 150,000 or even more. Practically overnight the problems of recruiting, equipping, supplying and paying the royal armies multiplied to the point where the traditional mechanisms simply became inadequate; the irresistible consequence was the progressive subordination of the military to the civilian arm of government.

Yet there was no way in which the government's response could match the speed with which the situation developed. Although the notoriously unreliable companies of *gendarmerie* were more or less phased out, the difficulties associated with them were by no means overcome. By 1642 the core of the army consisted of 15 regiments created through the welding together of smaller contingents of soldiers. But the chain of command remained far from systematized and the regimental commanders – the colonels – retained a far-reaching degree of autonomy. In return for a commission they undertook to supply an agreed number of men, selling the posts of company commanders to captains, who then set about raising troops by the means they found most acceptable. For the captains the whole exercise remained a source of profit which could be derived in a number of ways: by falsifying the numbers of soldiers recruited, under-supplying the troops with services and provisions, by withholding part or even all of the wages and by the traditional method of pillaging the countryside which enabled the thoroughly brutalized troops to compensate for their own treatment. Generals and provincial governors could be equally wayward, sometimes altering route marches and billets as they pleased. In wartime the regimental forces were supplemented by mercenary troops – perhaps constituting a third of the total – whilst the feudal levy continued to be used, albeit somewhat erratically. During the Thirty Years War 'the fighting force ... had to be cobbled together with an almost prodigal delegation of powers.'[4]

Perhaps the most important technical improvement during this period was the introduction of the *étapes* or staging posts designed to ensure that provisions were readily available to troops in the field. Of course in order to create them it was necessary to make financial levies. Guyenne had to find 50,000 *livres* in 1641 and 250,000 the following year. Nevertheless there was merit in the view that this helped lessen the disorders of the soldiery, and from about this time *étapes* were developed in Dauphiné, the Lyonnais, Guyenne and elsewhere. In 1643 instructions were given for the establishment of *étapes* in eight northern *généralités* and a few months later for the creation of the necessary funds in each province. Maintaining the now huge armies in the field remained however a formidable problem, especially when supply lines became stretched. Inability to supply the troops in Catalonia in 1652 contributed directly to the loss of the French foothold in that province. Dependence on private suppliers and carters, who had to be encouraged by exemptions from tolls, did not help to overcome the difficulties. Hospital arrangements likewise stretched financial and administrative resources to the limit. Although legislation of 1629 held the commanders responsible for establishing hospitals, very few did so and hospital provision was mostly organized on the spot by the requisition of buildings or through the services of the religious houses.

[4] C. Jones, 'The Military Revolution and the Professionalisation of the French Army', in M. Duffy, ed., *The Military Revolution and the State* (Exeter, University of Exeter, 1980), p.30.

It was the attempt to grapple with such problems that spawned perhaps the most significant development of all. This lay in the assumption of military powers by those celebrated royal agents, the intendants. Precursors of the intendants can be found in the *commissaires* of the sixteenth century and even earlier who were dispatched to the provinces to deal with this revolt, ensure the collection of that tax or investigate specific complaints. From the time of Henry IV there also existed a number of *intendants de l'armée* who were frequently men of military excellence and well equipped to deal with the growing logistical and technical problems. But the major development of the intendancy as a generalized institution conferring comprehensive powers of police, justice and finance on the incumbents came in the mid seventeenth century. Between 1617 and 1627 intendants were in fact present in only 12 provinces and then for only part of the time. It was another 10 years before they became permanent representatives of the crown in virtually every province and a few more before the crystallization of the general principle that there should be one intendant in each *généralité* in the *pays d'élections* and one for each province elsewhere.

This chronology constitutes more than adequate grounds for assuming a direct causal link between the rapid extension and systematization of the intendancies and escalating military need. Any doubt on this matter is certainly dispelled by an examination of their functions which reveal how easily and continuously the intendants moved between civilian and military duties. From 1643 to 1648 no commissions were issued to intendants which did not confer some military responsibilities. These were not limited to such matters as negotiating with suppliers, organizing the *étapes* or hospital care but extended to advising on campaign routes, fortifications and to assisting with recruitment. From 1638 the provincial intendants became responsible for raising the *subsistance* – a tax imposed in cash or kind for the winter quarter – and eventually acquired complete administrative control over any armies billeted in their jurisdiction during the winter season. That contemporaries appreciated the close connection between the intendancies and military need was clearly shown in the Fronde when, compelled by public hostility to withdraw them, the government was none the less able to retain those in the frontier provinces. From 1653 the intendants slowly reappeared, frequently in the guise of military commissioners.

The return of the intendants was essential above all for the maintenance of discipline in the armies themselves. For perhaps the major problem posed by the vast and rapid expansion of the forces at the crown's disposition was how to deploy this unprecedented concentration of brute force without it getting out of hand. Fear of disorder in the armed forces became one of the most insistent elements in government thinking. The attendant desire for royal agents powerful and impartial enough to deal with the military commanders was expressed perfectly by article 81 of the reforming ordinance known as the Code Michaud in 1629; this forbade the appointment of anyone as a provincial or army intendant who had connections with the commanders in the region concerned. As the investigative and disciplinary powers of the intendants increased there were indeed many governors and captains who had cause for regret. Those engaged in defrauding the paymaster with false muster rolls, in illicit trade or disorderly conduct did so at the risk of investigation and summary punishment. A certain Captain Gastigues was prosecuted for allowing his troops to take eight months' winter quarter instead of the statutory four! The intendants of the frontier province of Picardy seem to have spent most of their time and energy coping with questions of military discipline and were more than willing to apply the full severity of the law. A lieutenant in the regiment of Bullion was executed for pillaging and governors of strongholds who surrendered too readily were also condemned to death. Although the intendants could not quite so easily utilize their powers against the commanders-in-chief, the lesser governors and middle-ranking officers were, for the first time, effectively subject to public law.

   This was a crucial stage in the crown's achievement of a 'monopoly of violence': a paradoxical process whereby a regime born out of warfare, sustained by brutally coercive measures, began to insist that war was too complex, too costly and too dangerous to be left to the generals.

Money, Money, Money

In the opening decade of the seventeenth century war expenditure was usually less than 5 million *livres* per annum. By the 1620s it averaged 16 million, by 1635 it reached 33 million and after 1640 rose to over 38 million a year. What this meant for the population at large can be seen in the staggering increases in the estimated yields from the direct taxes (the *taille* supplemented by the *taillon, subsistance* and *étape*); 10 million in 1610, 36 million in 1635, these mounted to a gigantic 72.6 million in 1643 before falling to 56 million on the eve of the Fronde. There was also a significant if less spectacular rise in the various indirect taxes managed by the tax farmers. Savage though the increase in the tax burden was, the problems for the regime would have been relatively slight if this had been the whole story. Theoretically the revenue from the principal taxes was more than enough to meet both the civil and military expenditure of the government, yet this was far from being so. In the first place the figures for the *taille* contain a considerable element of fantasy, there being no way in which the tax-paying population could meet the demands made of them. Everywhere arrears began to pile up. In 1641 the *élection* of Loches owed no less than 1 million *livres* accumulated since 1632. Two years later it was calculated that the *généralité* of Bourges owed 2.5 million going back six years. Secondly the fact that many payments were made locally continued to have a profound effect on the net receipts of the *épargne*. In the 10 years from 1626 those from the *taille* were actually less than at any moment in the previous 25 years; in 1635 less than one sixth of the amount levied found its way to the treasury. The tax farms also experienced a series of crises as the disruption of trade and the general misery of the population undermined both ease of collection and capacity to pay. In 1632 the *gabelle* provided just 1.5 million. These difficulties were then compounded by a policy of over-leasing which was in turn followed by remissions of rent to save the tax farmers from bankruptcy. Between 1637 and 1641 the *aides* teetered on the edge of collapse. During the

Fronde some farmers simply abandoned their leases. For a period in 1652 the government was obliged to administer the five consolidated tax farms of northern France itself. When it did find a consortium of financiers willing to assume responsibility, the initial lease was for a derisory 1.9 million *livres*.

The inevitable outcome of these difficulties was an ever greater reliance on extraordinary taxes, fiscal expedients and private credit. Venality of office, temporarily abolished in 1618 in accordance with earlier promises, was restored as the wars against the Huguenots got underway, subsequently assuming a vital rôle in royal finances; during the 1630s the *parties casuelles* provided no less than a quarter of the total revenues. By contrast the contribution of the *taille* had dropped from 50 per cent to a mere 10 per cent. Even more significant was the growth in income from the extraordinary taxes which, by the late 1630s, yielded approximately one half of the total. Prior to 1619 extraordinary revenues had averaged about 7.5 million each year but by the 1620s this had risen to 11.4 million, in the 1630s to 40.7 million and during the next decade to over 53 million. Although it should be borne in mind that these averages are inflated by one or two particularly bad years – in 1635 extraordinary revenues totalled an amazing 156 million *livres* – they clearly reveal the tightening grip of the *traitants* with whom the crown negotiated the new impositions that provided the bulk of this income. One of the major items negotiated with the *traitants* was the sale of government *rentes* or bonds. In 1634 8 million *livres* of *rentes* were issued on the *taille* and 3 million on the *gabelle*. Such policies of course simply mortgaged the future revenue of the crown. Not only did the *rentiers* have to be paid interest but the *traitants* claimed 25 per cent interest, or even more, on their transactions. Moreover the flooding of the market with *rentes* dramatically reduced their value and the expected yield never materialized. Similarly the market for offices also became saturated and from 1642 income from the *parties casuelles* dropped significantly. A bad situation was now made worse by recourse to large-scale borrowing in anticipation of future revenues which were assigned to financiers who would provide ready cash. By 1645 income from the *taille* had been anticipated as far ahead as 1647 and in 1648 loans were secured against the revenues of 1650 and 1651. Compelled to renege on its contracts during the political crisis of 1648 and thus precipitate the already incipient bankruptcy, the subsequent recovery of the regency government owed much to the willingness of the financiers to maintain their support. Between 1650 and 1654 the revenue from extraordinary taxation rose to an unprecedented 63 per cent of the total, the market was flooded with yet more *rentes* and even the customs revenues were anticipated by further loan contracts. Colbert estimated that by 1661 the total indebtedness of the crown amounted to 451 million *livres* (380 million if adjusted to 1600 prices). Even if he were guilty of a little hyperbole, it was more than justified by the enormity of the fiscal problems facing the crown.

Long before the full effects of the Thirty Years War were felt it was already apparent that the government could no longer afford to allow the resources and revenues of the realm to be diverted or continue to tolerate the host of exemptions claimed by privileged provinces, towns or corporate bodies. Under Henry IV the Auvergne had to ward off an attempt to introduce the *gabelle* from which it had earlier purchased its freedom, whilst in the Agenais the Estates became embroiled in a bitter struggle against proposals for new tariffs and tolls on the Dordogne and Garonne. However it was the campaigns against the Huguenots that really opened up the way for a significant extension of the royal fisc. Victory brought with it for the first time effective control over the provinces and ports of the west, many of which, if they were not actually exempt from royal taxes, had proved very reluctant to establish the appropriate customs offices. Of greatest value to the government was the access which it gained to the rich salt pans of Saintonge and Aunis. Ironically it was able to utilize a salt tax originally levied by the Huguenots known as the '*trente cinq sols de Brouage*' to undermine the otherwise privileged status of these regions. Between 1633 and 1655 the weight of this tax doubled. In addition officers were created to supervise the measuring of the salt at the various bureaux, a process which culminated in the creation of a sovereign court at La Rochelle in 1639 with jurisdiction 'over all the proceedings civil or criminal which pertain to the salt marshes of the town and government of Brouage.' Even the Ile de Ré, traditionally free of all taxes, recognized as a *pays d'étranger* to be outside the customs boundaries of the realm, was subjected to both salt and wine taxes. In neighbouring Guyenne the *parlement* of Bordeaux had to engage in a long running battle with the farmers of the *convoi et comptablie*, a number of originally distinct customs and subsidies; it even went so far as to execute one of the fiscal agents but was unable to prevent the institutionalization of this farm which in time became the biggest provider of revenue in the province. Regions where royal control was more effective suffered correspondingly. Normandy, already overtaxed by comparison with other provinces, saw its theoretical right to consent to taxation simply swept aside by the *élus*. In 1631 the Estates accorded 473,000 *livres* in *taille* on the *généralité* of Caen but over a million was actually collected.

Crucial for the fortunes of the monarchy was its ability to exploit and control the towns. The practice of appealing to them for assistance or simply imposing forced loans was nothing new. Even before the end of the civil wars a major centre like Rouen began to feel the adverse effects of royal fiscalism; a 5 per cent surtax on cloth in 1582 was followed four years later by new taxes on paper and playing cards so hefty that they apparently provoked the emigration of some of the manufacturers. Yet these impositions were of little consequence compared with those that subsequently not only rendered many municipalities bankrupt but destroyed any capacity to resist the government. Amiens, which lost all its privileges in 1597 because of its alleged failure to resist the Spanish, was one of the first victims; reduced to insolvency by demands for war subsidies, new taxes on trade and the need to purchase its own municipal offices from the king, its budget was completely out of balance by 1626. Perfectly loyal towns suffered the same fate. Bourges, the home of the monarchy during the worst days of the Hundred Years War and well rewarded for its loyalty, suffered a steady erosion of its fiscal privileges. Faced with Sully's *pancarte* (5 per cent sales tax) the municipality conducted a partially successful resistance but none the less had to agree to an annual subsidy of 4,500 *livres* instead. On the death of Henry IV it refused to pay any more but the intervention of the governor quickly ended this display of resistance. By 1633 the town's liquid assets were so diminished that it could not even purchase the office of municipal treasurer from the crown. For failing to do so it was punished by the seizure of its remaining funds. Four years later communal properties were sold in order to cope with outstanding debts.

Gradually the attack on the towns assumed a more generalized character. From 1636 they suffered a series of forced loans, taxes on the well-to-do (*luxe des aisés*) and an attempt to revive the *pancarte*. None was particularly successful and all aroused great opposition, which may have contributed to the government's decision in 1647 to seize municipal funds in order to redeem its own desperate plight. Although the towns were given authority to replenish their treasuries by increasing the *octrois* many were in no position to do so and themselves resorted to loans. As towns slid into bankruptcy the government seized the opportunity to send *commissaires* or intendants to investigate their finances and preside over the liquidation of the debts. This had already occurred in some towns of Provence and Dauphiné in the time of Sully and under Richelieu the practice became widespread. In 1631 *commissaires* were dispatched with orders to verify the debts of the towns and communities of Languedoc, even where this had already been done by the royal council or provincial Estates. Similar investigations followed in the other great *pays d'états* – Provence, Dauphiné, Burgundy – whilst less comprehensive ones were made in Guyenne, Auvergne, Champagne and elsewhere. Whether the council expected to unearth untaxed wealth behind the debts of the towns is not clear; they certainly provided a means of extending royal authority and further developing the functions of the intendants.

If necessary the work of the royal agents could be reinforced by direct political intervention. Resistance to the *pancarte* provided Henry IV with the opportunity to reduce the consultate of Limoges from twelve to six. A similar fate overtook the Dijon authorities in 1631. The franchise was also restricted severely and henceforth the mayor was to be chosen by the king from a list of three names, thus exploiting a device which was not uncommon in the constitution of the northern towns. Increasingly the intendants, sometimes in conjunction with provincial governors, were empowered to intervene in municipal elections. The governor and the intendant suspended the elections at Aix-en-Provence in 1634–5 and again in 1647–8, appointing the municipal officials themselves. Despite its formidable array of privileges Marseille found its elections suspended annually from 1643 to 1645. In 1656 riots in Angers against a new tax brought the intendant to the town with troops; he immediately proposed a new constitution for the town and for the next two years the mayor and *échevins* were simply imposed. Some towns resisted more successfully than others and some retained important economic privileges, notably the trading monopolies of certain key ports, but this could not obscure the general and progressive destruction of their fiscal and political autonomy.

By comparison with the urban communities the clergy and nobility remained highly privileged orders; but even they did not escape from royal determination to raise money wherever possible. The decennial assemblies of the clergy regularly renewed their financial contract with the crown, although not always with good grace. In addition they were put under intense pressure to increase the amount of the 'free gift'. In 1621 when the bi-annual assembly, whose brief was merely to check the accounts, was asked for a hefty loan it took four months of continuous pressure and two enforced moves of location before it finally agreed. Three million *livres* were to be raised from the sale of ecclesiastical offices, the *tithe*, and taxes on benefices. In 1628 Richelieu ordered the clergy to assemble at Poitiers to provide assistance for the siege of La Rochelle. This irregular process did not encourage them to be generous and when, after one enforced move of location and pressure from the pope, they still offered only 2 million *livres* the king was incensed. Again the clergy gave way, finally agreeing to find 3 million by yet more sales of office and taxes on benefices. By 1640 Richelieu however was asking for twice the amount, no less than 6 million *livres*. By dint of manipulating and intimidating the assembled clerics, the first 4 million was forthcoming without undue difficulty. But the opposition to the payment of any further amount obliged Richelieu to act with his characteristic ruthlessness. In June, after three months of fruitless endeavour, he overcame the opposition by the simple expedient of expelling six recalcitrant bishops from the assembly. Shaken by this dramatic and unprecedented infringement of their liberties, the delegates managed to find 5.5 million *livres*.

The nobility had no comparable means of resistance as that afforded to the clergy by their regular assemblies. Although no frontal attack was made on their tax privileges, measures were introduced to prevent abuse. As early as 1600 legislation was enacted to ensure that all tenants both of ecclesiastical and noble *seigneurs* were on the tax roles. This was repeated in 1634 and 1640 and reinforced by regulations limiting the amount of land on which a noble could claim exemption. At the same time extensive investigations were instigated into the validity of noble titles in order to try to reduce the numbers claiming exemption from the *taille*. Although such investigations never yielded much in the way of financial benefit to the crown, as most holders of dubious titles were not very rich, the manner of their execution caused no little irritation. In 1634 and 1635 the Estates of Normandy complained of the actions of the tax farmers and the *trésoriers* responsible for carrying out verification of noble titles. Searches made by agents of the *gabelles* who entered the houses of the nobility were alo a constant cause of complaint.

Perhaps the biggest single infringement of noble rights took place in Dauphiné where there occurred a protracted and bitter conflict between the second and third estates over whether the *taille* was *personnelle* or *réelle*. Eventually the third estate who objected to the ability of the nobility to buy up property and remove it from the fiscal system by virtue of their personal status, won the argument. In 1634 the *taille* was declared *réelle*; henceforth exemption would be determined by the status of the land rather than that of the owner. Moreover the government was able to exploit the dispute to dispense with the Estates, which were never summoned after 1628 and in which the third estate, their victory achieved, lost any real interest. The nobility of Dauphiné were eventually permitted to assemble in 1638 but the only concession they obtained was the right to appeal to the intendant against decisions of the fiscal agents.

Of all the groups who felt the force of the government's fiscal policies the *officiers* are the most interesting because, not only were they exempt from the *taille*, but they also constituted a crucial element in the state administration. Their ambivalent position as both exploiters and exploited can be illustrated in a number of ways. Most obvious was the trenchant opposition of existing office-holders to the creation of new offices which devalued their own. The *parlement* of Aix-en-Provence for instance conducted almost perpetual guerrilla warfare over this issue. In 1628 it had to contend with the creation of no less than 37 new offices in the provincial *cour des comptes*. Four years later a confrontation developed over the decision to create two entirely new *sénéchaussée* courts which the *parlementaires* refused to ratify until 1638. In 1641 the *parlement* learnt that it was to be saddled with a new *chambre des requêtes* consisting of two presidents, 14 magistrates, one *procureur* and 20 lesser personnel. Open conflict erupted with the intendant and in 1645 10 of the most recalcitrant magistrates were suspended from office. Worse befell in January 1648 with the proposed establishment of a *semestre* – an additional corps of 95 officers who were to alternate with the existing magistrates every six months. A similar fate had already overtaken the *parlement* of Rouen which had likewise been engaged in a long struggle against the imposition of new offices. The *parlement* of Bordeaux by contrast was able to purchase the withdrawal of 12 new councillorships in 1639 on payment of 400,000 *livres*.

That was one way to raise a forced loan. Equally effective was the practice of either suspending the payment of salaries or offering a future increase in salaries in return for an immediate contribution. Sometimes suspension of salaries was accompanied by suspension of payment of interest on the *rentes*, which was a double blow to the thousands of *officiers* who were also *rentiers*. In 1645 the payment of both was reduced by 50 per cent and by more in the years that followed. Even before this it was estimated that the salaries of the Parisian *parlementaires* were 1,200,000 *livres* in arrears; in 1648 the *élus* complained that they had paid over 200 million into the royal coffers since 1620. A far more risky method of exploiting the office-holders was by manipulation of the *paulette*. When it was re-established in 1621 the financial conditions were extremely heavy, amounting to the imposition of a loan of 5 per cent of the value of an office supplemented by annual payments of 1 per cent. Such was the opposition that the terms were subsequently modified for members of the sovereign courts and other principal officers who were required to pay only the annual levy. Inevitably lesser office-holders found that they had to make good the loss to the crown with an even higher loan of 6.66 per cent. In fact the government had arrived at a most effective method of dividing and exploiting its own agents. In 1636 when the king extended the term of the *paulette* for six years on condition that the annual payments for 1637 and 1638 be paid in advance, the sovereign courts were exempted.

However this tactic had its limitations, for the *parlements* were not only offended by the infringement of their members' rights as office-holders but also in their capacity as judicial bodies which claimed the right to register all legislation including financial proposals. Although the government could proceed without registration this undoubtedly made tax collection much more difficult. From 1636 the *parlement* of Paris increasingly refused to ratify new tax proposals or so modified them that their value was destroyed. In reply the crown resorted to *lettres de jussion* to enforce its will or simply circumvented the *parlement* by turning to the usually less troublesome *cour des aides* or *chambre des comptes*. Yet even here support could not be guaranteed. The *comptes* itself had grown increasingly irritated by the practice of preventing public scrutiny of the disbursements to the financiers by recording them in the *comptants* (secret expenses) of the royal council. By 1644 the accounting officials were prepared to join with other sovereign bodies in opposing the ratification of financial edicts. In desperation, as the financial situation worsened, the government resorted to two *lits de justice* – one in September 1645 and again in January 1648 – to force some 25 edicts through *parlement*. Not only was this quite unprecedented during a regency, but the crisis was then compounded by the decision of April 1648 to suspend the *gages* of all the officers throughout the realm, with the exception of the Parisian *parlementaires*, in return for the renewal of the *paulette*. It was this crude threat to the patrimonial interests of the office-holders which finally precipitated the Fronde.

Undoubtedly the search for ever-increasing sums of money brought the crown into conflict with a multiplicity of privileged groups and corporations. The net result was to intensify the authoritarian stance of the government and many of the incidents that were precipitated had a significant political dimension. In particular there was a discernible shift in the relationship between the crown and municipalities. Yet, that said, the durability of many of the fiscal measures was limited. Indeed it was inherent in the situation that permanent alterations could be avoided by paying up. Above all the mere multiplication of fiscal expedients in an essentially *ad hoc* way did nothing to overcome the lack of uniformity in the fiscal administration which so inhibited the development of a truly effective tax-raising machinery. If anything the consolidation of five of the major custom taxes of northern France into one farm (*cinq grosses fermes*) by Henry IV confirmed the fiscal separation of north and south. In any event there still remained 19 separate duties levied along the length of the internal tariff wall. Nor did the mere multiplication of taxes, however onerous, in itself do anything to overcome the fiscal and political divide between the *pays d'états* and the *pays d'élections*. On the contrary, although the *pays d'états* could not escape entirely from the mounting burdens (particularly the *étapes* and other military obligations), the fact that the government had to negotiate with them for both the *taille* and any additional *don gratuit* certainly enabled them to escape comparatively lightly. In 1620 Provence paid a pathetic 170,000 *livres* in *tailles* and Languedoc a mere 223,900.

Sully was the first minister to grapple seriously with this problem, apparently wishing to create *élections* in the major *pays d'états* and to introduce *cours des aides* where none existed. Perhaps because royal backing was lacking for such a radical reform, he concentrated his efforts in the end on Guyenne where the provincial Estates (as opposed to the local assemblies) were not particularly vigorous and where *élections* already existed in the Bordelais. After a softening-up process involving the dispatch of *commissaires* and the installation of a chamber of justice to investigate tax frauds in the region, legislation was introduced in 1603 establishing eight new *élections*. Such was the resistance that the new officers were unable to begin work until 1609 and thereafter life was made so difficult for them that it became impossible for the regency government to resist the pressure for their suspension. However that was not the end of the matter. In September 1621, taking advantage of his triumphant military progress through Guyenne to Montauban, Louis ordered the re-establishment of the *élections*. The edict did not require the abolition of either the provincial or local Estates and indeed they continued to meet in some localities down to 1630 or so. However their functions were effectively usurped by the *élus*, and co-operation between the various communities became increasingly difficult, particularly as the privileged orders displayed no real interest in the assemblies. The provincial Estates of Guyenne met for the last time in 1635.

During the course of 1628 and 1629 the government, undoubtedly encouraged by its victory over the Huguenots, decided that the moment had come to bring the remaining *pays d'états* into line. In close succession edicts were issued introducing *élections* in Dauphiné, Burgundy, Provence and Languedoc. Only in Dauphiné, where, as has been observed, the government was able to take advantage of the rivalries between the second and third estates, was the policy successful. Maybe the relative apathy of the third estate was also encouraged by the fact that a truncated form of assembly dominated by the towns did survive. In the other three provinces by contrast the resistance was immense, involving major uprisings in Dijon and Aix, and culminating in Languedoc in the alliance of 1632 between the Estates and the provincial governor, Montmorency, who was also conspiring with Gaston d'Orléans against the king. The first reaction of the government was to punish Dijon by the lost of its privileges, to deprive Aix of its status as provincial capital and to exile its *parlement*. Yet Richelieu fairly quickly agreed to withdraw the *élections* in return for substantial cash payments and to restore the privileges of the two cities. Whilst the rebellion of Montmorency cost him his head, and thus broke the ancient connection of that family with Languedoc, the scale of the revolt none the less forced the crown to compromise. By the Edict of Béziers (October 1632) the *élections* were suppressed. On the other hand the rôle of the royal *trésoriers* at the meetings of Estates was enhanced and the levels of various contributions raised. In addition the Estates were reduced to meeting for only 15 days a year and their scope for dispensing monetary gratifications limited.

Richelieu's abandonment of the attempt to extend *élections* has been attributed by Russell Major to his 'indifference to institutions' and a desire to raise revenue quickly. It was, it is argued, the keeper of the seals, Marillac, who was the thorough-going absolutist and whose policy was reversed after his fall in 1630.[5] At best the evidence for this is circumstantial but even if it

---

[5] J.R. Major, *Representative Government in Early Modern France* (New Haven, Yale University Press, 1980), pp.618 ff.

were conceded that a difference of approach did exist between the two men, it hardly follows that Richelieu's triumph over Marillac involved a retreat from absolutist policies. Indeed, there were very good and well-understood reasons for not regarding the creation of *élections* as a panacea for the government's financial problems or as the best method for developing fiscal uniformity, for as Major himself shows such a policy required the establishment of hundreds of additional venal office-holders, with all the disadvantages that entailed. After the installation of the *élections* in Rouergue, the cost of sustaining the financial administration rose to over 27,000 *livres* per annum compared with the 8,000 that the local Estates had previously spent on their entire activities. In Dauphiné the administrative costs of the fiscal machinery doubled. The abortive proposals for Languedoc involved the creation of 700 new officials and would have produced a tenfold increase in administrative overheads. Moreover this estimate takes no account of the almost inevitable diversion of revenues that would have followed. *Élus* were renowned for their inefficiency and corruption. Some were actually non-resident; others made assessments without even bothering to undertake the obligatory tour of inspection. They undertaxed the parishes where they had connections and overtaxed those that had the temerity to challenge them at law. Like all other officials they lined their own pockets. At Saintes the *élus* netted 81,000 *livres* in two years from law suits alone. To multiply the number of such officials was merely to multiply the burdens on the labouring population for limited financial advantages and at the cost of a great deal of aggravation. By 1648 there were no less than 3,000 treasurers and *élus*, generally agreed to be more than enough.

The more radical solution to the problems facing the crown was not the creation of yet more venal office-holders but the dispatch of *commissaires* or intendants whose powers and authority depended solely on the commissions they held from the royal council. As early as 1598 such agents had in fact been sent into at least nine *généralités* with instructions to re-allocate the *taille* and to investigate the alleged malpractices of the financial officials. They were also empowered to assess the capacity of the parishes to pay. Whilst this investigation lasted for only a year, it became the model for subsequent attempts to overcome the shortcomings of the treasurers and *élus*. A similar effort was made in six *généralités* in 1623, and in 1634 in all the *pays d'élections*. From 1635 concern grew in government circles about the ability of the officers to meet the urgent fiscal needs of the country. During 1635 and 1636 *commissaires* were in operation in a number of *généralités* exercising the functions of assessment and levying of taxes normally undertaken by the financial officials. Their investigations were sometimes amazingly thorough; at Alençon the intendant checked the tax rolls back to 1600. The intendants also assumed responsibility for the forced loan on the towns in 1637, the *subsistance* of 1638, the *taxe des aisés* of 1639 and the *pancarte* of 1641. In November of that year royal intentions were clearly spelt out in the edict for the levying of the *taille*; this enumerated the complaints about the inequitable distribution of the *taille* and the partiality of the officers, threatening to transfer their functions to the intendants should matters not improve. Barely given time to respond, the officers were finally deprived of their authority over the *taille* in August 1642. Henceforth, except for the period during the

Fronde when the intendancies were suppressed, the treasurers and *élus* were merely the subordinate agents of the intendants. The latter assumed complete responsibility for all the direct taxes, with full powers to preside over the distribution of the *taille*, to verify the accounts of the receivers and a determining voice in the *bureaux des finances*.

Economic Nationalism and State Intervention

In 1506 an edict was issued forbidding the export of all money and bullion save specie of inferior quality. This was followed during the reign of Francis I by attempts to persuade the towns to accept a number of restrictions designed to achieve the same end. Thus the crown wished to impose a ban on the import of English cloth, to control the influx of spices and drugs, and to require French merchants to pay for two thirds of foreign purchases with French goods. Despite the largely negative response from the municipal authorities, which were fearful of injuring their own activities, the years that followed saw the multiplication of restrictive legislation covering a growing list of commodities. Tariffs on silk and other fine materials were also supplemented by measures to limit the wearing of luxury apparel to those of the appropriate status. The burgeoning sense of national economic interest revealed by such legislation was underpinned by the widespread conviction that it was both possible and desirable for France to dispense with the service of foreigners. Claude de Seyssel articulated the belief that was to permeate French economic theory and practice for two centuries when he declared France to be 'so abundant in wealth that she can much more easily do without her neighbours than they can do without her.' From mid century the attempt to give substance to this claim was reflected in a series of privileges bestowed on a variety of textile producers in order to foster domestic manufacturers. The government also began to manifest its concern for the quality of French products. In 1571 it issued an edict which fixed the length, width and number of threads for different types of cloth, thus anticipating the preoccupation with the details of textile production that was later so central to Colbert's activity.

Indeed all the key elements of what was subsequently described as mercantilism – the desire for self-sufficiency, discriminatory tariffs, protection of domestic manufacture – were in evidence prior to the reign of Henry IV. Moreover it was increasingly understood that the responsibility for the generation of these policies had to lie with the government. However it was only with the fading of the sixteenth century that all these elements were brought together in a generalized body of theory and practice which was to make France the country of state intervention *par excellence*. The most significant indication of a change of tempo and quality came in 1601 with the creation of the commission of commerce together with the appointment of Barthélemy de Laffemas, erstwhile *valet de chambre* to the king, as *contrôleur général de commerce*. Laffemas, an assiduous propagandist for government supervision of every aspect of economic activity, envisaged the creation of *bureaux des manufactures* in every major town through which the work of the merchant and craft gilds could be controlled. Although this was decidedly over-ambitious and although the commission of commerce lost impetus within a few years, there is no doubt that as a result of Laffemas's endeavours the level of state involvement was substantially increased. Members of the commission investigated innumerable proposals presented by entrepreneurs and offered or declined assistance as they deemed fit. A variety of entrepreneurs, involved in a wide range of activities from rug and tapestry manufacture to soap- and glass-making, benefited from privileges and material support. At the same time the number of gilds increased, thus bringing merchants and craftsmen within the framework of corporate bodies and subject to statutes which regulated everything from the training of apprentices to the manufacturing process itself. Where necessary statutes were amended or edicts – such as that banning the use of indigo in dyeing – introduced. Above all Laffemas directed his efforts towards the creation of an indigenous silk industry in France; whilst the inhibitants of the northern provinces proved immensely reluctant to turn land over to mulberry trees, in the south Laffemas achieved a major success and within a few years silk manufacture was well established. The early years of the seventeenth century saw also the appearance of the first state-sponsored trading ventures. In 1604 one Sieur de Monts and associates received a monopoly for 10 years of all trading rights over a large stretch of the Arcadian coast including the St Lawrence river. The government stipulated that in return his company should take out 100 colonists a year to 'New France'. The same year saw the founding of the French East India Company whose shareholders, on payment of the requisite 3,000 *livres*, obtained a 15-year monopoly of trade with the Indies. One further, but by no means insignificant, area of government activity was undertaken by Sully in his capacity as *grand voyer* which gave him responsibility for the development and upkeep of the highways. Expenditure on roads rose during his period of office from 14,000 *livres* to over a million per annum. Measures were also undertaken to improve the navigability of the waterways, the most famous project being that for the building of a canal between the Seine and the Loire, not however completed until 1640.

In part this intensification and extension of government intervention reflected the opportunities that came with the restoration of peace. Fundamentally, however, it was a manifestation of the growing realization that, far from progressing towards self-sufficiency, France was actually becoming increasingly dependent on its rivals, the English and, above all, the Dutch who were fast emerging as the dominant maritime and commercial nation. Immensely beneficial as the emergence of the Dutch republic was to the French for its rôle in undermining Spanish hegemony, the economic consequences were far less welcome. Amsterdam now became not merely the focal point of the commercial activity of northern Europe but also the centre of a maritime empire stretching from the Baltic to the Mediterranean and beyond. By the end of the century the Dutch had taken Seville without firing a shot, thus drawing into the orbit of Amsterdam the huge prize of Spanish America along with the merchants of Antwerp.[6] The effects of this relatively

[6] F. Braudel, *The Mediterannean and the Mediterannean World in the Age of Philip II* (2 vols., London, Collins, 1972–3) I, pp.636 ff.

rapid and dramatic shift of economic power on the French were almost entirely adverse. One of its most obvious consequences was the dislocation of the French system of currency which since 1575 had been adjusted to cope with the veritable flood of silver from Spanish America. With the last decade of the century the situation was rapidly reversed and the inland regions and mints of eastern France were quickly denuded of silver specie. Even the western ports began to encounter difficulties as the Dutch tightened their grip on the Atlantic trade and on the supplies of available silver. Finally the government was compelled to abandon accounting in silver and by 1607 copper had become the basis of the French currency. It was a formidable blow to a policy designed to increase the amount of circulating specie within the realm.

The shift away from the Mediterranean to the Atlantic, which was both reflected in, and reinforced by, the movement of silver, accentuated the regional imbalances within France. The slackening of trade along the eastern corridors of France already noted in the 1580s, was not paralleled in the western parts, benefiting as they did from the blossoming Atlantic trade. Even Rouen whose economic activity was violently disrupted during the period of League domination and the ensuing military campaigns in Normandy, seems to have recovered fairly quickly. By 1600 the birth rate was back to the 1585 levels, foreign merchants returned and the number of master craftsmen increased once more. For La Rochelle, protected by its walls and comprehensive privileges, the opening decades of the seventeenth century were years of immense prosperity. Yet little of the benefit, as the dwindling supply of silver specie shows, was passed on to the crown or felt outside the immediate hinterland of the ports. Partly this was a consequence of their fiscal privileges and partly because so much of their trade was not in French hands. Complaints about the Dutch presence in everything from the grain to the textile trade were rife. La Rochelle remained dependent on the Flemings (the general name for all inhabitants of the Low Countries) for ships of over 10 tons for its cannon, for expertise in sugar refining, and it preferred Dutch ropes to those made in the town. Moreover the disparity between the performance of the French and Dutch was such that in a variety of fields the government itself was obliged to have recourse to them, enticing them with privileges and promises of naturalization, to bring their skills and resources to France. Dutchmen or Flemings were called upon to do everything from draining marshes to providing the manpower and ships for the East Indies Company, notwithstanding the fact that the latter was established in direct competition with the Dutch EIC founded in 1602.

By comparison England as yet offered a challenge of somewhat lesser proportions. Nevertheless concern about the penetration of the French market by English woollens has already been noted from the early sixteenth century. In 1572 a treaty was agreed between the two countries to reduce the areas of friction. By the concessions which it granted to English merchants it seems to have created only more problems. From 1600 the French began to confiscate defective merchandise which culminated in a minor crisis when English cloth worth £75,000 was seized in Rouen. Tempers were further inflamed by English attempts to claim fishing rights up to 100 miles out to sea. Nor were French sensitivities reassured by the foundation in quick succession of the Virginia Company (1600) and the English EIC (1602). Laffemas observed bitterly that whilst French goods were no longer sold on the English market, their old hats, boots and shoes had free access to France.

It is then in the context of both the actual and the perceived threat to French aspirations created by the rapid rise of the Dutch and the English that the growth of state intervention should be seen. Nothing reveals this more clearly than the instructions sent by the king at the behest of the commission of commerce for the regulation of the manufacture of fustians at Rouen. Some measures were necessary he explained since:

> the workers . . . and those who employ them caring more for their own gain than for the public good do not sell them as they ought to either in length or width or in workmanship and inner worth, and in addition, they have not the skill to finish and dye them like those which are finished and dyed in foreign countries, and principally England: because of which it is to be feared that the French scorning them altogether will have recourse to foreigners and that this manufacture will be abandoned.[7]

Fear of foreign competition and the need to improve the quality of French produce was thus directly linked to the accusation that French producers cared little for the public good in order to justify tighter control.

On the death of Henry IV, Laffemas and Sully (who in any event had been less than wholehearted in his support for some of the controller's schemes), fell from power. Even before then many of these schemes had foundered in the face of insuperable financial difficulties or the hostility of vested interests. The company for trade in 'New France' aroused the anger of excluded merchants and the Paris hatters who complained so bitterly about the increased cost of fur that the monopoly was rescinded after only three years. The EIC never really came to life at all. Whilst manufacturers might welcome restrictions on imports, these impinged on the interests of the wholesale traders; thus the ban on silk imports fell foul of the Lyon merchant community. Lyon was also at the forefront of resistance to the edict of 1597 requiring that all merchants and craftsmen should be organized in gilds, and managed to secure recognition of its traditional freedom from them. Even proposals for the improvement of the highways ran into opposition. The Estates of Burgundy requested that no change should be made in the procedures for maintaining roads, whilst those of Languedoc in 1602 flatly declared that there was no money for the repair of bridges; they were even unwilling to establish a safe harbour at Sète and the project was abandoned.

Such difficulties, and the general loosening of authority during the regency, seem however to have reinforced rather than destroyed the search for comprehensive solutions to the country's economic problems. Certainly nothing was more comprehensive than the extraordinary scheme for a gigantic trading company put before the royal council in 1613 by François du

[7] C.W. Cole, *Colbert and a Century of French Mercantilism* (2 vols., Hamden, Archon Books, 1964) I, pp.52–3.

Noyer. Modelled after companies in Seville, Lisbon, Genoa, Amsterdam and London, the new body was to be given extensive rights over both domestic and foreign trade as well as manufacturing. The draft proposals ran to 63 clauses, giving the company amongst other things the power to construct quays along the Seine, build tanneries and slaughterhouses, rights over abandoned quarries in or near Paris, the right to capture vagabonds and transport them to the colonies, the sole right to run public coaches, to supervise all dyeing, to have a monopoly for the production of playing cards and authority to verify the quality of all fabrics for export. All this was in addition to the essential business of maintaining 45 vessels on the sea. Although du Noyer's proposals attracted the support of the government and he inherited Laffemas's office of *contrôleur*, there was no way such a grandiose conception could be implemented. Failing to gain the co-operation of the major cities as he had hoped, du Noyer gradually reduced his horizons, turning to the Estates of Brittany for assistance. Even this was denied, although du Noyer continued to tout his schemes around for years

Within two years of de Noyer's ambitious proposals there also appeared Antoine de Montchrétien's *Traité de l'économie politique*. Celebrated for its pioneering use of the term 'political economy' this work brought together a mass of ideas for the regeneration of manufactures and the development of trade, and culminated in a discourse on the rôle of the crown. 'The most royal task which your majesties can undertake', he declared, 'is to restore order where it has been destroyed, to regulate the mechanical arts which are in a monstrous state of confusion, to re-establish trade and commerce which have been interrupted and troubled for so long.' Without such an effort France would not meet the challenge of its rivals whose threatening presence is reflected in virtually every page of the book. The Dutch, Montchrétien observed, 'dominate the linen trade, the English that in woollens, whilst France is even dependent on Germans for scythes. We are the foreigners here and foreigners are the citizens.' It was necessary to retaliate with the sort of measures imposed on Frenchmen elsewhere. Montchrétien noted with particular approval the regulations covering commercial transactions in London: 'very precise at the expense of our own which are full of licence and liberty.' Much tighter control of foreign vessels was required and French ships should be used in preference to foreign ones. He also commended the financial assistance given by the English crown for the construction of large ships, and urged the government to follow the profitable example of the Dutch in creating an East India Company. Of course a war fleet was essential if French interests on the high seas were to be protected.

With this observation Montchrétien alighted on a huge problem for the French government. Far from being able to defend its merchants at sea, it barely had control of its own coastline. At the beginning of the century authority in this sphere as in so many others was fragmented. The admiral of France controlled only the coast of Normandy and Picardy, whilst three other admirals claimed extensive privileges together with the lucrative revenues they brought. In addition there were a host of lesser claims for a share in maritime matters. At Les Sables d'Olonne the duc de Thouars contrived to divert the revenues of the admiral for his own benefit, whilst the *parlement* of Bordeaux strove continuously to retain a right of appeal from the admiralty of Guyenne. During times of crisis the Rochelais established their own admiralty. In 1620–2 this abrogated the right to levy taxes, authority over prizes, the power to direct merchants and commandeer their ships. Moreover the Rochelais fleet was bigger and more powerful than that of the crown which consisted of a few Mediterranean galleys, useless in the rougher waters of the Atlantic. For years Rochelais privateers dominated the seaboard, intimidating the merchants of Bordeaux and harassing shipping in the English Channel. Rochelais vessels, frequently armed to the teeth, were also regularly sighted in the St Lawrence in defiance of trading privileges given to others.

An initial step towards the administrative centralization of the marine was taken in 1613 when the duc de Montmorency acquired the admiralty of Guyenne from the Coligny family, to which he added those of France and Brittany inherited from his uncle. Despite the objections of the *parlements* he styled himself grand admiral or admiral general of France. In 1620 Montmorency also bought the post of viceroy of New France from Condé. By this time it was becoming clear that any progress which might be made towards central control would be impeded by the *force majeure* of the Rochelais and their allies. When a reasonable royal fleet was finally assembled in Brittany in early 1625 it was captured almost in its entirety by Soubise, brother of the duc de Rohan. Ironically it was only as a result of the alliances negotiated with Holland in April 1624 and with England (sealed by the marriage of Charles I to Henrietta Maria the following May) that the government was able to gain the military initiative. With 12 vessels lent by these strange new friends, on the 14 September Montmorency engaged and finally defeated the Rochelais fleet. Richelieu repaid the duke by abolishing his post of grand admiral and personally assuming the title and office of *grand-maître et surintendant de la navigation et commerce de France*. This completed the centralization of naval administration and gave Richelieu authority over the movement of merchant ships as well. The principal justification of the move however lay in the declared intention to create 'a powerful and well-regulated company to undertake general commerce by sea and land' and 'without which neighbours and foreigners will not be able to dispense to the honour and grandeur of our state, the profit and growth of the public interest.' Next the cardinal presented his plans to the Assembly of Notables which was summoned in late 1626. Carefully chosen though this gathering of prelates, magnates and leading magistrates was, there is no doubting their genuine approval of the idea of trading companies and the creation of an Atlantic fleet of 45 vessels. 'On the power of the sea', declared the archbishop of Bordeaux, 'depends the lowering of the pride of England, Holland and Spain . . . and the ruin of the Huguenots.'

The linking of domestic and foreign issues was perceptive. Victory over La Rochelle not only brought with it access to the lucrative trade in wine and salt but also opened up the way for greater government intervention in maritime affairs. Amongst the many clauses of the Code Michaud of 1629 there were those stipulating that all French sailors abroad were to return home and cease to serve foreigners, a census of seamen and sailors should be made, no ship was to sail without royal permission, foreign ships were not to be loaded except with salt, shipwreck rights were to be abolished and the *grand-maître* was to ensure the improvement of harbours and other facilities. Over-ambitious and over-detailed though it was, the aspirations reflected in the Code Michaud were not entirely disappointed. The naval budget rose from 1.5 million *livres* in 1626 to 3 or 4 million between 1628 and 1642. Naval arsenals were developed at Havre, Brest and Brouage. By 1640 Richelieu had 40 or 50 galleys at his disposal and perhaps 35 ships of the line in the Atlantic. Commissioners were regularly dispatched to the ports to improve efficiency and reduce the fraudulent practices of the local officials. At the same time Richelieu put much effort into a variety of trading and colonial enterprises. A number were more or less stillborn. Nevertheless companies were revived or established which ensured for France a presence however tenuous in Canada, the West and East Indies and elsewhere.

Although the cardinal's main interest lay in commerce and the navy, the now well-established pattern of government intervention in manufacturing also continued. Under his aegis regulations were issued covering the activities of leather workers, parchment makers, tanners, gold- and silversmiths, butchers, masons, plaster makers and paper makers. Further attempts were made to improve the performance of the crucial textile industry. In 1639 the government issued an edict for the control of all woollens and of the dyeing thereof, which required the establishment of inspectors in every town and city. The opposition was enormous and in Rouen so violent that troops had to be called up.

However the intense activity of the cardinal and his associates cannot obscure the fact that at the end of the day the fundamental objectives of the government remained unfulfilled. English and Dutch commercial and colonial superiority constituted an unyielding fact of life. The Baltic trade was virtually monopolized by them, whilst in the East Indies French ventures encountered their unremitting resistance. The Company of New France formed in 1628 suffered from internal dissension and English interlopers. By 1642 there were only 200 settlers in New France as opposed to the projected 4,000. The settlements in the West Indies depended on Dutch supplies. At home Dutchmen were still called upon for assistance with draining marshes and the establishment of sugar refineries. Tapestry production depended not only on Dutch but also Italian skill. Moreover the requirement of France's anti-Spanish foreign policy made it difficult to sustain outright hostility towards the Dutch; in the critical year of 1635, despite vociferous protests, Dutch merchants acquired the same rights as native ones in French ports. The fragility of Richelieu's achievements and the extent to which progress depended on the drive and initiative of individual ministers, was revealed within a short time of his death. Ship construction virtually petered out; by 1660 the navy was reduced to perhaps 20 vessels, not all fit for service. Between 1648 and 1661 no commander went to sea more than three times, whilst 6,000 sailors still served abroad. The merchant fleet also lagged far behind its rivals. In his *Le commerce honorable* (1646) Jean Eon estimated that France had barely 600 ships to compare with the Dutch 10,000. This was reflected in an annual trade deficit of 9 million *livres*, 5 million of which Eon thought stemmed from the adverse relationship with the Dutch. Modern scholarship would seem to bear him out; in 1651 for instance only 24 per cent of the shipping tonnage passing through Bordeaux was French, the vast majority of the larger vessels being foreign.

Eon and his contemporaries were thus preoccupied with exactly the same problems as their predecessors at the beginning of the century. On the eve of the Fronde the *parlement* of Paris complained that 'woollens and silks of all sorts and types are no longer made in this kingdom as they used to be because of those that the Dutch and English merchants bring into it'. Moreover the solutions propounded for overcoming foreign superiority changed not at all. In 1654 it was suggested that the Commission of Commerce be revived. In 1659 Focuquet ordered an imposition of 50 *sous* on every ton carried by foreign vessels. Foreign vessels were deemed to be those with a crew less than two thirds French. The mind boggles at what the state required of its local officials and the problems of enforcing such a decree. Economic self-sufficiency rested like a mirage on the road ahead, luring the government on to ever greater endeavours in hitherto unprecedented attempts at manipulating and stimulating all the manifold aspects of economic activity. Failure simply reinforced the insistence on authoritarian solutions. Nothing reveals this more sharply than the response to the problems generated by the steady rise in the incidence of vagabondage and destitution. The ravages of civil wars, combined with the mounting pressure on the land, from firstly a rising population and then the *rentier* activities of the urban notables, had produced a massive influx of indigent poor into the towns. Aggravated by the widening gulf between those in a position to profit from inflation, scarcity and privilege and those with nothing but their labour to sell, urban poverty outgrew the capacity of traditional forms of charitable endeavour. The mercantilists anxious to utilize the human resources of the realm dreamt up typically grandiose schemes to set the poor to work. Laffemas devoted two pamphlets to the problem, eventually proposing the establishment of workhouses financed by entrepreneurs and merchants. Du Noyer envisaged the distribution of tickets which would enable the poor to find work through employment bureaux. Those without tickets would be shut away. Some of the mercantilists' aims were fulfilled locally at Lyon where in 1614 an *hôpital-général* was established offering limited relief to those unable to work and some training to those who could.

However the relative stagnation of the economy precluded the possibility of any significant reduction in the number of the idle poor; and as time passed the emphasis in the remedies shifted from a desire to offer gainful employment to the need to preserve public order and decency. Richelieu felt that it was necessary to confine the unemployed poor because otherwise they simply resorted to begging, which deprived the deserving poor of bread. In the years of mounting unrest which culminated in the Fronde, this repressive tone grew even more insistent. Leadership of the movement for reform also passed to the Company of the Holy Sacrament, a rather unpleasant and secretive offshoot of the counter reformation. Its members, draw from the urban élites in perhaps 60 localities, regarded themselves as the guardians of clerical discipline and public morality. Their attitude towards poverty which they regarded as a sign of moral laxity, bore an uncanny resemblance to that of English Puritans. Licentiousness, drunkenness, profanity, begging and vagabondage were all lumped together as anti-social misdemeanours. The obvious solution was to remove the poor from the streets and give them a good dose of hard labour and religous instruction. In Paris the members of the Company together with many leading magistrates (who may or may not have been members) began to press vigorously for the establishment of a general hospital on the Lyon model, finally achieving their aim in 1656. An edict was issued amalgamating the administration of five existing hospitals dealing variously with beggars, the aged and infirm, prostitutes, orphans, foundlings, the insane and pregnant or nursing mothers. From the following year the poor were forcibly detained by the socially constituted 'archers of the poor' and subjected to a 'regular discipline of prayers, sermons, forced labour and, if needed, floggings'.[8] By 1661 there were some 5,000 internees and a number of similar institutions had been set up in the provinces. The following year a royal edict ordered their establishment in every town and large village 'in order to contain beggars and to instruct them in piety and the Christian religion'.[9]

The Contradictions of Emergent Absolutism

The net result of the religious, military and economic pressures analysed in the preceding pages was a further concentration of power at the centre and a corresponding, albeit variable, reduction in the autonomy of representative institutions, municipalities and corporate bodies ranging from the *parlements* to the gilds. Most obvious was the demise of the Estates-General after 1614–15 and the fading away of the provincial Estates in Guyenne, Dauphiné and Normandy, together with their replacement by less representative bodies in Burgundy and Provence. With the Estates-General also went any lingering hope of establishing the principle of no taxation without representation. Indeed the idea tended to disappear from the writings of the jurists. The principal agent through which the concentration of authority was effected was the intendant, whose truly comprehensive responsibilities, embracing everything from the surveillance of the Huguenots to the provision of army supplies, impinged on those of all the existing bodies without exception. In addition the development of the intendancies did something to diminish the administrative disparity between the *pays d'élections* and the *pays d'états*. The general rule became one *intendant* per *généralité* in the former and one per province in the latter.

However it was not just the scope of the intendant's authority which made him such a significant figure, for in distinction to the existing *officiers* he held his post by virtue of a royal commission and not through purchase. From the 1620s the commission invariably included powers of justice, police and finance, thus precluding the separation of executive and judicial functions

[8] O. Ranum, *Paris in the Age of Absolutism* (New York, Wiley, 1968), p.243.
[9] C. Lis and H. Soly, *Poverty and Capitalism in Pre-Industrial Europe* (Hassocks, Harvester Press, 1979), p.122.

which was to characterize more liberal regimes. The intendant wielded an administrative form of justice designed to get things done; it had little to do with a sense of equity, natural justice, or the traditional view so admirably expressed by Seyssel that justice constituted a restraint on royal power. On the contrary, the intendants were directly and solely responsible to the royal council. This body was itself in the process of transformation, tending to subdivide into specialist units. To the inner council, known from 1643 as the *conseil d'en haut,* were called only a handful of the chief ministers and royal advisers. Two lesser councils, the *conseil privé* and the *conseil d'état et des finances* were both presided over by the chancellor and had a much larger, essentially similar membership. Technically the former acted as a supreme court of appeal and adjudicated on disputes between lesser courts, whilst the latter, as its name implies, dealt essentially with financial matters; but despite attempts to delineate responsibilities, the line of demarcation remained unclear. In addition there appeared in mid century the *conseil des dépêches* consisting of the chancellor and ministers, which received dispatches from the provinces. Hesitant though these changes were, they nevertheless constituted an attempt to respond to the vast increase in government business and the need to break it down into manageable categories and to separate broad policy-making from routine administration. One consequence of the growing reliance on the professional administrators who staffed the councils was a reduction in the rôle and influence of the princes of the blood.

The clearest manifestation of these tendencies was the emergence of the two secretaries of state for foreign affairs and for war, together with the *surintendants des finances,* as the linchpins of the central administration, each responsible for embryonic government ministries. Ministers of finances were appointed in the late sixteenth century but a continuous line of *surintendants* is traceable only from 1619. Unlike the *surintendant,* who became the most powerful figure in the government after the chief minister, the secretaries of state were not originally ministers in their own right. They developed out of the scribes appointed to deal with council correspondence; four in number by the mid sixteenth century, they each had responsibility for a group of provinces. Only slowly did they assume more specialized functions and achieve the ministerial status which would assure access to the inner council; or, more accurately, it became customary for those appointed as ministers to purchase the appropriate secretaryship, for these charges retained their venal character. The department of foreign affairs was the first to take shape, assisted by the prolonged direction of Villeroy who occupied the secretaryship under four kings from Charles IX to Louis XIII. Subsequently Richelieu's personal supervision of foreign policy somewhat retarded the evolution of an independent ministry. By contrast, although a secretary of state for war did not appear until 1624, this department developed steadily with the onset of the Thirty Years War. The appointment in 1635 of Sublet de Noyers, succeeded in 1643 by the celebrated Michel le Tellier, marked the onset of a period of dynamic reforming activity which was reflected in the military developments noted earlier.

Government decisions were thus channelled through the secretaries of state who, more and more, dealt directly with the intendants, sending them instructions, requests for information and replying to their reports. These developments involved not simply a further reduction of the checks on monarchical authority, but the emergence of a bureaucratic as opposed to a patrimonial form of administration; that is to say, a system with a clear chain of command in which the office had become distinct from the office-holder and in which 'experts' operated according to institutionalized precedents. Paradoxically this resulted in a lessening of the direct involvement of the king and chief ministers (Richelieu and Mazarin rarely attended the lesser councils) and a simultaneous strengthening of the grip of the royal council over other elements of the body politic.

The most politically sensitive facet of this bureaucratic thrust lay in the way it brought to the fore the contentious question of the relationship between the royal council and its agents on the one hand and the sovereign courts, notably the *parlement* of Paris, on the other; for the development of the intendancies involved the delegation of sovereign judicial powers by commission and frequently without the verification of the *parlement*. In 1626, learning that some *maîtres des requêtes* had accepted commissions as intendants, the *parlement* expressly prohibited any person 'of whatever quality and condition they might be of executing any commission or of performing any act of justice by virtue of letters bearing an attribution of jurisdiction.... which have not been verified in the court'.[10] Far from being intimidated by such utterances the government made it quite clear that it regarded them as an unacceptable limitation of royal sovereignty. The Code Michaud of 1629 included proposals for the establishment of a special judicial commission in the provinces (*grands jours*) and the creation of a permanent chamber to investigate financial malpractice. Forced, albeit after seven months of filibustering, to register the code, the magistrates were quite unable to prevent Richelieu resorting to the use of hand-picked panels of judges whenever he felt it appropriate. Such commissions were employed to impose the death penalty on the comte de Chalais (1626), Montmorency (1632) and Cinq-Mars (1642). The most notorious of all was the *chambre de l'arsenal*; created in 1631 to deal with counterfeiters and similar criminals, it was abruptly transformed, without the approval of the *parlement*, into a tribunal meting out summary justice to political offenders. For several months the magistrates refused to recognize the chamber or register the edict establishing it. Finally compelled to submit to the will of Louis XIII and his chief minister, five of their most recalcitrant members were temporarily exiled, whilst the deputation that made the arduous winter journey to find the king at Metz suffered a humiliating rebuke. They were, said Louis, established only to judge between master Pierre and master Jean, and if they did not confine themselves to such matters their claws would be cut to the quick. For the next four years the *chambre de l'arsenal* dispensed summary justice without hindrance, becoming legendary for its disregard of legal norms or the status and privileges of those arrested. Sometimes it was not even felt necessary to

[10] J.H. Kitchens, 'Judicial commissions and the parlement of Paris', *French Historical Studies* XII (1982), p.328. This article provides the most succinct summary of the issues at stake.

have recourse to any legal procedures. The abbé de St Cyran, erstwhile confidant of Richelieu but increasingly disaffected by the government's foreign policy and suspect for his Jansenist sympathies, was simply confined in the chateau of Vincennes for four years without ever being brought to trial. In the aftermath of the Norman rebellion of 1639 the chancellor dispensed justice personally and by mere oral decision.

Not only did the *parlementaires* retreat on the question of judicial commissions and the associated extension of the powers of the intendants but in 1641 they were finally obliged by a *lit de justice* to register an edict reducing their capacity to comment on affairs of state. Henceforth decrees of a political rather than a financial or judicial nature were to be registered without prior deliberation.

With the advent of the regency of Anne of Austria in 1643 the *parlements* renewed their protests but although the government agreed to abolish the *chambre de l'arsenal*, it showed no inclination to give way on the general principle of commissioned justice and conciliar supremacy. Nothing made this plainer than its continuation of the practice of annulling and suspending the decisions of the *parlement* by royal decree or the removal (*évocation*) of suits from its jurisdiction. This might be done in order to protect someone from investigation or if the crown felt that legal proceedings were impinging on its own interest. Resort to such manoeuvres along with the use of *lits de justice* increased steadily in the decade preceding the Fronde.

Formally the crown's position was not untenable for there was no doubt that the king was the fount of all justice. Judicial commissions had a long history going back to the fifteenth century when they had frequently been used for political purposes. On the other hand there was also a widespread body of opinion which held them to be contrary to custom and inimical to the interests of a monarchy whose legitimacy depended on the proper administration of justice. On occasion the crown itself had even forbidden the use of *commissaires*, as by the Edict of Blois in 1579. Similarly the circumstances in which the crown could intervene in the procedures of the sovereign courts had been limited by the Edict of Moulins in 1562. Yet in 1656 the magistrates were able to compile a list of nearly 200 *évocations* made since 1645 in violation of the ordinances.

Moreover in order to defend the increasingly arbitrary style of government against its critics, royal ministers and propagandists went beyond a simple exposition of royal sovereignty. Richelieu argued that whereas the due process of law must normally be observed, in cases affecting the interests of the state this was neither appropriate nor desirable. Marillac justifying the proliferation of offices whose vexatious character he recognized, declared that 'the inconvenience of an individual is to be preferred to that of a family, that of a family to a town, that of a town to a province, that of a province to a kingdom.... Necessity is above the laws'. In some tracts the distinction between the ethics pertaining to affairs of state and those governing society in general became quite explicit. Machon in his appropriately titled *Apologie pour Machiavelle* (1643), written at Richelieu's behest, noted that 'the quality [of the prince] dispenses him from thousands of subjections that are inseparable from private persons ... there being nothing more certain than that the justice, virtue and integrity of the sovereign function entirely otherwise than those of individuals'. Such sentiments carried political commentators a long way from the tradition of Seyssel which not only emphasized the institutional limitations on the king but constantly stressed the obligation to rule justly and his duties as father of the people. The practical implications of these ideas were sharply revealed with the arrest of the most obstreperous magistrates in 1649 which the chancellor defended on the grounds that 'in the government of the state it is more expedient that a hundred innocent persons suffer than the state perish by fault of the individual'. Corporate and personal loyalties were it seems to be subordin-ated to loyalty to the state. Not even the pleading of Gaston d'Orléans could save Montmorency from the scaffold, and the unfortunate de Thou who loyally concealed the involvement of d'Orléans in the Cinq-Mars conspiracy was executed for complicity. The traditional notion of a body politic whose harmonious regulation was ensured through the agency of a virtuous and just prince, appreciative of the force of custom and privilege, was apparently about to succomb to an impersonal and bureaucratic state machine which levelled all before it.

Such a conclusion would however he misconceived, for not only was the bureaucratic impulse still hemmed in by powerful institutional constraints in the form of provincial Estates and *parlements*, together with the persistent lack of judicial and fiscal uniformity, but it was itself distorted by the traditional structures within which it operated. A cursory examination of the key agents of the crown suffices to show that even they embodied highly contradictory tendencies. The secretaries of state for instance still bought their offices and treated them as part of the family patrimony. Thus the Phélypeaux family provided a succession of nine secretaries between 1610 and 1777, an exceptional case but illustrative of the nature of the system. For a new minister the business of buying out the incumbent officer could be quite prolonged. Nor would he automatically take over the archives of his predecessors for these were still regarded as personal rather than state property, a fact which clearly illuminates the extent to which the office fell short of being a truly bureaucratic one. Similar observations can be made about the intendants. Although their posts were non-venal, they were overwhelmingly drawn from the *maîtres des requêtes* whose offices were venal. Moreover the normal route to these was via a *parlement*; thus of the 128 intendants appointed by Richelieu and Mazarin, 56 had spent part of their careers in the *parlement* of Paris and 25 in the provincial sovereign courts. In addition the intendants like every corporate group in French society developed close family ties amongst themselves which, in some cases, also extended into the highest reaches of the state apparatus. Chancellor Séguier, formerly an intendant himself, had connections with at least eight others, one of whom was his nephew for whom he obtained the position at Riom in 1647–8. *Surintendant* Bouthillier was also linked to six intendants. Moreover a number of the intendants who were without exception members of the *noblesse de robe* retained close connections, sometimes over several generations, with the great 'families of the sword'. Back in the sixteenth century the Séguiers combined service to the Nevers with parliamentary affairs, as well as acting as lawyers and creditors to the Montmorencys. In the 1620s a Séguier held the post of intendant in Epernon's army in his government of Limousin, Angoumois and Saintonge. Among the clients of Henri II de Condé was Théodore de Nesmond, *maître de requêtes* and chief of the prince's council in Paris, who subsequently served both as a *commissaire* in Languedoc and as intendant of justice in Condé's army. In 1632 he was appointed intendant in Lorraine where the prince was army commander and later governor. Claude Machault also followed Condé around as he progressed from one governorship to another. His loyalty brought him a place in the royal council.

The fact that no less than 11 provincial governors were dismissed or exiled by Richelieu cannot therefore be attributed to any fundamental antagonism between the great nobles of the sword and a rising class of bureaucrats. Despite the inevitable conflicts that erupted either over personal issues or questions of policy, intendants and governors co-operated closely. Champigny travelled round Provence with Governor Alais in 1643 and together they selected a town council for the troublesome city of Marseille. In February they rushed to Arles to put down a violent factional struggle. In Dauphiné the intendant and governor were to be found in 1644 dealing with a revolt over the *taille*, and together they pursued a line which was at odds with that of the *parlement* of Grenoble and the *présidial* of Valence. When the duc de Ventadour was confronted with a revolt of the inhabitants of Limoges he appealed to the government for the assistance of an intendant. In Languedoc two intendants sat in Schomberg's council which discussed policy on a wide variety of issues ranging from grain prices to Protestant worship. When Schomberg learnt that he was to be deprived of one intendant for a while he warned that without him his commands would not be executed and disorder would follow. There is therefore considerable justification for the view of one recent scholar that far from polarizing the intendants and governors into antagonistic groups 'the construction of the absolutist state concided with a tightening of the bonds between the old patrimonial élites and the very class of lawyers that were introducing bureaucratic procedures into local government.'[11]

Were such social analysis extended to every category of royal officials and to all sections of the privileged strata, it would serve only to confirm the enduring power of patrimonial and personal ties. Effective government continued to hinge as much on ability to manipulate them and to dispense or withhold patronage, as it did on bureaucratic procedures and mechanisms. Nothing reveals this more clearly than Richelieu's relationships with the secretaries of state whose subordination was a consequence of his monopoly of patronage rather than his formal superiority as chief minister. All the secretaries were in some way personally dependent on Richelieu. In return for loyal service the cardinal augmented their incomes, facilitated advantageous marriages and provided offices and pensions for their dependents. Richelieu even paid the purchase price of the secretaryship on behalf of Sublet de Noyers, whilst Claude de Bullion was rewarded for his earlier

[11] R.R. Harding, *The Anatomy of a Power Elite. The provincial governors of early modern France* (New Haven, Yale University Press, 1972), p.190.

fidelity by the prodigious fortune he amassed as *surintendant*. His entire family also benefited; one son became a magistrate in the *parlement* of Paris; another received a special dispensation to replace his brother in Metz when the latter acquired a major ecclesiastical benefice. Bullion's own brother obtained an intendancy in 1635. Richelieu also ensured that when Raymond Phélypeaux died in 1629 his office passed to his son and not to an alternative candidate favoured by the keeper of the seals, Marillac. It was of course Richelieu's victory over Marillac and the conspiratorial group around the queen mother and Gaston d'Orléans on the famous Day of Dupes (11 November 1631) that ensured his personal dominance. He immediately consolidated his position by promoting his supporters not only at court but also to the provincial governorships vacated by Orléans' clients.

In the years that followed, Richelieu's system of patronage acquired the most extraordinary dimensions, in turn succeeded and perhaps outshone, by that of Mazarin who had at his disposition one of the largest personal fortunes of the entire century. The significance of this development for the consolidation of royal authority may be seen by reference to two particularly separatist provinces — Brittany and Provence. In the former Richelieu made no attempt to undermine either Estates or *parlement* through major institutional innovation. He did however assume the governorship himself, whilst his cousin the marquis de la Meilleraye was appointed lieutenant-general at Nantes. He carefully cultivated a number of bishops and abbots and a certain baron de Pontchâteau, who allegedly brought a hundred lesser nobles to the Estates of 1636. Even the *procureur syndic* of the Estates was a Richelieu client. Between 1632 and 1640 the *don gratuit* rose from 1.5 million to 2 million *livres* and in addition the government accepted 400,000 *livres* in return for the suppression of some venal offices in the *parlement*. The cardinal also received a personal gift of 100,000 *livres* from each meeting of the Estates, which might just have had a bearing on his approach to the province. Be that as it may, La Meilleraye was able to retain the loyalty of the Bretons during the Fronde. Provence by contrast proved much more difficult. In the first place it was blessed with a series of recalcitrant governors who were determined to consolidate their own power bases: Charles de Guise, in office since 1594 but forced into exile in 1631, Vitry dismissed in 1637, and Condé's cousin the duc d'Alais who was arrested by Mazarin in 1652. To offset the pretensions of the governors the crown needed the *parlement* of Aix; but this posed its own problems because the attempt to impose *élections* on the province and then to smother the *parlement* in new offices which culminated in the *semestre* of 1647, generated a powerful and violent resistance amongst the magistrates. In the event, it was the one time anti-Mazarinist president of the *parlement*, the baron d'Oppède, who came to the crown's aid. Persuading Mazarin that his own clientele and credit in Provence outshone those of his rival president, he managed to secure the post of first president. Then, making good his assurance, he utilized his wealth and connections to break down the various centres of resistance. These included the major towns of Draguignan, Marseille and Carpentras where he assiduously built up his influence through the election of friends and relatives as municipal magistrates. In 1664 his younger brother was appointed bishop of Toulon, later becoming one of the two *procureurs* of the general assembly of the communities. During 1658 a cousin also occupied the second position, whilst yet another was for a time *syndic* of the nobility. D'Oppède was also careful to lend 30,000 *livres* to the duc de Vendôme, legitimized son of Henry IV and father of the new governor Mercoeur. During the frequent absences of the latter d'Oppède himself acted as governor. Moreover, in face of the opposition to the installation of an intendant, he also took over this rôle; he was acting intendant of justice without title until he died in 1671. This extraordinary concentration of power was exploited so ruthlessly – to implement unregistered edicts, to raise illegal taxes, to billet troops on Aix and to interfere in municipal elections – that the crown barely needed a proper intendant.

Yet however remarkable and effective the patronage systems developed by the chief ministers proved to be, they involved a reciprocal recognition of the interests of the provincial clienteles. In return for their services the d'Oppèdes and those like them expected and obtained confirmation of their wealth, privilege and status as well as a not inconsiderable degree of political influence. Patrimonial mechanisms of social control by their very nature thus imposed certain constraints on the exercise of royal authority and critically affected the capacity of the crown to override vested interest in the name of rational policy. This was true even in relation to the army where, notwithstanding the growing presence of the intendants, the traditional power bases of the commanders displayed great resilience. Louis XIII on replacing one commander by his son declared that had the regiment been given to anyone else 'it would have completely disbanded because all the captains were from his region and were kinsmen or friends of the deceased'.[12] It is perhaps however in the context of the government's relationships with the clergy, formalized as it was by the regular national assemblies, that the power of privilege can be perceived most clearly. For here the chief ministers were constrained to go beyond the routine promotion of clients and relatives to key benefices, the manipulation of elections and the distribution of funds; in addition the government had to provide constantly reiterated and formal guarantees of the clergy's fiscal and feudal privileges. In 1624 a threat to withdraw from the financial contract with the crown sufficed to produce a confirmation of exemption from the *taille* which was repeated in subsequent years. At the celebrated meeting of 1641 when Richelieu resorted to the forcible eviction of a number of obdurate bishops, the clergy nevertheless obtained an array of edicts of both particular and general significance. Thus the towns of Dauphiné and Provence which were attempting to avoid payment of rents to ecclesiastical landlords were ordered to pay, as were those Norman farmers who claimed exemption from the tithe; by contrast the bishop and archbishops of Narbonne and Montpellier had their own freedom from salt duties confirmed. Various judicial rights and rights of precedence were also upheld. In 1645 the clergy refused even to discuss the *don gratuit* before a number of grievances about the activities of tax farmers and intendants were considered. There followed a series of decrees maintaining their traditional immunities. Again in 1657 the assembly secured a clear and

---

[12] Major, *Representative Government*, p.620.

comprehensive exemption from the *taille, gabelle* and also from the *aides* and other custom dues on their own produce. Such was the price of their relative political docility and continuing financial assistance.

In one fundamental respect the crown's own policies actually extended the scale of privilege and intensified the attachment to patrimonial interests. This was through the multiplication of venal and hereditary offices which created new possibilities for the consolidation of family fortunes and for upward social and political mobility. In a major way the crown mortgaged its future to the office-holders and created structures which could only impede a full deployment of royal power. This was particularly true of the complex fiscal apparatus where the *officiers* operated simultaneously as royal agents and as private tax farmers and financiers, effectively lending the king his own money. Occasionally the government instigated investigations into the malpractices of the financiers and the Code Michaud even proposed a permanent chamber of justice for this purpose. It never came to fruition and although some lesser financiers did end their careers in prison, in general the worst that happened was the imposition of fairly moderate fines; these were then collected by other financiers, thus doing nothing at all to free the government from its dependence on them. It has even been suggested that the generalization of the intendancies was a consequence of the need to ensure the rapid flow of funds to maintain the confidence of the financiers. As the *taille* was farmed out from 1637 onwards, at roughly the same time as the intendants were becoming established nearly everywhere, this view has a certain merit. In the years that followed one of the most prevalent and bitter accusations levelled against the intendants was that they were merely the creatures of the great financiers. Indeed it was not unknown for the intendants to levy the *taille* with the assistance of tax farmers' agents, and when, after the interlude of the Fronde, the intendants were fully re-established in 1653 it was also in order that the crown could meet its contracts with the financiers concluded in July of that year.

The fiscal policies of the crown were also inimical to its economic as well as its political aspirations. Sale of office was almost universally recognized as harmful for the way in which it diverted capital from productive investment into usurous channels, transforming merchants and entrepreneurs into rentiers in the process. In addition, as was also understood, the proliferation of office constituted a huge burden on the productive classes. In one sense it was nothing more than a device for passing on to them the fiscal demands of the crown, thus compelling the lower orders to sustain the privileged status of their social superiors. Moreover, so pressing was the government's financial plight, that even measures designed to stimulate and regulate the economy could all too easily degenerate into attempts to raise cash, thus multiplying the burdens yet again. There was clearly a fiscal element in the legislation requiring all merchants and entrepreneurs to be members of gilds, for a payment to the crown was specified. Similarly inspection of produce to ensure its quality had to be paid for. It was also quickly learned that the necessary offices for this purpose could be sold. The inspectors of beer, required in every town, became venal, as did the measurers and carriers of charcoal and wood, together with the perhaps more essential inspectors of iron. Tariffs ostensibly introduced to protect domestic manufacture were subject to similar distortion and, particularly under Mazarin, to sharp fluctuations as the government sought to ease its problems. Of course further funds could be raised by allowing certain trades or communities to purchase exemption from the general regulations. This was perhaps the ultimate nonsense within the framework of an economic policy which was supposed to involve the subordination of the private interest to the common good.

It would however be a mistake to evalute government policy in terms of a clearly defined absolutist perspective. On the contrary, it should by now be clear that the evolution of the absolutist state was not the result of the consistent application of a new view of government or society, but a pragmatic, frequently *ad hoc* and contradictory attempt to *restore* royal authority in the context of a rapidly changing world. Inasmuch as the government had a defined programme, it was the essentially conservative one reflected in a series of major ordinances between that of Orléans in 1561 and the Code Michaud of 1629. Indeed in some respects there was a continuity of thought and approach stretching back to the earlier reforming edicts of Villers-Cotterêts (1539) and Blois (1499). Outstanding was the persistent expression of a desire to have cheaper and more effective justice, reduce or abolish venality, minimize the corruption of officials, reduce pensions, and limit tax exemptions; restoration of commerce loomed large with hopes of a unitary system of weights and measures and greater freedom for domestic trade. Concern about the capacity of the clergy and the need to improve public morality was a recurrent theme. Whilst the ordinances showed an increasing determination to do away with private associations and leagues, they equally reveal a desire to preserve the legitimate social privileges of the nobility, their access to office and to restrict the influx of newcomers which was debasing the order. Few, if any, of the government objectives did not find a response amongst significant sections of the populace; indeed many of them emanated from the express wishes of the delegates summoned to the meetings of Estates-General that met down to 1615 and by the notables at the assemblies of 1617 and 1626. It has recently been pointed out that there was a close resemblance between the reforms proposed by the three estates in 1614–15 and the views contained in Richelieu's *Testament Politique*.[13] Of course the *Testament* was almost certainly composed with the benefit of hindsight, but that it represented very clearly the initial aspirations of the cardinal is indicated by his proposals made for the Reformation of the Kingdom in 1625. At that time he wished to reorganize the councils, albeit without depriving the nobility of their influence, to reduce the bureaucracy and the salaries of officials, abolish venality, redeem the domain and, whilst limiting the size of the household, to give the nobility a monopoly of positions both there and in the army. The inspiration of the *cahiers* of 1614–15 is unmistakeable, as is the remarkably conservative and un-absolutist tone of the document.

Moreover the ideological framework, the world view, within which these

[13] J.M. Hayden, *France and the Estates-General of 1614* (Cambridge, CUP, 1974), pp.215–16.

policies were framed was a thoroughly traditional one based on acceptance of the divinely ordained universe in which a chain of being progressed from the lowliest inanimate object to God on high, and in which the function of monarchy was to preserve the human rungs of the universal hierarchy. What emerges from the propaganda pamphlets published as the onslaught on the Huguenots reached its climax, was an intense commitment to heal the body politic, to restore the social hierarchy as it was understood to have been, with a reformed clergy, satisfied nobility and a blostered merchant community all making their appropriate contribution. Of course many writers incorporated in their picture the notion derived from Bodin's *Six Books of a Commonweal* (1576) of sovereignty as the untrammelled capacity to make law which no subject had the right to resist. Yet it should not be assumed that Bodin or those that followed him simply replaced the concept of the king as the just and virtuous father of his people with that of the sovereign legislator. On the contrary Bodin was quite clear that precisely because the king was cast in the image of God and responsible to Him alone, it was necessary to rule with moderation and justice, allowing due scope to Estates and *parlement* alike.[14] Those like Cardin le Bret who were profoundly influenced by Bodin followed a similar line. In his *Souveraineté des Rois* written in 1632 Le Bret simultaneously extolled the absolute sovereignty of the king and the obligation on him to rule justly. Kings, he declared, ought to take wise counsel and certainly should not change laws without due care; they should treat customs and also the *parlements* with respect, for these represented the 'majesty of justice.' Both the Estates-General and the provincial Estates had a rôle to play in exalting the monarchy. Kings never appeared with greater presence and magnificence than they did when 'accompanied by all the princes of their council and the greatest seigneurs of their court they opened the Estates'. The purpose of such assemblies where there existed 'a close liaison between the head and the members, between the king and his subjects' was to proceed to the reformation of the realm.

It can thus be seen that the dualism in French political ideas with their simultaneous insistence on the absolute and yet limited character of kingship persisted into the seventeenth century even in writers commonly regarded as essentially absolutist. Indeed the world view of people like Le Bret was little different from that of Seyssel. On the other hand, as we have seen, there was also a tendency to justify the increasingly authoritarian character of government policy by making a distinction between the morality which governed affairs of state and that which pertained to ordinary mortals. This tendency became even more marked as the government sought to defend its anti-Spanish foreign policy against the substantial body of opinion which found the resort to Protestant alliances for a war against a major Catholic power morally repugnant. Criticism of official policy came at one moment or another from across the entire spectrum of Catholic conviction, from Jesuit to Jansenist. The response of the government propagandists was a paradoxical

[14] My assessment of Bodin, which differs from that of most recent writers, is developed in D. Parker, 'Law, society and the state in the thought of Jean Bodin', *Journal of the History of Political Thought* 2 (1980), pp.253–85.

attempt to justify Reason of State by anchoring it to Divine Right. Thus Machon in his *Apologie pour Machiavelle* (1643) sought to show that Machiavellian principles in politics were entirely compatible with those of a Christian monarchy. Changes made by kings even if not comprehensible, apparently unjust and contrary to Christian morality, were to be accepted as originating in Heaven. Whatever the king did was bound to be just for it was rendered so 'by the sole fact of his commanding it'. Such arguments undoubtedly compounded the already manifest contradictions within French monarchical theory, generating a considerable degree of scepticism in intellectual circles. Nevertheless in the short term these contradictions were not resolved through the elaboration of a modern or secular view of the state, but by a renewed insistence on the divinity of the king that brooked no argument. Those that insisted on challenging official wisdom and morality could suffer a dire fate. One only has to mention Michel de Marillac, Richelieu's unfortunate rival for power, whose demand for peace, retrenchment and reform brought him from high office to a death in prison, Mathieu de Morgues, erstwhile royal propagandist whose subsequent satirical invective against the manipulation of religion in an unworthy cause made him the most prestigious victim of the *chambre de l'arsenal*, and the abbé de St Cyran who sat out Richelieu's last years in confinement.

Despite the cardinal's unassailable position, such episodes illustrate the acute tensions that his policies generated within the highest reaches of French society and the failure of the crown to control totally those powerful religious impulses which, paradoxically, were so vital to the restoration of its own authority. Particularly disturbing to the orthodox pragmatic gallicanism of government circles was the persistent tendency for the widespread preoccupation with inward spirituality and personal salvation to spill over into a critique of worldly politics or into semi-clandestine activity. The most striking illustration of the latter phenomenon was the Company of the Holy Sacrament which penetrated deep into the world of the urban upper classes and with which Marillac himself was associated. In one way its insistence on personal discipline, public morality and good order corresponded to the interests of the state, but its secrecy and fanaticism were alarming, whilst its expanding grip on the provision of charity irritated the regular clergy. Ironically the Company's contribution to the great confinement of the Parisian poor probably facilitated Mazarin's decision in 1660 to ban all secret societies. It survived only a few more years.

Part rivals, part fellow-travellers with the Company of the Holy Sacrament were the Jansenists. The focal points of their activities were the famous convent of Port Royal at Paris and its rural but male offshoot, Port Royal des Champs founded in 1637 by a group of lay *solitaires*. Like the Company, the Jansenists had a sympathetic following in well-to-do and influential quarters; indeed the puritanical austerity of the *solitaires*, involving rejection of their own background and royal service in favour of devotion and manual labour, was partly what made them seem so subversive. This retreat from society might have been tolerable, although St Cyran certainly did not help his cause by turning down a bishopric in order to act as mentor and guide to the nuns of Port Royal; in addition however the Jansenists were tainted by their criticisms of the government's foreign policy and by the protection they received from some of the most incorrigible *Frondeurs* like the libertine Madame de Longueville and the unscrupulous de Retz who sought nothing more than his cardinal's hat. All of this was compounded by the fact that the Jansenists were identified with a theology that not only set them apart from mainstream Catholicism but appeared to make them little better than Huguenots. It was in fact St Cyran who introduced the works of Jansen to Port Royal. Like Bérulle before him, St Cyran had long been concerned about the easy mechanical routine of confession and repentance followed immediately by communion; in the teachings of St Augustine as presented by Jansen he found support for his belief that true contrition and inner cleanliness could not be so achieved but required the penetration of the human spirit with God's Grace. This was dangerous ground, reviving ancient controversies over free will and predestination, and it struck right at the heart of the teaching of the Jesuits who by this time had become the principal educators of the upper classes including the royal family. In 1643 Antoine Arnauld, brother of Angélique, abbess of Port Royal, published his *De la Fréquente Communion* which was in essence an attack on the laxity of the Jesuits in the matter of confession and communion and on the idea that these offered some guarantee of salvation. From this moment the theological debates grew in intensity and bitterness. In 1653 the pope issued a bull condemning five propositions allegedly contained in Jansen's *Augustinus*. Pascal whose own sister had joined the nuns of Port Royal, then intervened with his celebrated *Lettres Provinciales* which appeared throughout 1656. These constituted a devastating onslaught on the ethical standards of the Jesuits, their willingness to compromise Christian principles in the interests of realpolitik and their use of casuistry to avoid problems of individual conscience. The following year the pope issued another, even more comprehensive, indictment of the *Augustinus* and instructed the French clergy to sign a formulary of acceptance on pain of being brought before a panel of French bishops and charged with heresy.

Unfortunately for both king and pope the *parlement* then refused to register the bull; not, as is sometimes suggested, because of its religious sympathies (a few magistrates were Jansenists) but on straightforward gallican grounds. According to Séguier the court believed that 'the bull establishes an inquisition in France and it believes that the king wishes to take away the *appel comme d'abus*'.[15] Although Mazarin finally secured registration of the bull in a *lit de justice* it was accompanied by letters from the papal nuncio assuring the *parlement* that there was no intention to extend the powers of the French prelates. To ensure that this concession was well publicized the *avocat général* Talon delivered a speech maintaining the judicial authority of *parlement* and warning the pope not to interfere in France's religious affairs. That the magistrates' fears were not unreasonable became clear when a Jansenist bishop lodged an *appel comme d'abus* against the instruction of the cathedral chapter of Beauvais to sign the formulary; the royal council evoked

[15] A. Hamscher, *The Parlement of Paris After the Fronde* (Pittsburgh, University of Pittsburgh Press, 1976), p.114.

the case causing such uproar that judgment was postponed and the formulary remained a dead letter.

This was the ultimate irony. For now the crown, having been buffetted around by these turbulent religious currents, was prevented from controlling them by a *parlement* which itself claimed to be the true guardian of the general interest. Although the impasse both on the religious and the parlementary front was to further intensify the search for absolutist solutions, nothing pinpoints more neatly the contradictory nature of the pressures at work and, indeed, of the crown's response to them.

3

The Limits of Resistance

Not surprisingly the rapid and frequently brutal extension of royal power and the accompanying massive increase in taxation provoked widespread discontent. The three decades after 1620 were ones of almost permanent unrest involving every section of the population. At one moment or another grandees, provincial nobles, officers high and low, urban patriciates and artisans, peasants and labourers all showed a willingness to resist royal pressure and intimidation with violence. Riots against the soldiery, the fiscal and judicial agents of the crown and against those local authorities who sought to deflect the burdens onto the backs of the less fortunate became almost everyday occurrences.

Frequently these endemic and essentially spontaneous eruptions blossomed into large-scale, organized rebellion. A portent of things to come was the revolt of Aix in September 1630 against the imposition of the *élus* and proposed increases in salt taxes, at a moment when plague and high grain prices were generating widespread unrest. For several weeks a powerful coalition of militant *parlementaires* and elements of the populace made the provincial capital unsafe for the intendants and those suspected of colluding with the government. Order was not finally restored until Condé arrived with an army early in 1631 and negotiated with the Estates a price for the withdrawal of the *élus*. Next it was the turn of Languedoc to rise against similar measures and in 1632 the Estates lent their support to Montmorency's ill-fated rebellion. Again the *élus* were withdrawn. The first of a series of major uprisings which were to sweep through the western provinces began in 1635 when a new tax on wine sold in taverns was announced in Bordeaux. Two months of violent agitation followed during which the authorities periodically lost control of the popular quarters of the city, recovering them only by dint of superior firepower after prolonged bouts of fighting. Moreover unrest broke out almost immediately in Périgueux and Agen. In the latter town it was particularly brutal causing the deaths of 15 notables, virtually all associated with the royal fisc; other officials were lucky to escape with the destruction of their urban and rural properties or the pillaging of their goods and cattle. Further north in the southern regions of Saintonge and Angoumois – a region of dispersed hamlets populated by wine and hemp workers – resistance to the mounting burdens of the *taille*, wine taxes and the demands of the military culminated in the summer of 1636 in one of the most remarkable peasant insurrections. Again the principal victims were fiscal agents, but in contrast to the violent urban upsurge of Agen, the revolt of the countryside was characterized by its discipline and organization. The basis for this was a series of popular assemblies, announced in advance and summoned by the tocsin. In June 4,000 insurgents gathered at Blanzac, perhaps 10,000 at La Couronne. According to various reports between 12,000 and 40,000 peasants were in arms; although they did not all serve at once as a rota was established to ensure that the fields were not left unattended. The peasant forces blocked Cognac and Angoulême, compelled the local nobility to march at their head and rendered ineffective the tax-collecting machinery. From Saintonge and Angoumois the revolt spread into Poitou, Limousin and as far as Berry. Although troops were dispatched to the region in July under the duc de la Force, the rebels were allowed to present their grievances in return for disarming. Nothing however was really settled and the following year a comparable movement swept through the Périgord, involving an assault on Périgueux itself and the occupation of Bergerac by contingents of peasants. An assembly 7,000–8,000 strong elected a local noble, La Mothe la Forêt, as leader in May 1637 with the title of 'General of the Communes of Périgord'. However after suffering severe losses in a confrontation at La Sauvetat with an army under the duc de Lavelette, the resistance became very divided and La Mothe abandoned Bergerac without a struggle. Nevertheless peasant bands continued to infest the region for years to come, whilst tax evasion became a way of life. In the winter of 1643 after a series of bad harvests and persistent refusal by the peasantry to pay the *taille*, the lesser nobility of Saintonge and Angoumois themselves took action to bring attention to the intolerable burdens imposed on the region. A general assembly of nobles at Lusignan had to be dispersed by force.

As the revolts of the central western provinces ebbed away, the ground was being laid for perhaps the most celebrated uprising of the century – that of the Norman Nu-Pieds of 1639, when for a period of four and a half months a large part of the Cotentin peninsula slipped from royal control. At the same time there were major revolts in both Rouen and Caen. Normandy had been groaning for years under a disproportionately large share of the tax burden. Passive resistance to the payments of the *taille* was widespread. St Lô and Coutances had experienced revolts against leather taxes from the 1620s. In 1636 the *parlement* of Rouen, angered by the non-payment of wages, manipulation of the *paulette*, and the creation of new offices took the side of the tanners in a dispute over a new tax on leather. Opposition also came from the *cour des aides* of Rouen. The following year the officers of the *élection* at Caen simply refused to implement government demands. Attacks on suspected grain hoarders and on detachments of soldiers were also reported. Matters finally came to a head with the rumour in July 1639 that a full *gabelle* was to be imposed on those regions of Normandy which paid only the *quart-bouillon*. The revolt began at Avranches with assaults on those suspected of carrying the new edicts, on the *bureau des finances*, and the office of the *cinq grosses fermes*. From there it spread outwards and eventually a well-organized army composed largely of salt workers and wood carriers, directed by a few priests with noble assistance and perhaps 20,000 strong, assumed control of the region between Avranches and Coutances. A smaller army led by a noble and two lawyers operated in the Mantilly region. At Caen and Rouen the authorities adopted a fairly passive stance in face of disturbances led by the cloth and textile workers. Only with the arrival of crack troops under Marshal Gassion in December was the peasant army finally beaten and dispersed. Some of the rebel leaders were executed or exiled. In January 1640 Chancellor Séguier came to Rouen, suspended the *parlement*, the *cour des aides* and the municipal officers, and instigated proceedings against the rebels. As late as September 14 were condemned to death at Bayeaux, on which a heavy fine was also imposed.

It is doubtful whether such repression was effective. Arrears of *tailles* continued for years and on its re-establishment the *parlement* of Rouen simply returned to a policy of prevarication. From 1643 to 1645 revolt was endemic throughout the west and south and some parts of the north. Best documented was the anti-*taille* rebellion in Villefranche-sur-Rouergue. On the 2 June 1643 a crowd of twelve hundred peasants invaded the town armed with picks and muskets, compelling the intendant to declare a reduction in taxes. Assemblies were organized in the neighbouring villages. It took some 10 months and a general amnesty before a semblance of tranquillity was restored. According to the intendant many of the local officers, notably in the *présidial* of Villefranche, were guilty of complicity. Somewhat different in its social complexion was the rising two years later at Montpellier. On this occasion crowds of women, accompanied by artisans and refugees from the countryside, barricaded the streets and sacked the houses of the fiscal agents and their relatives, killing several in the process.

It is against this turbulent background that the Frondes of 1648–53 must be set. The events of these years which forced the government and royal family out of Paris and Mazarin into temporary exile, were not, as is sometimes suggested, the result of Mazarin's incompetence but the consequence of the financial and political impasse into which he had been driven. Certainly the railroading of unpalatable fiscal measures through the *parlement* was provocative, particularly as many of the measures adversely affected the interests of the Parisian property-owners and traders, thus uniting them behind the magistrates; and the attempt to browbeat the office-holders by making the renewal of the *paulette* conditional on a forced loan whilst withholding it entirely from the *maîtres des requêtes*, proved totally counterproductive. It was this which precipitated the famous and unprecedented union of the Parisian sovereign courts in the Chambre de St Louis on 13 May 1648 to discuss their grievances. Yet from the government viewpoint the alternatives were not obvious. Royal revenues had been anticipated for several years and the capacity of the labouring population to meet additional demands was strictly limited, if not exhausted. Not only was the resort to yet more fiscal expedients at the expense of those who could pay almost unavoidable, but so also was the need to reassure royal creditors by obtaining ratification of the new taxes.

Once the representatives of the sovereign courts had convened in the Chambre de St Louis it became very difficult for the government to retreat without appearing to accept a major constitutional innovation. However the political confrontation now produced precisely the collapse of confidence amongst the financiers that the government was seeking to avoid. Their refusal to make new loans before matters had been resolved proved to be amply justified; for when the Chambre de St Louis produced its proposals for reform it was readily apparent that they amounted to nothing less than a demand for the reduction of the whole apparatus of war finance. Amongst other measures the officers demanded a reduction of the *taille* by 25 per cent, an end to the practice of farming it out and its return to the auspices of the *trésoriers* and *élus*; new taxes and new offices were to be introduced in accordance with the proper procedure, whilst the payment of *rentes* was to be restored and subject to judicial supervision. The effective destruction of the powers of the intendants implicit in these proposals was completed by a demand that all special commissions which had not been duly verified by the courts were to be suppressed. There was also a call for observance of the restrictions on the power of the royal council to evoke proceedings from the courts.

Effectively bankrupt and with no obvious remedy, the government was forced to revoke its contracts with the financiers, and to endeavour to placate the magistrates with some concessions. Particelli d'Hemery, the *surintendant*, was dismissed and at the end of July in a farcical travesty of a *lit de justice*, the government restored some of the *parlement*'s fiscal authority. This however was insufficient to prevent the *parlement* announcing an investigation into the affairs of several financiers. Fearful of the complete collapse of its financial support, pressurized by those with investments in the loan contracts, and perhaps encouraged by the victory of Condé over the Spanish at Lens, on 22 August the government determined to use force. Four days later two parlementary militants, Broussel and Blancmesnil, a president in the *enquêtes*, were arrested. It was a mistake. Immediately barricades went up throughout Paris and the regent was obliged to release her prisoners. On the 13 September the royal household left the city apparently with renewed resolve to use force, but its isolation was such that it was in the end compelled to negotiate. Most of the outstanding demands of the *parlementaires* were conceded by the declaration of 22 October and ratified two days later. An uneasy calm descended on the capital but it was clear that the crown could simply not afford to stand by the agreement; particularly as both the *comptes* and the *aides* continued severely to amend its financial legislation. Early in 1649 the royal household once more departed for St Germain, ordered the recall of the armies of Condé and Turenne from Flanders and the Rhine, and the blockade of the capital. On 8 January *parlement* responded by declaring Mazarin an enemy of the king and state and the following day resolved to set up a fund for the levying of troops. Some magnates, including Condé's brother the prince de Conti, the duc de Longueville governor of Normandy, and the prince de Marsillac subsequently announced their attachment to the magistrates' cause and numbers of lesser nobles began to converge on Paris.

Meanwhile the situation in the provinces had also been fast deteriorating. The *parlements* of Aix and Rouen were involved in a bitter resistance to the *semestres* imposed on them, a struggle compounded in Provence by the intense antagonism felt towards the governor, the duc d'Alais. News of the royal flight to St Germain served only to precipitate matters. On 29 January 1649 in a remarkably successful and almost bloodless coup, Alais together with the intendant and the duc de Richelieu were all arrested. A bourgeois guard was created for the defence of Aix which was virtually sealed off, whilst deputies were dispatched to muster support from the other towns of Provence and the *parlement* of Paris. In Bordeaux which became the other great provincial centre of the Fronde, the repressive activities of the governor, the duc d'Epernon, similarly helped to bring simmering passions to the boil. Emboldened by events in Paris the *parlement* had quickly prohibited the raising of taxes not previously ratified by itself. It went on to revoke additional offices created by the government and to declare that the intendant would not be obeyed unless his orders were first approved by the *parlement*. It also suppressed the *présidiaux* in a number of adjacent communities. These measures designed to reassert the *parlement*'s sovereign jurisdiction were accompanied by reductions in import taxes and the *taille*. Construed by many as an encouragement to defy the fiscal agents, such decisions inevitably generated episodes of mounting disorder. Early in 1649 Epernon began to prepare the Château Trompette, his stronghold within the city, for the anticipated confrontation. It was not however until March that the *parlement* took major steps to organize the increasingly agitated populace, creating a council of finance to raise funds, a council of police to oversee the city's defences, and an army 20,000-strong divided into 36 companies each commanded by a *parlementaire*. Although at Rouen there was no comparable organization, the *parlement* likewise took steps to exclude royalist forces.

By March however the Parisian *parlementaires* who had assumed effective leadership of the defence of their city were preparing to negotiate a settlement with the crown. The government was also predisposed to negotiate by the daunting coalition of forces ranged against it and the growing unrest in the provinces. By the peace of Rueil (11 March 1649) mutual disarmament was agreed, whilst in exchange for a general amnesty the contentious decrees of the *parlement* issued since early January were annulled. Otherwise the treaty by accepting the earlier agreement of 1648 gave the magistrates almost everything they had sought, particularly as a clause allowing the government to borrow money for two years was subsequently rejected by the *parlement*. A separate and similarly concessionary settlement was made with the *parlement* of Aix where, as at Rouen, the *semestre* was withdrawn. Alais, released from confinement, left the city as fast as he could go.

In contrast the settlement of March 1649 gave the dissident nobility nothing by way of the governorships, pensions and political influence to which they aspired. Even those who had loyally defended the royal cause now began to be troublesome. In Provence Alais determined to have his revenge over the Aixois, maintained the troops who should have been disbanded, levied illegal taxes to support them, interfered in municipal elections and harassed the inhabitants. Inexorably, despite the efforts of royal mediators, the province slid into civil war. In Guyenne where no settlement had been concluded, the conflict between the independent-minded governor and Bordeaux likewise escalated, spreading out into larger and larger tracts of the countryside, but with inconclusive results. Most serious for Mazarin, however, was the problem posed by Louis II de Condé who, justifiably disgruntled by the failure to compensate him for his distinguished services and loyalty, had retreated to his governorship of Burgundy. The prince was also extremely concerned about a proposed marriage alliance between the duc de Vendôme and one of Mazarin's nieces. Such an alliance would give the cardinal the sort of connection and base amongst the French nobility that he clearly lacked. In early October Mazarin agreed with Condé not to marry off any of his nieces or nephews without the prince's permission. At the same time Condé began to develop plans for a marriage between Anne de Poussart de Vigean to the duc de Richelieu who controlled Le Havre, perhaps the most powerful stronghold in the realm. Just as in 1616 when the prestige and influence of a prince of Condé proved intolerable to a regency government, so it was now. On 18 January 1650 in an almost uncanny re-enactment of the events of 1616, Condé together with Conti and Longueville were arrested.

Civil war was now unavoidable. The prince's family and associates began to mobilize their support. By May his wife, the duc de la Rochefoucauld, and the duc de Bouillon made their way to Bordeaux where a reluctant *parlement*, which had itself come to terms with Mazarin, gave way to popular pressure to receive them. With this base assured, the Condéans then negotiated a treaty with Philip IV of Spain. In the north-east the duchesse de Longueville and Turenne, who constantly changed sides, had already concluded an agreement with the governor of the Spanish Netherlands. Despite Spanish assistance for the rebels, Mazarin was able to contain their forces and the summer's campaigns resolved very little. Commitment to the prince's cause was, to say the least, lukewarm amongst other sections of the population. Nevertheless the demand for the three prisoners' release provided a common platform for all those who sought the departure of the cardinal. By the beginning of 1651 the clergy, the *parlement*, and an assembly of lesser nobles which gathered in Paris, were all exerting pressure to this end. It also provided the basis for a coalition between the Condéans, the rival faction of Frondeurs associated with de Retz, and Gaston d'Orléans who had become increasingly vexed by the cardinal's management of affairs. Thoroughly isolated, Mazarin went to Le Havre, released the princes and then fled to Cologne where he stayed until the end of the year. His influence over the regent however remained undiminished and despite renewed threats of violence the Condéans were unable to consolidate a grip on the government; and with the declaration of the king's majority on 8 September Mazarin was able to restore his clients to ministerial office. Undeterred by the royal majority Condé withdrew to Guyenne to continue his resistance. Gaston d'Orléans was also provoked by the return of Mazarin into an alliance with the prince. In the spring of 1652 Condé's troops advanced on Paris, causing immense distress to the countryside for miles around. On 2 July they suffered a particularly bloody defeat in the Faubourg St Antoine at the hands of Turenne who had once again changed sides. Nevertheless Condé duly penetrated the city and attempted to force both *parlement* and municipality to endorse his rebellion. Violent disturbances followed during which a number of municipal officers were 'massacred' at the *hôtel de ville*. A puppet administration for the city was then established with Broussel as mayor.

However, its arbitrary and repressive nature steadily forfeited what popular support there was and confirmed the general reluctance to endure all the privations of yet another blockade of the city. On the 14 October, taking advantage of Condé's absence the royalists in a neatly engineered coup facilitated also by the voluntary second exile of Mazarin, recovered control of Paris. The king returned to his capital a week later, whilst Condé offered his services to the Spanish crown.

In Bordeaux however the flames of revolt were far from quenched. Although in October 1650 the city had successfully withstood the determined attempts of the royal forces to take it and indeed obtained a favourable settlement which included the dismissal of Epernon, the struggle left it exhausted and divided. Many of the notables were already suspect because of their initial reluctance to join with the Condéans and matters were made worse when the *parlement* began to levy heavy taxes in order to cope with the city's accumulated debts. Rumours of Epernon's possible return further exacerbated these tensions. By the middle of 1651 a popular organization known as the *Ormée* had taken shape. Support for it grew steadily and by the spring of the following year it was demanding the expulsion of those *parlementaires* suspected of failing to give adequate support to Condé. When the *parlement* banned public assemblies the Ormée defied the instruction and in May there occurred the first armed clashes. In June the thoroughly intimidated *parlement* agreed to suspend its sessions and the Ormée seized effective control of the city, reducing the various municipal bodies to mere appendages of its own organization; this was quite sophisticated with a 500-strong general assembly, its own organs for the administration of justice and control of commerce, all supervised by an executive body, the *chambre de trente*. At its height the Ormée probably had the active support of a quarter of the population; the extent of its achievement is shown by the fact that it did not finally succumb until July 1653, nearly a year after the king regained Paris. By this time it was totally isolated, the royal army was within a kilometre of the city walls and internal dissensions precluded further resistance.

Given the scale and mounting intensity of the resistance to royal policies in the first half of the seventeenth century, the question of why the crown was able to emerge victorious and consolidate its position is a crucial one. At times it seemed quite possible that under the impact of factional rivalries the realm would succumb once again to prolonged civil strife; at others it appeared perhaps more likely that the system of war finance would be dismantled and the monarchy subjected to constitutional constraints. Mazarin certainly feared that France might follow the same path as Cromwellian England. As it was, neither of these possibilities materialized; and in retrospect the cardinal's anxieties can be seen to reflect an understandable concern for his personal safety rather than an accurate appraisal of wider political realities.

Indeed one of the most remarkable aspects of the Frondes was the capacity of the financial system, the bankruptcy of 1648 notwithstanding, to survive the strains imposed on it and to keep the government afloat. Part of the explanation for this lay in the ever-deepening ties which bound the interests of the state to those of the financiers. Mazarin whose fortune grew to a colossal 37 million *livres* was the personification of this trend, for much of his wealth derived from earlier activities as a *munitionnaire*, loans to the state and the profits of office. In 1648 he was able both to draw on private resources to keep the government going and also to take advantage of his intimate connections with the financial world. For their part the financiers had a great deal to fear from a parlementary victory and a number undoubtedly made efforts to transfer funds to St Germain when the court fled there. In the spring of 1649 Mazarin utilized his connections with European financiers to raise 800,000 *livres* in order to buy off Turenne's army which was poised to relieve the royal blockade of Paris. Three years later when once again the government had lost control of the capital, and despite the virtual collapse of the tax farms, it was still able to anticipate revenues by borrowing. By the autumn of 1652 almost all the direct taxes for the following years had been anticipated with loans from major financiers who were now clearly confident of a royal victory. By contrast the prince of Condé had the utmost difficulty raising taxes from a resentful population and consequently remained heavily dependent on Spanish backing.

Such dependence on foreign support indicates why a return to the type of civil strife characteristic of the previous century was unlikely, if not impossible; for it was a consequence of the fast-declining ability of the magnates to raise whole regions behind them, already apparent in 1614–15 when Montmorency and Nevers vainly tried to generate support for Henri II de Condé. Even the last ill-fated insurrection of Montmorency in 1632, which did at least elicit the support of the Languedoc Estates, was hampered by the lack of response from significant sections of the urban élites, notably the *parlementaires* of Toulouse. During the Fronde similar problems arose. For instance when the prince de Marsillac, about to become the duc de la Rochefoucauld and presently governor of Poitou, supported by the prince de Tarente, eldest son of the duc de la Tremouille, and the comte de Daugnon, governor of Brouage, attempted to raise the western provinces they met with great resistance. At Cognac the lesser nobility actually formed an alliance with the municipality, obliging Marsillac to besiege the town. It is true that, as in Normandy in 1649, the nobility might lend support to the governor, but equally true that, as in the same province the very next year, they might withdraw it. Even Condé in Burgundy was able to arouse only the most half-hearted response despite his distribution of largesse; and as we have seen, at Bordeaux it was the populace that insisted on a welcome for his wife against the wishes of the authorities. The extensive clienteles and organized parties which the nobility had utilized in former times were, apparently, no longer at their disposition.

Whilst the reasons for this profoundly significant development are still in need of much clarification, their general character can be discerned without undue difficulty. Part of the explanation lies in the action taken by the government to break the local power of the great nobles. Most conspicuous was the steady reduction in minor governorships together with the destruction of the strongholds that sustained them, a process which lasted from the 1590s to the 1630s. Accelerated by the victory over the Huguenots in the

1620s, the last major clearance of fortresses came in the aftermath of the rebellion of 1632, when more than 100 chateaux and urban citadels were demolished in Languedoc. However the most significant aspect of royal policy was that it clearly accorded with the wishes of the provincial authorities who frequently requested and paid for the cost of demolition. Under Henry IV and Louis XIII the Estates of Brittany, Béarn, Rouergue, Provence and probably elsewhere all sought permission to carry out this work. In 1614 the cahier of the third estate included a demand for the razing of every stronghold except those on the frontiers.

This clearly reflected a deep-seated revulsion against the military power of the nobility or rather against the purposes for which it was employed. The antagonism of the urban patriciates towards the magnates surfaced even where their interests were closely linked. Thus Rohan who more than proved his loyalty to the Huguenot cause was asked on one occasion to leave La Rochelle, whilst his brother, always regarded as a wayward adventurer, found himself refused entry in 1625 when he returned in triumph with the captured royal fleet. In March 1631 Dijon simply shut its gates when the provincial governor, the duc de Bellegarde, attempted to involve it in the conspiracy of Gaston d'Orléans. In Dijon, of course, the *parlement* played a critical rôle, its attitude reflecting the widespread hostility amongst the magistracy towards the pretensions of the magnates. During the Fronde, as has already been noted, the bitter rivalry between governors and *parlements* was a major element in the disorder which overcame both Provence and Guyenne. Troublesome as these rivalries were for the government, they had the immense advantage of precluding the formation of old-style parties around the governors. Moreover, although the common hatred of Mazarin brought the *parlement* of Paris to urge the release of the princes, it consistently refused to enter a formal alliance with them. The devastation of the Parisian countryside and Condé's repressive rule in Paris – itself a manifestation of lack of public support – only served to confirm the notables in their attitudes.

Without control of the urban communities and the co-operation of the officers, the magnates could not so readily appropriate royal revenues or draw on commercial wealth. Indeed it was precisely the attempt to exploit the resources of La Rochelle that fuelled resentment amongst the townsmen towards their noble allies. When the Protestant assembly drew up its famous constitution in May 1620, it was significant that the military commanders were expressly forbidden to divert revenues without its assent or to engage in other forms of profiteering.

Even more indicative of changing times than the antagonism between urban notables and magnates, was the growing divide between greater and lesser nobility. There was after all a world of difference in power, status and wealth between a great duke whose annual revenue might reach a quarter of a million *livres* and a provincial *seigneur* with an income of 500 *livres* or even less. The interests of the latter were essentially bound up with those of his tenants and the locality, whereas the former was concerned to preserve an influence on government together with access to the court and king. As the pressure on the countryside intensified the lesser nobility became increasingly critical of those whose privileged position not only allowed them to escape but also to benefit from the enormous sums that were being drained away and channelled through the state apparatus. The anxieties of the lesser nobility were clearly revealed at the Estates-General of 1614–15 when they requested that no pensions or other gifts should be bestowed at the behest 'of the princes and seigneurs of your kingdom so that those who have them will be entirely bound to your majesty'. During the Fronde Mazarin was able to exploit this antipathy to the great and powerful in his own interests, allowing in 1649 an assembly of nobility to present its grievances. Amongst these were objections to the favours bestowed on upstarts like the duc de la Roche-foucauld and the depredations of the military governors. When the faction around the duc de Beaufort sought to gain access to the assembly it was made plain to him that 'it did not want anything to do with the princes and even less with the chief of the Frondeurs'. Equally interesting in the light of the failure of the princes to raise the western provinces, was the request made two years later by the nobility of Angoumois that certain taxes on the wine trade granted to La Tremouille should be withdrawn.

Paradoxically such complaints far from being a testimony to the uncon-trollable licence of the governors, actually mirrored their further incorpora-tion into the patronage system of the crown. This was also reflected in the marked tendency after the civil wars for the governors to take up residence in Paris. Out of 39 governors appointed between 1605 and 1650 only six spent extended periods in their governments; two thirds of those appointed between 1627 and 1650 were in Paris when they died. There they built fine houses, rode about in magnificent carriages (the governor of Champagne ordered 15 at once), attended the court and, despite their ostensible disdain for such matters, invested in offices, tax farms and loans to the state. There were even magnates, fearful for their investments, who actually urged Mazarin to stand firm against the *parlement*. In part a reflection of the diminishing material benefits of residence in the provinces, these develop-ments could only further reduce the capacity of the governors to retain their allegiance at moments of crisis. As the ties between the magnates and the regions were weakened, so the fine balance between the advantages and disadvantages of the system of governors tipped in favour of the crown. There is little doubt for instance that, save when in revolt themselves, the governors and other grandees fulfilled their obligation to preserve law and order, intervening in the disturbances of the populace, leading the armies dispatched to intimidate or repress, and co-operating on a daily basis with the intendants. Moreover, when in 1620 the Protestant grandees were given what proved to be the last major opportunity to place themselves at the head of an organized party they declined to do so. Of the generals appointed to command the 'departments' established by the Huguenot assembly, only Rohan and his brother showed real commitment to the cause. Bouillon and the duc de Thouars retired almost immediately, Lesdiguières abjured for grace and favour in the royal service, whilst the duc de la Force and Gaspard de Coligny were not long in deciding to accept their marshals' batons from the king.

In part this devastating blow to the Protestant cause was just one more consequence of the fact that loyalty to the crown was rapidly becoming more profitable than rebellion. But it also flowed from the naturally conservative attitude of the nobility who, when the crunch came in the early 1620s, could not bring themselves to defy the king by leading a movement widely condemned as republican. The effectiveness of this accusation actually lay in its inaccuracy, for seventeenth-century rebels from whatever quarter they came were more than anxious to avow their royalist beliefs. None of the movements of resistance displayed more than a superficial familiarity with republican ideas and none generated any sort of ideological alternative to that of divine-right monarchy. If the diminished effectiveness of the aristocratic clienteles rendered unlikely a return to the prolonged civil strife of the previous century, the lack of a radical perspective surely precluded the possibility of rebellion turning into revolution. Indeed the preoccupation with limited and sectional interest characteristic of even the major revolts almost guaranteed victory to the monarchy as it was the only institution which could effectively claim to represent the common good.

Of the conservative and sectarian attitudes of the nobility there is no doubt. In the Fronde the main objectives of the magnates were to wrest control of the council from Mazarin and to protect the military and material bases of their lineages with the usual positions, pensions and marriage alliances. Thus in 1649 Conti sought a place in the council of state and a fortress in his governorship of Champagne. Longueville similarly wanted a fortress in his governorship of Normandy and the right to resign his position in favour of his sons. Then there were the claims for governorships by those denied them; Beaufort demanded Brittany for his father the duc de Vendôme, disgraced in 1626; Frédéric Maurice Bouillon who had been accused of complicity in the Cinq Mars conspiracy of 1642 wanted Auvergne, whilst his elder brother Turenne had his eye on Alsace. Although their demand for peace with Spain did give the revolt of the nobles a political flavour, for many of them this was simply a tactic designed to consolidate support and make life difficult for Mazarin. However as long as the Cardinal retained the initiative the very nature of the magnates' objectives left them open to bribery. Thus, in February 1652 as Condé was gathering his forces for the march on Paris, Turenne and Bouillon were bought off, elevated to the status of sovereign princes and given the duchies of Albret and Château Thierry. Turenne, whose military prowess rivalled that of the great Condé, assumed command of the royal forces, which it has been said was 'perhaps the single most important factor in the defeat of the princes'.[1] As ever the nobility were engaged in a constant rivalry for the spoils of the system and, united only in their dislike of Mazarin, they operated in a world of rapidly shifting alliances and opportunistic manoeuvring. Whether the magnates could have formed a workable government seems dubious; for when they finally occupied Paris they found it difficult to agree amongst themselves, let alone carry the populace with them. Beaufort went so far as to shoot the duc de Nemours because of a disagreement in their council. In defeat the nobles, with the exception of Condé, were more than happy to settle for the payment of their

[1] R.J. Bonney, 'Cardinal Mazarin and the great nobility during the Fronde', *English Historical Review* XCVI (1981), p.828.

debts incurred during the rebellion, new pensions and governorships. Gaston d'Orléans, Longueville and La Rochefoucauld retained their positions in Languedoc, Normandy and Poitou, Conti obtained Guyenne, and Mercoeur Provence. Turenne was additionally rewarded with the Limousin. When Condé finally returned to the fold in 1659 he was restored to his governorship of Burgundy which necessitated a further redistribution.

In contrast to the sectional demands of the nobility, those of the *parlement* of Paris expressed the interests of all those adversely affected by the fiscal policies of the crown. Moreover its objections to arbitrary taxation and insistence that financial edicts should be subject to scrutiny and ratification, clearly raised significant constitutional issues. Yet the magistrates never moved, as the English parliament did, beyond a conservative defence of their constitutional powers. The sovereignty of the monarch was never challenged; nor was any attempt made to elaborate fundamental laws which could overrule the royal prerogative and there was barely an echo of the theories of elective monarchy so widely disseminated at the end of the sixteenth century. On the contrary, the *parlement* simply claimed in time-honoured fashion that its authority to oppose the crown came from the crown itself. At the *lit de justice* of October 1648 the *avocat-général* Talon put the case:

> The opposition of our votes, the respectful resistance which we bring to bear in public affairs must not be interpreted as disobedience but rather as a necessary result of the exercise of our office and the fulfilling of our obligations and certainly the king's majesty is not diminished by his having to respect the decrees of his kingdom, by doing so he governs in the words of the scriptures a lawful kingdom.[2]

This viewpoint was shared by virtually all the magistrates, even the most militant, and it clearly reveals the continuing dualism in French political thought with its emphasis on the absolute yet limited power of the king. Such a position of course fudged the issue of where the authority of the king stopped and that of the *parlement* began; when asked if it was their intention to challenge the absolute nature of royal authority, the *parlementaires* invariably took two deferential steps backwards. Their declared enemy was Mazarin. A decree of 1617 which had forbidden foreigners from holding office was resurrected and read out in *parlement* on 22 September 1648, reiterated in February 1651, and even confirmed in a somewhat modified form by royal declaration. But because *parlement* never challenged the authority of the regent and because Anne resolutely refused to sacrifice Mazarin, it proved impossible to dislodge him. Nor was the *parlement* prepared to conduct a war of aggression against the crown which could have resolved the issue by force. After the court fled from Paris at the end of 1648, the *parlement* took the view that it was conducting a legitimate defence of the capital against a government which had succumbed to evil advice. In addition many of the magistrates possessed extensive estates throughout the Parisian region and risked their ruin if the war escalated.

[2] J.H. Shennan, *The Parlement of Paris* (London, Eyre & Spottiswoode, 1968), p.268.

A major weakness in the *parlement*'s position was that it was neither a representative nor, despite the extent of its jurisdiction, a national body. Indeed it was most careful not to trespass on the rights of its sister courts or to become too involved in their affairs. The grievances of the latter were handled with due care for the legal niceties and for the *parlement*'s own position. Thus when asked by their colleagues at Aix and Rouen to help in the struggle against the *semestres* the *parlementaires* refrained from issuing decrees countermanding them but agreed to raise the issue with the regent. When the *trésoriers, élus* and lesser judicial officers of Poitou offered to take up arms on the *parlement*'s behalf they were thanked politely and advised to stick to the legal channels. Conversely, the fact that only the *parlements* of Bordeaux and Toulouse followed the lead of Paris in outlawing Mazarin was a cause of much irritation. The magistrates of Metz remonstrated against Mazarin only when they discovered that his place of exile at Cologne was uncomfortably close to their jurisdiction. Dijon and Grenoble took their time. Yet by the summer of 1650 it was the Parisian magistrates, anxious to settle with Mazarin, who were becoming vexed at the stubbornness of their southern counterparts. Toulouse, Aix and Bordeaux ceased writing to them for assistance and when delegations arrived from Aix and Bordeaux the following year they directed their appeals to the regent.

Although many of the demands of the Parisian magistrates did have implications for the country at large, they were always tempered by a preoccupation with their own corporate and patrimonial interests. One of their most illuminating decisions was that to abandon a general investigation of the financiers, which could have been construed as trespassing on the royal prerogative, in favour of legal proceedings where individual magistrates had a grievance. The limited legalist and sectional attitudes of the *parlement* were even more marked amongst the provincial sovereign courts and the lesser corps of *officiers*. Of the 15 major grievances presented by the *parlement* of Aix, 12 concerned their privileges as a corporate body or as members of the social élite: suppression of new offices, payment of wages, access to free salt, a reduction in *évocations*, exemption from military billeting, as well as requests for positions for their supporters, all received prominence alongside the demand for the dismissal of the governor and intendant. Only three of the grievances revealed a concern for traditional provincial liberties or the general interest.[3] Inevitably such sectarian attitudes led the various bodies into conflict with each other. Indeed one of the central demands of the *parlement* of Bordeaux was for the suppression of the *cour des aides* established at Agen in 1629. In Provence the *cour des comptes* quarrelled incessantly with both the *trésoriers* and the *parlement* over matters of precedence and authority. Although the financial officers shared a common hatred of the intendants they were themselves acutely divided. Both the *trésoriers* and the *élus* had formed associations – the *élus* as long ago as 1599 – to protect their interests, and during the Frondes the two bodies spent as much time fighting each

---

[3] S. Kettering, *Judicial Politics and Urban Revolt in Seventeenth-Century France. The parlement of Aix 1628–1659* (Princeton, Princeton University Press, 1978), pp.276–7. See also S. Kettering, 'A provincial parlement during the Fronde', *European Studies Review* xi (1981), pp.151–69.

other as the government. Throughout France the *élus* refused the *trésoriers* access to their bureaux, resisted the execution of their orders and appealed against them to the *cours des aides*. These were only too willing to support the *élus* because of their own objections to the claims of the *trésoriers* to constitute sovereign bodies. For similar reasons the *trésoriers* ran into difficulties with the *comptes* and also some of the *parlements*: that of Toulouse intervened to reduce the level of *taille* in the *généralité* of Montauban by 900,000 *livres*. Such antagonism towards the *élus* was deftly exploited in 1652 by the government in order to facilitate the gradual reintroduction of the intendants. At Paris too the heady days of the union of the sovereign courts soon passed; the *maîtres des requêtes* declined to co-operate in the military defence of the capital partly because of the dominating rôle of the *parlement*; during the time of the final negotiations with Mazarin both the *comptes* and *aides* also withdrew for the same reason.

Thus constrained by the traditional ideological framework within which justifications of resistance were couched and severely inhibited by its sectarian basis, the opposition of the *officiers* was fundamentally little different from that of the magnates; for it amounted not to a demand for a new system but to a competition amongst rival groups for the most privileged positions within the state apparatus. There was no objection to venality in principle, merely to the way in which it was manipulated to extort cash and to the creation of new offices which devalued the existing ones. Opposition to royal fiscalism degenerated into a battle for control of the financial administration, each contending group claiming in virtually identical language that it alone was sufficiently competent and trustworthy to merit the king's confidence. Such an analysis can be extended to embrace the resistance of the towns to the undermining of their political and financial autonomy. Divided from each other by corporate and economic rivalries, the towns displayed virtually no sense of solidarity. Even their manifold objections to state intervention in economic matters failed to bring them together. Those who protested about monopoly trading companies invariably did so because of their own exclusion or because of the consequential infringement of their traditional activities. The merchant community was not even united in its attitude towards restrictive tariffs; those aimed at English and Dutch textiles in 1648 contributed to a bitter tariff war which in turn provoked complaints from the wine interests in Guyenne and the Loire as well as the Parisian merchants. The latter did in fact go beyond a sectarian defence of their own position, declaring that 'the ebb and flow of mutual aid produces the abundance in which consists the repose and felicity of peoples'. Yet others, particularly in manufacturing, continued to demand protection thus delaying a generalized attack on the principles and practice of mercantilism.

In any event the development of a truly bourgeois opposition was greatly retarded because of the penetration of the municipal governing bodies by royal officers, a tendency reinforced by the widespread flight from productive and commercial activity into office and land. Although the loyalty of the *officiers* could not of course be assured, their growing influence had a divisive and debilitating effect on the urban communities. At Orléans where the municipality supported the *parlement* of Paris the *présidial* loyally continued to take orders from the chancellor; in Auvergne the royal officers who controlled Riom did all they could to undermine the *échevins* of the rival town of Clermont. Where urban revolt *was* headed by *officiers* they were unlikely to generate solidarity. When the *parlementaires* of Aix appealed in 1630 and again in 1649 for support from the other towns of Provence it was not forthcoming. Indeed the merchants of Marseille actually sided with the governor Alais, whilst the *parlement* found its support in the faction around the lieutenant of the admiralty who was in constant conflict with the Marseillais over their claims to tax exemptions. The urban élites were just as divided by corporate and factional rivalry as any section of French society. Moreover any semblance of democratic control by the inhabitants had long since disappeared in most towns. Either through the extension of venality to municipal office or through systems of co-option which transformed the town councils into self-perpetuating oligarchies, the influence of the populace had been largely removed. The immediate objective of the urban ruling groups was to preserve their privileged position from both the attacks of the government and the lower orders. Conservative in both their social and political attitudes, the relationship of the urban élites to the crown was therefore highly ambivalent. Resentful of the restrictions imposed on them, particularly as it affected their ability to enrich themselves at public expense, the urban notables, like the *parlement*, never denied that the source of their authority was the crown. The organization of deputations to Paris in search of confirmation of privileges or to plead a case before the royal council was a major activity of urban communities; ironically, they were invariably an occasion for the intensification of factional struggle as inclusion in such deputations was usually a profitable business. Those dispatched from Toulouse in 1643 to the duc d'Orléans, governor of Languedoc, with instructions to plead the city's exemption from the *tailles* secured instead their own installation as *capitouls* (*échevins*).

Inadvertently, of course, the factional rivalries within the ruling groups encouraged the agitation of the *menu peuple* and gave them the opportunity to press their own grievances. But frightening as the disturbances of the populace could be, they too failed to provide the basis for a radical ideology of revolt. The main objective of both rural and urban crowds was to get rid of the hated *gabeleurs* – the general name given to anyone associated with the royal fisc or who was even erroneously suspected of such an association. Virtually all the victims of popular upheavals came into this category and the typical cry of the insurgents was 'long live the king without the *gabelle*'. As this suggests, the populace shared the royalism of their betters. Such political ideas as could be detected – and these were probably fed into the movements by their literate and moderately well-to-do leaders – expressed a desire to return to an imaginary golden age, to defend traditional liberties, and to resist the evil advisers of the king. Nothing was more likely to spark off resistance to paying taxes than the news, imaginary or real, that the government had granted a reduction. When news of the concessions made to the *parlement* in the summer of 1648 reached the provinces whole communities simply refused to pay their arrears.

The basic conservatism of the popular forces can be seen even in the revolt of the Ormée, undoubtedly the most organized and most politically conscious revolt of the *menu peuple* during the entire century.[4] Although the Ormists effectively supplanted both the *parlement* of Bordeaux and the municipal institutions, there was never any suggestion of disengagement from the monarchy. Indeed the crowd saw in the monarchy and also in the princes their natural allies against a corrupt and exclusive oligarchy. Ormée tracts did contain quite a sophisticated defence of democracy but it was counterposed to aristocracy not to monarchy. Popular assemblies were defended on the grounds that they existed long before the *parlement* and reflected the natural tendency of human beings to organize themselves in communities in order to secure 'all the goods they need whether for survival or pleasure'. Yet although this argument depended on an acceptance of natural equality, the Ormists were unable to free themselves entirely from a corporate and hierarchical world. The corporations of the *parlement* and municipality may have been rejected but not the principle of corporate organization itself. Thus the preamble to the Ormée's covenant asserted 'that being bourgeois we have deliberative as well as consultative privileges in the assemblies of the communal government'; and in its rather gild-like protection of the interests of its members, the Ormée itself displayed a highly corporate sense of identity. Moreover if there was a theoretical attachment to the principle of natural equality, there was no question of abolishing the distinction between masters and servants. True, when the Ormée finally turned in desperation to the English for help there was some flirtation with republican ideas, but this served only to intensify the deep divisions developing within its ranks, revealing the extent to which such notions fitted ill in the French context. Certainly the hopes of some of the Ormists that the Bordelais had shown the way for the rest of the kingdom to recover 'the liberties lost in the course of centuries' were totally misconceived.

Indeed the complete isolation of Bordeaux in the last months of the Frondes illustrates perfectly the extent to which resistance to the crown was handicapped by the unintegrated nature of French society either at a political or economic level. Above all, the various elements which came into conflict with the crown lacked a permanent national representative assembly to assist in the process of overcoming sectional differences and developing a sense of common interest. Moreover although there was some pressure from the lesser nobility and the clergy during the Fronde for the summoning of an Estates-General, the *parlements* resisted the proposal for which there was not great enthusiasm. Lack of political unity was reinforced by the low level of economic development which precluded the rapid evolution of classes capable of sustaining a general struggle against the monarchy. Most obviously, the fact that the towns existed as relatively isolated enclaves, the focal points of a multitude of local economies, inhibited the coalescence of either popular or bourgeois movements of protest. Occasionally one town did take its cue from another, as at Agen in 1635 when news came of events down river at Bordeaux, but mostly the urban uprisings were fragmented by time

---

[4] The material on the Ormée is drawn from S. Westrich, *The Ormée* (Baltimore, Johns Hopkins University Press, 1979).

and geography. This was also true of the peasant uprisings. Given what we know about the general lack of mobility between rural communities, most inhabitants rarely straying more than a few miles from their birthplace, the major rebellions of 1636 and 1639 did mobilize the population over an impressively large area. Yet even at its height that of the *Nu-Pieds* raised only the southern parts of Normandy and some parishes close to its heart never moved. In Provence there were an estimated 250 disturbances of one sort or another between 1600 and 1660, yet none compared with the sustained revolts of the western provinces, and probably only a sixth of the rural communities were ever affected.

What is particularly remarkable about the resistance to the crown in the period after 1630 is the absence of the one factor that might conceivably have furnished it with both a distinctive ideology and a means of forging a degree of unity: the Protestant religion. After all this had proved its worth in providing the conviction and organization necessary to overthrow the rulers of both Holland and Scotland, whilst in England Puritanism played an absolutely crucial rôle in welding popular and bourgeois opposition into a force capable of challenging the crown. Moreover, as has been observed, in the 1570s the Huguenots themselves had espoused justifications of resistance rooted in both historical argument and ideas of natural liberty. Yet by the late 1620s despite the grim determination of La Rochelle to preserve its political and economic independence, it was apparent that the Huguenots had neither the capacity nor the will to conduct an offensive against the monarchy. In 1628 La Rochelle was just as isolated and just as dependent on English support as Bordeaux was to be in 1653. French Protestantism had already been confined to its provincial outposts, and even here it failed to penetrate the key sections of the administrative apparatus, notably the *parlements*. With the significant exceptions of the Cévennes and the Vivarais, it also failed to make any impact on the mass of the rural population. The Catholic resilience of a largely illiterate peasantry whose rhythms of existence were governed by the passing of the seasons and the associated religious festivities proved insuperable. Strangely such success as was achieved in the reduction of saints' days and the sometimes turbulent celebrations of the *confréries*, was the work of the state and the *dévots* rather than the Huguenots. Failure to break out of its isolation inevitably accentuated the social and factional rivalries which beset the Protestant movement, leaving it hesitant and divided in the face of royal intimidation and the power of the counter-reformation.

Yet this does not fully explain the way in which the Huguenots reneged on their radical past to become pragmatic, conservative and profoundly royalist. Pushed into rebellion in 1620, they adopted a strikingly defensive posture. When the Assembly of 1621 published its manifesto it proved to be little more than a list of grievances, accusing the Jesuits of plotting their destruction, complaining of events in Béarn, of troop movements in Poitou, about the removal of tax bureaux from Protestant strongholds and so on. Indeed throughout the 1620s only one Protestant writer, de la Milletière, produced any rationale of a philosophical sort justifying resistance to the king. Even this had its limitations because he merely reiterated the traditional view that as kings are cast in the image of God they are obliged to observe the dictates of natural and divine justice. In part such conservatism derived from the fact that in order to respond to the Jesuit apologists for papal supremacy the Protestants became defenders of divine right, arguing that the king received his power directly from God and from God alone. One of the most paradoxical episodes in religious history occurred when in the after-math of the Estates-General of 1614–15 the Huguenots made a central issue of the failure of the government to endorse the celebrated first article of the third estate with its trenchant gallican defence of the absolute sovereignty of the king. Moreover, given the widespread acceptance of gallican views and the increasingly anti-Spanish orientation of official policy, it proved impossible for the Huguenots to follow in the footsteps of their Dutch and Scottish counterparts and claim a place of honour as defenders of the true national interest. Not that it should be supposed that the Huguenots' royalism flowed essentially from a particular conjuncture of circumstances or juxtaposition of events; for the French Protestants were not merely royalist but conservative in a much deeper sense. In many ways the espousal of radical theories in the 1570s was an aberration generated by the massacre of St Bartholomew and soon regretted; even the tracts of that decade were careful to limit the rights of resistance to the established representatives of the people or the magistracy. Popular rebellion was certainly not countenanced. Indeed the attitude of the Protestant leadership to anything that smacked of democracy was made abundantly clear by the determined efforts to defeat the originally quite strong congregationalist tendencies within the Church. These gave way to the more authoritarian views of Beza and the individual congregations were subordinated to a hierarchical system of provincial and national synods. The attachment to hierarchy and order went so far that, from the beginning of the seventeenth century, there were pastors who began to suggest that bishops were not, in principle, a bad idea. This clearly distanced the Huguenots from the English Puritans, whose anti-episcopal sentiments were a vital ingredient in their assault on the entire establishment. With alarm but considerable accuracy the Synod of Charenton in 1644 condemned the Independent movement in England as not only prejudicial to the word of God but also to the state.

These powerful conservative tendencies clearly reflected the domination of the Protestant movement by the nobles and urban patriciates. In part this was a consequence of the general dependence on them for military leadership throughout the years of open conflict. Yet it was also a reflection of the limited political rôle of the lower classes. There was just no equivalent in France to the 'middling' class of independent small producers and yeomen farmers who provided the backbone of the New Model Army and much of the driving force behind the English revolution. Even in those French towns where the artisans were numerically superior they remained vastly under-represented in both municipality and consistory. It is true that in 1613 the lesser bourgeois of La Rochelle, resentful of their exclusion from office, overthrew the established constitution and endeavoured to secure a more militant posture *vis-à-vis* the central government. Remarkably successful, this municipal revolution inevitably had the effect of reinforcing the predisposition of the oligarchs to compromise with the crown. They certainly welcomed the royal insistence on the restoration of the status quo at the peace of Montpellier in 1622; and the decisive defeat of the Rochelais fleet in 1625, whilst the mayor was dithering in the hope of negotiations with Richelieu, must be attributed to loss of nerve as much as to lack of resources. Ideologically ill-equipped to withstand the onslaught that followed, the Huguenots subsequently retreated into a stoical piety enabling them to live through the travails of this world in the hope of salvation hereafter. Nothing perhaps reveals more clearly the lack of a class basis for the generation of radical political or social ideas.

At the same time the Huguenot experience also indicates the extent to which class antagonism was a factor in undermining the unity of those opposed to the crown. For although the notables undoubtedly tried to utilize the discontent of the *menu peuple* for their own purposes, they could never be certain that it would not get out of hand. Politically conservative though they may have been, the labouring population were well aware that they were exploited and they knew who was exploiting them. In 1636 the peasantry of Angoumois complained that the *'officiers, sergents,* lawyers and *gros bourgeois* hold all the best land without paying the *taille*' thus throwing the burdens on to those least able to bear them. Because the 'said parishes, ecclesiastics, nobles and other *privilégiés* have many domains exempt from the *tailles* ... one can clearly see that nothing remains for the poor supplicants and that ... it has been necessary for 10 or 12 years to borrow or mortgage their property to the inhabitants of the said towns and the said *privilégiés*'. This sharp perception of the cause of their distress expressed itself in the irruptions of the peasantry into the towns, attacks on the fiscal agents and their offices, and sometimes the town halls. The antipathy of the countryside for the towns had unmistakable class overtones reflecting the resentment towards those who, in their dual capacities as officers and land-owners, dominated entire localities. In the poorer suburbs and artisan quarters of the towns the peasantry frequently joined forces with the urban crowds whose leaders shared their class feelings. As the municipal rebellions at Bordeaux and La Rochelle indicate, the hostility felt by those excluded from the increasingly entrenched oligarchies towards the rich and influential was a potent factor in urban politics. 'The actual cause of sedition', declared the *Apologie pour l'Ormée,* 'is the excessive wealth of the few.' Furthermore the Ormée took action based on this principle. Funds were obtained from its opponents to feed the poor and to compensate the families of those who had died in the fighting; grain hoarding was forbidden and, most significantly, rents were reduced by a quarter. Invariably the courts established by the Ormée took the side of the poor in their disputes with tax farmers, merchants and masters.

Undoubtedly the Ormée was the most remarkable expression of urban class conflict, exceptional in the level of its organization and clarity of purpose. Yet everywhere the municipal authorities existed in a constant state of apprehension about the possibility of popular disorder and violence. This was reflected not only in their attempts to prevent the tocsin being sounded or to shut the gates when disturbances threatened, but in their determined efforts to ensure that food was made available in the markets and that its supply was subject to the tightest regulations. Nothing was more likely to stir up trouble than food shortages and rumours that the rich were engaged in hoarding or manipulating the markets. Attempts by the notables to draw on popular support for their own purposes was a risky business. In Aix in 1630 the radical *parlementaires* having encouraged the populace to intervene discovered that things could go badly wrong; on 3 November there arrived an influx of peasantry from lands adjacent to the lands of the first consul of Aix. Not only was the consul's loyalty to the town suspect, but he had been engaged in bitter disputes with the peasants as a result of his refusal to allow them to gather wood on his lands. He had also used his office to prevent the citizens of Aix from doing likewise and was alleged to be a grain-hoarder as well. After subjecting the *bourgeois* to a night of terror, the following morning a sea of peasants and artisans streamed out of Aix in the direction of the consul's château. There was some pillaging of out-buildings and the peasants returned to their villages laden with firewood, furniture, salt and wheat. But when the artisans returned to Aix they found the militia had been mobilized and meetings and assemblies had been forbidden. Nine years later during the unrest in Normandy a crowd besieged the town hall of Rouen. Unable to find anyone willing to defend it, the municipality was obliged to bring in a detachment of nobles. Members of the bourgeois guard who should have been fulfilling this function were themselves involved in a violent assault on the house of a farmer of the *gabelle*; but as the conflict spread it became somewhat easier to persuade the militia to act and three days later it intervened to disperse a crowd attacking the house of a suspected *gabeleur* in which several merchants were meeting. Throughout, the *parlementaires* displayed a highly ambivalent attitude which may, as the government later alleged, have reflected a certain sympathy with the rebels, but it almost certainly stemmed from anxiety as well. The *procureur général* said that he neither wished to be hated by the people for being too severe or by the government for being too weak, thus articulating the dilemma of those sections of the ruling groups themselves in dispute with the government.

During the Fronde the limits to the willingness of the notables to go along with the movements of the *menu peuple* became very apparent. Most striking was the attitude of the *parlementaire* Broussel to the upheaval in Paris provoked by his arrest; no sooner had the rebellion of the artisans and lesser bourgeois achieved his release than he was urging them to dismantle the barricades. In the months that followed the *parlement* had to contend on several occasions with the turbulent crowds whipped up by those nobles who were against any settlement with Mazarin. But the effect of this was to emphasize the judges' conservative inclinations; on 9 January 1649 they moved with alacrity to restore calm during a demonstration at the town hall, thus finding themselves coming to the rescue of the Mazarinist municipal officers (the most significant group to remain loyal to the government). In Aix where the now much smaller faction of opposition magistrates once again brought the populace into play, they were nevertheless very careful, in contrast to 1630, to maintain a sure grip on developments. The success of their coup once ensured, the *parlementaires* issued decrees creating street patrols in each quarter of the city, ordered a general disarmament, forbade assemblies and instructed the shops to reopen. Guards were appointed inside and outside the *palais de justice* and chains were left across the streets at strategic points. Subsequently a bourgeois guard was created for each quarter and no one was allowed to enter or leave the city without permission. Finally the tax on flour was reduced and the export of grain from Provence forbidden.

In Bordeaux by contrast the municipal élite lost control of the situation with the dramatic consequences that have already been outlined. But as the Ormée consolidated its position its more substantial adherents began to get worried by the militant defence of the lower orders. Some of them, suspect for their lack of conviction and perhaps for collusion with the enemy, were expelled. These included a professor of mathematics, latterly tutor to the governor's family, and a president of the *cour des aides*. Merchant support also began to waver, for although trade was severely disrupted contributions to the cause were still expected. The grain merchants found 40,000 *livres*, the munitioneers 100,000, whilst a single banker provided no less than 100,000 *livres*. Inevitably as the Ormée assumed an ever more radical position its social basis narrowed and it was led into increasingly repressive attempts to maintain control. By December 1652 some merchants were confident enough to openly defy the leadership which also had to contend with conspiracies amongst the lesser *officiers*. In July 1653 faced with armed revolt the Ormists found they no longer had sufficient support even amongst the artisans to survive. The internal tensions within the Ormée indicate both the lack of social homogeneity of the various elements broadly categorized as 'popular' and at the same time the fear that it generated. Such fear pushed the notables back towards a compromise with the crown.

The widespread and endemic unrest which culminated in the Frondes thus proved unable to undermine the system of war finance, achieve the permanent withdrawal of the *intendants*, or to generate any movement towards a constitutional form of monarchy. Nor were the nobility able to plunge the realm back into the chaos of the sixteenth century. In the remaining years of Mazarin's ministry, particularly once war with Spain was renewed, the government resorted to its old practices. In 1653 14 fiscal edicts introducing extraordinary taxes, fees and new offices, were pushed through the *parlement* in a *lit de justice*. Suits continued to be evoked from *parlement* by the royal council. More *rentes* were floated threatening to devalue those already issued, together with proposals to limit payment of interest.

Yet on virtually all these matters there was a degree of compromise. The *parlement* continued to discuss the fiscal edicts for months after the *lit de justice* and achieved some modifications in the edicts. It put up such a ferocious resistance to an edict devaluing the coinage which the government had sent to the *cour des monnaies* that it was able, notwithstanding the exile of five members, to secure jurisdiction over the edict's implementation. The judges were thus in a position to render it more or less inoperative. In the years that followed, the *parlement* achieved yet more successes with the withdrawal or modifications of fiscal legislation. Chancellor Séguier noted the 'cessation of taxes that we have ordered through the councils' which he complained were 'powerless to sustain and execute what they judge necessary for the king's service'.[5] Similarly the government felt constrained to compromise on the question of *évocations*, returning some suits to the jurisdiction of *parlement* and reiterating promises that it would abide by the ordinances governing them. The entire question lay unresolved at the end of the regency. Above all the government was careful to offer the *parlementaires* the most favourable terms on the *rentes*, agreeing to pay their arrears of interest in full and giving them priority over all other rentiers. There was no further question of tampering with the *paulette* and threatening the patrimonial interests of the office-holders. A similar compromise was also made, as we have seen, with the magnates who received not only compensation for their 'expenses' during the Frondes but also the governorships which they claimed.

What the Frondes made clear was the mutual dependence of the central government and the dominant groups in both Parisian and provincial society. Apart from the fundamental fact, elucidated in the previous chapter, that the government remained enmeshed in a system in which patronage and clientage still counted for more than bureaucratic mechanisms of control, it was now abundantly plain that the crown and its opponents shared a common interest in maintaining law and order. If their own quarrels got out of control the consequences might prove unacceptable. The lesson was articulated by secretary of state Phélypeaux when he wrote to the *parlement* of Bordeaux in the aftermath of the Fronde, instructing it on its responsibility to maintain order so that 'revolts in our provinces and in our city of Bordeaux will be discouraged. A good example must be made in order to preserve everyone's obedience'. At the same time, as already described, Mazarin began establishing his ties with the dissident baron d'Oppède, who shortly became first president of the *parlement* of Aix, and in a similar manouevre in Burgundy Condé's clientele was outflanked when Bouchu, his principal supporter and first president of the *parlement* of Dijon, was appointed intendant. In 1658 Bouchu played an instrumental rôle in overcoming a minor crisis precipitated by the refusal of the Estates to make a grant to the crown and by the provincial *parlement*'s simultaneous demand for a union with that body.

Not that these tense and somewhat fudged compromises amongst the privileged sections of French society sufficed to still unrest amongst the population at large on whom the burden of the war with Spain continued to fall. During the Fronde collection of taxes had been brought to a halt in some parts of every *élection* in the realm and it simply proved impossible to recover the arrears. Throughout the 1650s much of the south-west remained in a state of tension with repeated attacks on the brigades sent to enforce payment. Further north in the *généralité* of Alençon 25 parishes in a single *élection* refused to appoint any collectors of the *taille* from 1647 to 1659. Most alarming for the government was the fact that powerful movements of

[5] A. Hamscher, *The Parlement of Paris After the Fronde* (Pittsburgh, University of Pittsburgh Press, 1976), p.98.

resistance extended into the central provinces. In May 1658 30 parishes of Berry and the Orléanais formed an illegal association which then sought the support of the towns. The efforts of the intendants of Orléans and Bourges to suppress the revolt only made matters worse. Troops were billetted on the recalcitrant parishes, whilst the two hapless intendants were recalled and never given intendancies again. They were perhaps a little unfortunate, for throughout much of France their colleagues struggled manfully but with limited success during the last years of the regency to discipline an exhausted but obdurate populace. Moreover, although the Peace of the Pyrenees (7 November 1659) opened up the way for the cancellation of some of the massive arrears, it also aroused expectations of further remissions which did little to encourage a more co-operative attitude.

4
The Triumph and Failure of French Absolutism

Power and Order Under Louis XIV

Louis XIV inherited a mass of unresolved problems. The *parlements* remained powerful representatives of vested interest, quite capable of obstructing the royal will. Where provincial Estates survived it was still necessary for the crown to bargain with them for its money grant and it could expect to receive precious little. Virtually nothing had been done to overcome the lack of uniformity in either the judicial or fiscal administration. If anything the Fronde simply confirmed government dependence on the financiers; despite the restoration of the intendants and the subordination of the treasurers, receivers and *élus*, many of these officials more than compensated for their demotion through their operations as tax farmers and creditors of the state. All of which was underpinned by the persistence of venal office-holding, widely recognized as a hindrance to sound administration. Moreover the strategic objectives of the crown were by no means near achievement. Although the political power of the Huguenots had been broken, they stubbornly persisted in the error of their ways and together with the equally obdurate Jansenists constituted an affront to the royalist attachment to religious conformity. Above all, the attempt to oust the Dutch from their commercial supremacy and make France economically self-sufficient had made no headway. The Dutch dominated the Baltic trade, remained the essential suppliers of the French West Indies, crowded into French ports and infringed on the rights of the trading companies which were almost in a state of collapse. Richelieu's efforts to develop the navy had petered out, whilst at home the French required Dutchmen to drain marshes, establish sugar refineries and introduce textile skills. Even the hitherto buoyant textile manufactures of Languedoc had begun to falter when from mid century their outlets in the Levant were penetrated by the superior products from Holland and England. Nor, despite the settlement of Westphalia in 1648 and the Treaty of the Pyrenees in 1659, was the Habsburg-Bourbon rivalry terminated. On the contrary, the Austrian Habsburgs never reconciled themselves to the transfer of sovereignty of the three bishoprics of Metz, Toul and Verdun to France, nor the ceding of the 10 towns of Alsace known as the *decapole*. The settlement furnished Louis XIV with a basis for continued interference in German affairs. His marriage with the Spanish infanta likewise created rather than diminished tensions, for, despite Maria Teresa's formal renunciation of her claims to Spanish territories, Louis was henceforth able to assert an interest in them. The French invasion of the Spanish

Netherlands in 1667 made it abundantly clear that the old antagonisms were by no means played out. It was but a curtain raiser for a further vast escalation of military conflict which eventually united the principal powers of Europe against the French king, imposing ever greater demands on both government and people.

On the other hand, if Louis inherited problems he also acquired the main instruments for coping with them. At his disposition were the essentials of a ministerial system of government backed up by the intendants. In addition Mazarin bequeathed to Louis a team of ministers from established robe backgrounds whose loyalty and expertise were considerable assets. Even Colbert, who joined the government after the debut of the reign, had been Mazarin's personal intendant, in which capacity he had developed close relations with many key figures of the financial world. Under the rigorous direction of Le Tellier and his son Louvois, the process of subordinating the army to civilian control had already begun, whilst the Fronde had confirmed the effective collapse of the independent military capacity of the magnates. The financial structures of the regime, for all their flaws, still maintained a remarkable capacity to sustain the military machine. Opposition to the political and social consequences of royal policies had run into a cul-de-sac, trapped by its failure to develop an alternative to the ideology of divine-right monarchy. As Louis's reign got under way, virtually all discussion about the nature and scope of public authority ceased; the jurists who for more than a century had been the prime movers in the prolonged and intense debate about such matters retreated into the intricacies of private law. After all, if everything the king did was bound to be just, there was very little room left for argument.

Louis's own education had prepared him admirably for his rôle of Most Christian King. From his youngest days he was steeped in religious ritual which led him to accept without question the yearly round of processions and the need for public displays of piety. Little concerned with theological subtleties, the young king and his queen dutifully washed the feet of 13 poor men and women on Thursdays, and on Holy Thursday and again after Easter he touched the sick. At the same time, without any sense of inconsistency, Louis was reared in the martial arts. An enthusiastic hunts-man, he rode and shot competently, learnt to handle a variety of combat weapons, to drill and acquired some knowledge of the art of fortification. Learning very young that his presence in the royal army was calculated to raise morale, his robust constitution stood him in good stead; although the days were gone when kings endangered themselves by leading their troops into open battle, Louis was used to spending entire days in the saddle, inspecting the outposts, camps and fortifications. Such practical experience was backed up by an interest in the increasingly complex administrative and logistical problems posed by large-scale warfare and by the teaching of the great Turenne. From Mazarin himself Louis obtained an insight into the wider diplomatic and political problems of the day and was well used to presiding over the royal council long before the cardinal's death. His dedication to the business of being king also appears to have owed much to Mazarin's insistent reminders: 'God has given you all the qualities of greatness ... you must put them to use', he wrote on one occasion, and on another more tersely 'You owe your God and your Gloire.'[1]

The ground was thus well prepared for the absolutism of Louis XIV. Its essential institutional, ideological and human ingredients were all there on his assumption of personal power. Both the problems facing the government and its responses to them were largely conditioned by the experience of the previous 60 years or so. But, in addition, there was a heightened determination to utilize the opportunity offered by the advent of a new king to insist on his untrammelled sovereignty. Louis himself began the process by announcing to the world his intention to rule without a first minister and by making it abundantly clear to his ministers that they were to be personally and solely responsible to him. Action quickly followed to ensure that they were men whom he could trust. Colbert successfully supplanted Foucquet at the ministry of finances, whilst Lionne eased de Brienne, suspect for his *dévot* and pro-Spanish sentiments, out of the ministry of foreign affairs. Although neither of the newcomers was able to acquire for some time the appropriate secretaryships, both were called to the *conseil d'en haut* alongside Le Tellier. Everyone else was more or less excluded, thus setting the pattern of concentrated authority at the centre which was to characterize the entire 55 years of Louis's personal rule. Throughout he appointed a total of only 17 ministers to the inner council, which was rarely larger than three and never exceeded five in number. The clergy and traditional nobility (with two exceptions) were never represented in the ministeriat; indeed it was drawn almost entirely from just three families, those of Le Tellier, Colbert and Phélypeaux. The fall of Foucquet was also followed by the abolition of the post of *surintendant* and its replacement by a new council, the *conseil royal des finances*. Superior to the existing council of finances, this was presided over by the king and confined to a small number of experienced royal agents. In effect the real authority in the new body lay with Colbert whose power never ceased to grow. In 1665 he acquired the post of *contrôleur général des finances*, formerly held by the *surintendant*'s principal assistant, transforming it into a truly ministerial office. Within four years he had also become secretary of state in charge of the navy, galleys, commerce, horse raising, and the waterways and forests, as well as superintendent of the king's buildings. By 1671 authority over the royal household and the general affairs of the clergy had also been added to his list of responsibilities. Whilst the office of *contrôleur-général* was thus upgraded, that of chancellor diminished in importance. From September 1661 the holder of this post no longer had automatic right of entry as a minister to the inner council nor to the new council of finances, whilst some of Colbert's new functions impinged on those traditionally associated with chancellorship.

These developments would have been in vain without an effort to limit and define more tightly the competence of other institutions in relation to the royal council. Above all, it was necessary to limit attempts by the *parlements* to utilize judicial procedures to veto or modify royal legislation, and to reassert the supremacy of the royal council. This was very quickly done by the royal

[1] J.B. Wolf, *Louis XIV* (London, Panther Books, 1970), p.107.

declaration of July 1661 which stipulated that decrees of the council were to have precedence over those of the *parlements*. In 1665 the point was reinforced when the *parlements* were dubbed 'superior' rather than 'sovereign' courts. Two years later there appeared the ordinance instructing the *parlements* henceforth to proceed immediately to the ratification of royal edicts without delaying for remonstrances. When a number of judges demanded a plenary session of the chambers to consider this, Louis not only exiled some of them but also ordered three to resign their offices. In 1673 the political subordination of the *parlements* was confirmed by the royal decision that remonstrances could be made only *after* the implementation of conciliar decrees. The government was much assisted in overcoming opposition by the support of its officials in the *parlement* of Paris. Foucquet, who had held the post of *procureur-général* simultaneously with his office of *surintendant* and had been prone to compromise, was replaced by the loyal Achille de Harlay, who was in turn succeeded by his son. The formerly unreliable *avocat-général* Talon became increasingly docile, possible having done some sort of deal with Colbert, whilst the first president Lamoignon, although not one of the *gens du roi*, did his best to restrain the more militant magistrates. Similar mechanisms of political control operated in the provincial courts. At Aix on the death of d'Oppède in 1671 the post of first president remained unfilled for two years before the government secured the installation of the provincial intendant as his successor. At Toulouse in 1673 it was the *avocat-général* who acquired the first presidency.

The provincial Estates were also subject to a fairly effective combination of intimidation and manipulation. To overcome the unwillingness of those of Brittany to part with funds Louis actually paid them a visit in 1661; in the years that followed they were carefully managed by the adherents of the duc de Rohan and their proceedings closely supervised by the provincial governor. An attempt in 1673 to make a grant conditional on the revocation of objectionable legislation was not only rebuffed but the Estates were also obliged to double the 2.6 million *livres* offered in order to secure its withdrawal. Moreover they proved powerless to obtain the suppression of new taxes on stamped documents, on tobacco and on pewter dishes, which contributed directly to the uprisings that swept Brittany two years later. Negotiations with the Estates of Languedoc were often vexatious, particularly as they insisted on attaching conditions to any grant, going so far in 1662 as to establish a committee to monitor the crown's fulfilment of its promises. Colbert, becoming weary of the haggling, eventually instructed the intendant in 1672 to inform the deputies of the exact sum required and then to secure approval within a single deliberation. By 1676 the crown was obtaining without demur a grant of 3 million *livres* compared with 1 million at the beginning of the reign, which itself had been only half of the amount requested.

The assembly of the clergy bowed even more rapidly to the royal will. During the Fronde it had actually refused a *don gratuit* and the assembly of 1655, after months of negotiation over the renewal of the financial contract as well, had produced a mere 600,000 *livres*. Moreover this was deemed an extraordinary gift towards the cost of the coronation and not a war subsidy.

Encouraged by the conclusion of peace, at their next assembly the clergy specified that their gift was a contribution towards the expense of the negotiations and the royal marriage. By contrast in 1665, although they conceded only 2.4 million as opposed to the requested 4 million *livres*, agreement came quite unprecedentedly in one session. Most importantly the *don gratuit* was transformed into a customary gift. The docility of the clergy was further revealed by the relative ease with which Louis had his way over the vexed question of the *régale*. This was the right to administer or appropriate the revenues of vacant bishoprics but it was not a practice which had any currency in a number of peripheral provinces. Both Richelieu and Mazarin had avoided a confrontation over this anomalous situation, but in 1665 Louis referred the matter to the *parlement* in the well-founded belief that it would sustain his claims. Although the assembly of 1670 fought something of a rearguard action, it was both unable and unwilling to conduct a prolonged resistance. In 1673 there followed the famous edict extending the *régale* to the whole country. Only two Languedoc bishops, both of Jansenist persuasion, persisted in opposing the measure thus becoming, with supreme irony, the principal defenders of papal claims in France. In the ensuing conflict however the clergy as a whole rallied to the side of the king. In 1680 Innocent XI refused to accept Louis's nominee as mother superior of the abbey of Charonne. In reply the king summoned an assembly of the clergy which, carefully chosen and handled, gave him all the support he needed by producing the celebrated Four Articles of 1682. These reasserted the supremacy of ecumenical councils over the pope and the autonomy of the French Church. The government subsequently declared that all college faculties and seminaries were to conduct a reading and exposition of the Articles every year and that all students of theology were to confirm their approval of them in writing. Those prelates who were not happy kept their counsel to themselves.

Of all the loci of authority in provincial France those that suffered most from the extension of royal power were the municipalities. By the beginning of Louis's reign their vitality was already considerably diminished as a result of the prolonged fiscal pressures upon them. Of the major centres only Marseille retained a truly autonomous position *vis-à-vis* the crown; and virtually one of Louis's first acts was to descend on Provence with an army in January 1660, occupy Marseille and suppress its ancient constitution. At the same time the municipal constitutions of Aix and Arles were remodelled. The day of independent municipalities was effectively over. Investigation of their debts by the intendants, which had been interrupted during the Fronde, gathered momentum. As municipal finances were brought under a semblance of control, measures were introduced to prevent the towns accumulating more debts. An edict of 1673 made it illegal for extraordinary expenditure to be authorized save by a reunion of the inhabitants which itself required the approval of the intendant. Effectively this destroyed the financial independence of the towns and was followed logically in 1691 by legislation empowering the intendant to verify municipal accounts; four years later even the repair of churches required authorization. Finally the principal municipal offices were transformed *en bloc* into venal ones. Towns like La Rochelle which had earlier suffered the suppression of these offices now had them re-established for sale. Occasionally a municipality managed to repurchase its offices but mostly they passed into the hands of the *officiers* of the local courts and tax bureaux.

When the ordinary methods of enforcing the royal will were likely to prove inadequate the government resorted, as in earlier times, to special commissions. The first of these was that established to try Foucquet on the manifestly ludicrous charge of treason. There followed the *chambre de justice* for the investigation of the financiers and, most notably, the *grands jours d'Auvergne*, a special itinerant court of assize dispatched to the Auvergne which remained a region of great lawlessness. Sessions of the court were held regularly in Clermont from September 1665 to January 1666. Not only did it pursue the troublesome members of the local nobility, but it upset the assembly of clergy by interfering in religious matters and some of the judiciary by attempting to reform the procedures of the local law courts. Sometimes the due process of law was dispensed with entirely and individuals were summarily imprisoned by royal command.

When all else failed Louis had at his disposition an unprecedented concentration of armed force which he was quite prepared to utilize. He certainly understood that a powerful army was not just for use against France's enemies, as the commission bestowed on Turenne at the outset of the reign reveals:

> We find ourselves obliged [it ran] for the conservation of the state as much as for its glory and reputation, to maintain ... in peace as well as in war a great number of troops, both infantry and cavalry, which will always be in good condition to act to keep our people in the obedience and respect they owe, to insure the peace and tranquillity that we have won.... and to aid our allies.[2]

The wisdom of this view was soon made clear. In the summer of 1662 during the course of an essentially anti-seigneurial uprising involving some 6,000 peasants of the Boulonnais, the local cavalry units were forced to retreat whilst the insurgents occupied some chateaux. Four hundred rebels were subsequently condemned to the galleys. Two years later a revolt of similar proportions, but anti-fiscal in nature, broke out in the deep south-west of the country. The peasantry led by a modest nobleman joined forces with the artisans of Bayonne, whilst the municipal authorities sent desperate requests for assistance; signs of rural discontent were evident in the area for years. In 1670 it was the turn of the Vivarais when a force of 4,600 regulars had to be dispatched to disperse yet another 5,000-strong peasant army which had already successfully confronted two companies of troops. However these incidents merely served as a prelude to the Breton uprisings of 1675 when it became necessary to take repressive action on a large scale. In the spring and summer of that year a series of anti-fiscal movements in Rennes accompanied by a violent anti-seigneurial movement in lower Brittany threw this key

[2] Wolf, *Louis XIV*, p.198.

maritime province into disorder. The government responded by billeting an army 6,000-strong in the region with strict instructions to live off the countryside. Then an even larger force was dispatched to install itself for the winter season. No wonder that in November of that year the Estates of Brittany granted the king 3 million *livres* without debate, or that the following year it sufficed only to threaten the Estates of Provence with troops to elicit a positive response from them too. A similar threat was also employed against the *parlement* of Brittany when it tried to obstruct the implementation of the government's new system of naval recruitment.

Louis was well aware however that it would not be expedient to rely entirely on force, whilst Colbert constantly exhorted his agents to refrain from coercive measures for the purposes of tax collection. The government also remained ever fearful of disorder within the army which, paradoxically, resulted in strict instructions to the generals to deal brutally with offenders. During one campaign five men found guilty of pillaging a church were condemned to be burnt alive before their fellows. A more effective solution to the disorders of the soldiers was to place them in barracks, which became increasingly common from the 1590s. The system of *étapes* was extended and magazines established in the frontier areas so that, theoretically at least, supplies were available every six miles. In 1704 the supplying of the army was centralized under the office of the director general of *fourrages et étapes*. Partly in response to the indecorous squabbling which broke out between senior commanders after the death of Turenne in July 1675, the chain of command within the army was also tightened up. A Table of Ranks was issued which not only established an officer hierarchy that was clear, but also a non-venal route for promotion, so doing something to help those who had ability but no money. The prestigious post of colonel general of the cavalry went the way of its equivalent for the infantry, suppressed in 1661, thus placing the military commanders under the direct authority of Louvois and the king. Although the troops themselves did not swear an oath of allegiance to the king, uniforms began to be provided by the state and the provision of arms and ammunition was slowly taken out of the hands of the commanders. The government also assumed some responsibility for the welfare of the soldiers and made efforts to improve the provision of hospital facilities. It even created in the *Hôtel des Invalides* a home for ex-soldiers, although this was probably as much motivated by the desire to keep them off the streets as by a sense of charitable obligation.

Perhaps the most significant and obtrusive extension of the state's military capacity lay in the creation in 1688 of a conscript militia which could be used to supplement the peacetime forces – themselves numbering a prodigious 100,000 or so. Each parish was obliged to provide one soldier by lottery, thus drawing the whole population into the bureaucratic-military complex by procedures which were themselves arbitrary and brutalizing. During the Spanish War of Succession the militia provided approximately 350,000 soldiers, nearly half the total, although evasion and desertion were widespread. Curiously enough, as a result of Colbert's influence, attempts to create an orderly system of recruitment for the navy had been under way in the western provinces from the middle 1660s. In the following decade the maritime classes as they were called were extended to Normandy, Picardy and Languedoc. The essence of the idea was to establish a complete roll of those able to serve at sea, which was then divided so that the sailors appeared for duty on a rota basis. Crews were to be checked and approved by admiralty clerks. One of Colbert's initial problems was that the influential duc de Beaufort who had acquired the post of grand master of the fleet, created and formerly held by Richelieu, utilized his position to obstruct the reforms. In June 1669 he even dismissed the *commissaire* sent to inspect his own crew and replaced him. Fortunately for Colbert, who had just assumed the secretaryship for the navy, Beaufort died in battle within a month. His post was subsequently suppressed and although that of admiral of France was re-established it was bestowed on the two-year-old bastard son of the king, the comte de Vermandois, thus leaving Colbert in supreme control. Commissaires were gradually introduced to deal with recruitment, discipline was improved with the introduction of naval court martials and measures taken to deal with the widespread problem of captains who treated their crews harshly or failed to pay and feed them properly. As in the army, control of supply and provisions was taken away from the captains who were increasingly constrained by the surveillance and disciplinary powers of the naval intendants. These measures were backed up by Colbert's willingness to inject funds into the navy. Under his auspices the naval budget rose from a mere 300,000 *livres* per annum to 12 million. Consisting of 20 fairly decrepit ships at the beginning of the reign, the fleet had grown by 1677 to 144 ships of the line, 50 supporting vessels and 34 galleys.

With the further consolidation of royal authority the bureaucratization of the regime also took another step forward. It is not without significance that from the reign of Louis XIV historians are so much better provided with information about the state of the provinces, the structure and size of the population, the development of manufacturing and so on. For the systematic investigation and copious documentation of such matters was largely the result of Colbert's success in extracting from the intendants a constant flow of information about every aspect of their wide-ranging activities. Whereas intendants previously stayed only three years in their provinces, they now settled for much longer: an average of five for those in the *pays d'élections* and practically double that in the *pays d'états*. They acquired permanent bureaux and staff. In 1710 the intendant of Alsace employed two secretaries and three specialized assistants and took on dozens of lesser agents to deal with specific matters. By this time it had also become the practice to appoint permanent *sub-délégués* to assist the intendants. Their numbers varied considerably but in 1700 the *généralité* of Moulins, for instance, boasted 30. The *sub-délégués* could provide a continuity of service exceeding that of an individual intendant; an *avocat* at the *présidial* of Limoges fulfilled such a function for 25 years. Although temporarily transformed into a venal office during the last 10 years of Louis's reign, the sub-delegacy possessed some clearly bureaucratic features. At ministerial level the same tendencies were in evidence. By the end of the century the ministry of foreign affairs, although the last to develop an independent existence, employed 50 resident bureaucrats, comprised a dozen specialized bureaux, directed a minimum of a dozen embassies abroad, in addition to numbers of secret agents, and consumed a basic budget of 1 million *livres*. Although the principal ambassadors, envoys and negotiators were drawn from the highest levels of French society and although control of the ministry remained very much a family affair, it did offer a career and training to those members of the nobility and upper bourgeoisie who filled the principal secretarial offices in the various bureaux. Usually such men served for life and were succeeded by their sons, venality of office promoting rather than hindering the notion of service to the state.

Even the world of the financiers was affected by the bureaucratic thrust. Colbert's desire to rationalize the labyrinthine financial system first led him to reduce the 19 different tolls on the periphery of the *cinq grosses fermes* to one import and one export duty. Subsequently it became the practice to lease out all the major indirect taxes (*gabelles, aides, traites, domaine* and the *cinq grosses fermes*) to a single consortium of financiers. This laid the foundation for the gradual development of the Company of Farmers General as one of the most powerful and effective of all corporate bodies. Consisting normally of about 40 principal financiers, it eventually spawned an extended hierarchy of directors, controllers, receivers and their assistants as well as a police force. Although a private organization with its own ethos, the Company was obliged, periodically, to negotiate its lease with the government and those whom it employed were in a sense state servants at one remove. At the same time as the position of the great financiers was thus institutionalized, the key treasureships of the *épargne* and the *parties casuelles* were deprived of their venal status to become revocable commissions.

Within Colbert's lifetime the benefits of consolidating the leases of the tax farms became apparent, their value rising from 44 million at the outset of the reign to over 65 million in 1680. It was indeed the steady rise in this income which enabled the *contrôleur général* to reduce the level of the *taille* in the heavily burdened *pays d'élections*. At the same time it was increased in the *pays d'états* by 50 per cent, thus doing something towards greater uniformity. In addition Colbert suppressed hundreds of useless offices, reduced the repayments on the *rentes* and through the *chambre de justice* effectively operated an undeclared bankruptcy, forcing tax farmers to disgorge their assets and redeeming many of the crown's obligations. Within six years its net revenues were doubled and for the first time since the beginning of the century the budget brought into balance. This rationalizing spirit also expressed itself in the law codes produced by a specially constituted council of justice which was largely inspired and guided by Colbert's uncle and councillor of state, Pussort. These covered civil procedure (1667), forest law (1669), criminal procedure (1670), land commerce (1673) and maritime law (1681). The code of civil law which set the pattern was intended to make justice less costly, more readily available and less subject to abuse; it thus attempted to define the procedures to be adopted by the courts at every stage of their business from the preliminary hearings to final appeal. Similarly the commercial ordinance strove to impose uniform practices throughout the land dealing with such matters as apprenticeship, banking and accounting procedures, bills of exchange, bankruptcy, merchant associations and much more besides. The code on maritime law covered naval recruitment, the jurisdiction of officers, the policing of the ports and fishing. A further code was issued for the navy in 1689.

All these developments undoubtedly reflected a further significant shift in the location of power. Indeed for the first time one has the impression that the centralizing forces had achieved ascendancy over the decentralizing elements in the body politic. The formal institutional restraints on the crown were much reduced, it had at its disposition a formidable administrative and coercive apparatus, whilst the capacity for resistance amongst the provincial élites had been immensely weakened. Yet it is also clear that there was little novel about the purposes to which this enhanced royal authority was put; indeed many of the Colbertian reforms were totally in keeping with long-expressed desires for greater uniformity in both the fiscal and judicial administration. What characterized the work of Louis XIV's government was not a search for new solutions but an attempt to ensure the clarification and systematic enforcement of established policies. This is most clearly illustrated by Colbert's application of mercantilist theories to the economic life of the country; for whilst there was nothing new about the underlying principles or the objectives of overcoming French subservience to the Dutch and English, Colbert's policies combined comprehensiveness with attention to detail in a quite extraordinary fashion and utilized every available technique of state intervention. The edicts of the late sixteenth century insisting that all craftsmen merchants should be organized in gilds were resuscitated and considerable headway was made in their implementation. At Paris the number of gilds rose from 60 to 129 by 1700; in Poitou gilds of those involved in cloth manufacture and dyeing developed in no less than 157 communities. Even in those regions of the *midi* where they had been rare, they began to develop. Between 1665 and 1670 about 30 trading and manufacturing companies were also founded. Best known are the monopoly trading companies of the East and West Indies, both founded in 1664, and the Company of the North established five years later. At the same time the first of a series of Levant companies also appeared. However the majority of Colbert's creations were concerned with textile production. One of these was a company for the manufacture of lace, created and granted a monopoly for nine years in 1665. In return for the monopoly and certain privileges such as exemption from the billeting of troops, the company was to develop production in eight towns and to train a work-force of 1,600 girls using women from Venice and Flanders to introduce the skills. Of greater concern to the government was the situation in the woollen cloth industry, for it had become abundantly clear that French cloths were unable to compete with the superior products of the Dutch and English. Foreign penetration of the domestic market was so great that the import of fine cloth became the biggest single factor contributing to France's adverse trade balance with her rivals. Colbert responded to this with measures intended to encourage production of cloth of the right quality and to assure its export. Carcassonne, the major centre of production in the south, was elevated to the status of *draperie-royale* and its *marchands-fabricants* organized into a single gild. The types of cloth which were to be made were to be specified and subject to the approval of duly appointed inspectors. Near Clermont-en-Lodève a royal manufactory was created with the intention of providing cloth suitable for the Levant market. The Levant company itself was obliged to export a certain amount of cloth and in 1683 it entered into an agreement with the royal establishment for its supplies. Government policy, it has recently been observed, was intended to ensure that 'specified clothiers, in specified towns, were to produce specified cloths, to be bought by specified companies, operating in specified ports and selling in specified markets.'[3]

By 1669 Colbert had introduced detailed regulations for the manufacture of textiles in no less than 30 centres. Fairly typical were those for cloth and serge production in Beauvais which ran to 58 clauses. Apart from the inevitable specification of the type and quality of cloth to be produced, these clauses covered everything from the organization of the gild, the use of apprentices, to the inspection of the final product. Thus masters who were obliged to be registered as members of the gild were not allowed to take more than two apprentices. The artisans themselves were to work for masters who lived in the town and its suburbs rather than outsiders. Wool was to be sold only in the market and those who bought it for resale were not allowed to commence business before 11 a.m. The gild office was to be open two hours daily for the inspection of cloth. Wardens were to visit the homes of the producers weekly. Every two months a general assembly of municipal officers, wardens and manufacturers was to be called 'to improve, perfect and bring good order to the industry, to prevent abuses and to send reports to M. Colbert.'[4] In 1669 the local regulations were supplemented by national ones for those areas without their own statutes. National regulations were also introduced to govern the dyeing of cloth which distinguished the procedures to be followed for fine cloths from those generally applicable. In similar style the legislation dealing with silk production at Tours, Lyon and Paris went into considerable technical detail limiting, for instance, the fabrics which could be mixed with silk and specifying the proportions for those where this was permitted. Although two thirds of such regulatory legislation concerned textiles, few manufacturing processes escaped entirely. Tar, paper and soap production were amongst the others affected, and Colbert's determined efforts to improve the communications network even went so far as to specify that in Normandy all roads were to be 24 feet wide, no trees were to be planted within 10 feet and carters were not to use more than four horses.

Enforcement of the manufacturing regulations on a daily basis was the work of the gild wardens. They were responsible to the municipal councils whose authority over manufacturing was enhanced by legislation bestowing powers of summary jurisdiction and control of the gild accounts. Councils were authorized to seize goods or impose fines for breaches of the regulations. A decree of 1670 declared that any defective goods were to be publicly exposed on a post nine feet high, with a sign indicating the culprit. Anyone who offended three times was to be attached to it by an iron collar. Not surprisingly townsmen frequently resisted the introduction of regulations. At

[3] J.K.J. Thomson, *Clermont-de-Lodève 1633–1789* (Cambridge, CUP, 1982), p.148.
[4] For the full text of the Beauvais regulations see C.W. Cole, *Colbert and a Century of French Mercantilism* (2 vols., Hamden, Archon Books, 1964) II, pp.377–81.

Rheims where the merchants and entrepreneurs proved particularly unco-operative, the new statutes were simply signed by the municipal officers at the behest of the royal agents. At Auxerre where Colbert wished to introduce the manufacture of French lace, it proved necessary to impose a change of mayor, and even then the authorities were long suspected of making little effort to promote the venture. Partly because of such difficulties, a corps of inspectors of manufactures was established. Some were attached to specified industries or ventures; in addition there was a general inspectorate, 34 strong by the end of the reign. Responsible to Colbert via the intendants, the function of the inspectors was to ensure the proper enforcement of the regulations, the functioning of the gild system and its officials. They were empowered to deal with disputes and instructed to let Colbert know who were the most responsive amongst the municipal officers.

Those who suffered most from the preoccupation with good order were not of course the urban notables, but the artisans. Indeed both central and local authorities shared a common interest in enforcing regulations which con-firmed the subordination of the spinners, carders, weavers, and other cloth workers to the interests of the well-to-do *marchands-fabricants*. Even without government intervention there is evidence to suggest that the gilds would have grown more enclosed and more hierarchical. It certainly seems to have become increasingly difficult for those who were not sons of masters to achieve this status, for in a period of economic difficulty the natural tendency was to close ranks. In some gilds there even developed a hierarchy of masters. In 1680 those of the *tissutiers-rubaniers* of Paris were divided into eight grades. At the same time organizations of journeymen and apprentices were forbidden. Strict regulations made it difficult for them to set up business on their own account and measures were taken to impose work discipline. The municipality of Lyon introduced very repressive regulations for the control of workers in the silk stocking industry. The first article required them to confess themselves and take communion at Easter, on all saints' days, at Christmas and on the four holy days of the Virgin. They were also to pray morning and evening in the place provided by the master. Swearing at work was forbidden, the workers were not to talk about what was being made or to take their tools home. A missed day's work could result in a fine, as might failure to observe the instructions about general behaviour, time allocated for meal breaks, and so on. At the royal manufactory of St Maur des Fosses near Paris similar measures were designed to ensure the discipline and servility of the workers. The first injunction to them was that at the start of labour they should stand before their looms to offer their work to God 'that he may bless it' and each was to make the sign of the cross.[5] This was followed by clauses which governed the rhythm of work for the rest of the day and the obligations of the artisans. The logical end product of this type of regime was the sort of enclosed settlement established at Villeneuvette, one of the foundations of the royal manufactory at Clermont-en-Lodève. Surrounded on three sides by walls and on the fourth by the river, it contained 66 houses for the labour force, a tavern, facilities for making bread, and a chapel as well as the

[5] Cole, *Colbert* 11, pp.453–5 for the full text.

equipment essential to all the processes involved in transforming raw wool into finished cloth. It was a complete community, a microcosm of Colbert's orderly and productive world.[6]

Essential to the creation of such order, as the codes of work discipline show, was the enforcement of religious conformity and devotion. Such regulations have a place not only in economic history but in that of the counter-reformation as well. Most obviously they compounded the difficulties of Protestant artisans in their struggle against discriminatory legislation. More subtly these measures contributed to the process of disciplining the general population in the interests of both Church and state. Efforts were also made by civil and ecclesiastical authorities to reduce the numbers of saints' days taken as holidays and with them the attendant disadvantages for both the economy and the tranquillity of the community. At the same time prohibitions against working on Sundays were reinforced. In addition the Church endeavoured to quell the more riotous forms of celebration associated with the *confréries*. One of the tasks of the bishop of the newly created diocese of La Rochelle (1648) was to draw up model statutes for the *confrèries* which were henceforth under strict episcopal surveillance. The Tridentine insistence on parochial conformity also appears to have made a somewhat belated impact. By the end of the century, Easter Communion probably became routine for the majority of the people in the major cities. At Paris it was also normal for children to be confirmed by the age of seven. Within the diocese of Paris churchgoers had the benefit of hearing the Mass in the vernacular and a simplified catechism; its emphasis shifted from complex theological issues to the fundamental truths derived from God's commandments and the teachings of the Church.

It is in this context that the revocation of the Edict of Nantes in 1685 must be seen. No doubt high politics and sheer expediency dictated the precise timing of this act, but it was the logical culmination of deep-seated pressures which expressed themselves in an insistence on total religious conformity. Naturally the clergy were to be forefront in working for this. As we have seen, they had successfully opposed the Edict of 1652 which had lifted the accumulated restrictions on the operation of the Edict of Nantes; but the concessions elicited from Mazarin merely whetted their appetite and from the moment of his accession Louis XIV was subjected to a barrage of anti-Huguenot propaganda and demands for even more repressive legislation. The clergy were rewarded with a series of edicts which *inter alia* forbade the pastors from wearing clerical dress outside church even for funerals, restricted the singing of psalms, inhibited correspondence between the local churches, prevented Huguenots presiding in municipal councils without permission, and compelled the children of mixed marriaged to be raised as Catholics. Gradually the Huguenots were excluded from gilds, from tax farms, from the magistracy and even from the medical profession. Their college at Nîmes was suppressed in 1664, that at Sedan in 1681 and the remainder in the next four years; the *chambres mi-parties* disappeared in 1679. For some time Louis seemingly persisted in the hope that a combination of intimidation and bribery might produce a 'peaceful' reunion of the faiths.

[6] Thomson, *Clermont-de-Lodève*, ch.6.

Such a solution was however precluded by the striking resilience of the Protestant minority. Louis may also have been impelled to resort to force by the need to make a gesture towards the pope, and his decision possibly reflected the increasing intensity of his own religious feelings. From the early 1680s he partook of more frequent communion and increasingly engaged in devotions to the Holy Sacrament. Certainly such piety was no impediment to the deployment of the troops. Within a year of being given his orders in 1681 the intendant of Poitou claimed 38,000 conversions. True his methods provoked such widespread disgust that he was recalled. But there was no change in policy. In the spring and summer of 1685 22,000 conversions were recorded in the *généralité* of Bordeaux alone; in August when the troops arrived at the Huguenot stronghold of Montauban they produced an estimated 17,000 converts, perhaps three quarters of the city's population. Moreover the violence spilled over the French frontiers into Savoy where the unwilling duke was forced to wage war on the small number of Protestants who lived along the mountainous frontier with France. Louis provided the troops. It was of course not difficult to cite biblical justifications for the use of violence for religious purposes or to find support in the writings of the Holy Fathers.

Much more difficult to deal with were the Jansenists. This was partly because their beliefs were not easily distinguishable from those of many more orthodox Catholics, who were nevertheless influenced by the pervasive currents of Augustinian pessimism; and for this reason the Jansenists were assured of a degree of protection by well-placed sympathizers. Moreover Louis's tense relationship with the papacy did not facilitate agreement on how to proceed against those he clearly regarded as both disloyal and heretical. The opening years of the reign did see an attempt to enforce the papal formulary condemning the five propositions of Jansen and an effort to disperse some of the nuns of Port Royal. But in 1668 the government was constrained to settle for a semantic compromise which allowed dissenting prelates to accept the formulary in acknowledgment of papal and royal authority, but without conceding that Jansen had actually enunciated the five allegedly heretical propositions. It was an uneasy peace, broken in 1678 by the publication of Quesnel's *Réflexions morales sur le nouveau testament*, which revived all the old controversies about the power of grace and the frailty of human effort. The following year the Jansenists were deprived of the support of the duchesse de Longueville who died and of the foreign minister Pomponne who fell from royal favour. The attack on Port Royal was thus renewed at precisely the same moment as the onslaught on the Huguenots gathered momentum. Port Royal was forbidden to receive further novices and the confessors, including Quesnel, retreated into exile. Despite the constant harassment in the years that followed, matters did not finally come to a head until 1705 when Louis, who had achieved a rapprochement with the pope, sought and obtained a papal bull which insisted on a full and unequivocal acceptance by the clergy of the controversial formulary. The handful of remaining nuns at Port Royal refused to accept it and four years later the convent was suppressed whilst the buildings at Port Royal des Champs were shortly destroyed.

Insistence on ideological conformity under Louis was not limited to religion; it extended over the entire spectrum of artistic and intellectual activity, involving a degree of government control unsurpassed before the twentieth century. To achieve the requisite conformity direct state intervention was combined with ministerial patronage and the dispensation of privileges to a variety of royal academies whose function was not only to glorify the monarchy but also to act as arbiters of taste. None of the methods were particularly new. Control of the press and assiduous exploitation of the limited official publications had been one of the hallmarks of Richelieu's regime. Indeed the Faculty of Theology had seen its powers of censorship transferred to the royal chancellory as early as 1563; Richelieu merely completed the process by depriving the Faculty of its residual authority to approve religious writings for publication. One only has to recall the fate of Mathieu de Morgues at the hands of the *Chambre de l'Arsenal* to appreciate the cardinal's resolve to control the printed word. Richelieu also founded the Royal Academy, partly as a means of recognizing those who served him faithfully and partly to develop agreed standards by which to judge the works of French writers. As far back as 1570 there had appeared a short-lived Academy of Music similarly brought into being with the express purpose of laying down general principles of musical style. In the midst of the miseries of the civil wars Catherine de Medici also exploited court spectacles, royal entries, masquerades and ballets to divert the nobility and elevate the monarchy in a clear anticipation of the great days of Versailles. The classical image of the king as emperor rather than saint was employed in popular representations from the reign of Francis, whilst the use of the sun emblem which Louis appropriated had been associated with French kings from the fourteenth century.

Yet, as in other matters, the government of Louis XIV revealed a capacity to harness these tendencies and exploit them in a systematic way. The dissemination of printed propaganda for instance by the end of the century had become a major responsibility of a department of the foreign ministry. The minister himself also developed a very close relationship with the lieutenant of police for Paris who was responsible for surveillance of the printing houses. These, in any event, were substantially reduced in number, whilst new gild members were barred and the smaller businesses made dependent on the larger ones. A similar exclusivity characterized the royal academies whether entirely new or formed from existing bodies. When the Academy of Dancing was launched in 1662 it provoked considerable opposition from the musicians' gild, which held the right to teach and award qualifications to both dancers and instrumentalists; the *roi du violons* appealed – unsuccessfully – to the *parlement*. The Academy of Painting founded in 1648 but remodelled in 1663–4 partly owed its origins to a struggle by a group of French artists to break away from the gilds of painters. Under Louis XIV it acquired a precisely defined hierarchy of officials and 12 full-time, state-funded professors. A monopoly over life drawing and other privileges set it on the way to becoming the supreme arbiter of the rules of painting and sculpture. It attracted so many students that examinations were introduced to sort them out. Chancellor of the Academy with the title of *premier peintre du roi*, at a salary of 3,000 *livres* per annum, was Charles le Brun, who became one of the most influential people at court and later at Versailles to which he contributed so richly. The Academy of Music (1669) was similarly associated with the composer Lully who, since the mid 1650s, had been responsible for the court ballets in which Louis himself danced.[7] After 1670 the king danced in no more ballets and Lully devoted his energies increasingly to operatic presentations. It was his academy's responsibility to provide musical entertainment for the court, in return for which it was allowed to give public performances. No other groups were allowed to sing 'any piece entirely in music ... without the permission of the said Sieur Lully'. Not surprisingly it became very difficult for musicians to gain employment without his patronage. Securing control of the *palais royal*, from which Molière's comedy troup was ousted, Lully supervised the production of two or three operas a year, ruling over his entourage like a musical despot, fixing the price of tickets, 'often collecting money himself at the door'. Despite the bitter hostility which his ruthless ambition and influence aroused, the enormous success of his operas and the support of the king not only ensured Lully's pre-eminence but also enabled him to make the Academy hereditary in his family.

The royal academies contributed to the elevation of the monarchy both directly and indirectly. Most immediate in its impact was the work of the Academy of Inscriptions and Medals founded in 1663. Its members, vetted by the king and protected by Colbert, were initially required to design tapestries, strike medals, and to make insignia for treasury documents. Their work gradually expanded to include the production of designs for painting, sculptures, fountains, ornaments, and the stage sets for operas; poets and painters sought their advice when in search of suitable themes for the glorification of the king. Charles Perrault as director assumed responsibility for the histories and accounts of royal ceremonies. A similarly direct form of propaganda emanated from Colbert's activities as superintendant of buildings. Under his auspices that remarkable team of Perrault, Lebrun, the architect Le Vaux, and the landscape gardener Le Nôtre indulged in a veritable architectural extravaganza. The Louvre and the Tuileries were continued, the Palais Royal improved, the Val de Grâce finished, the Invalides and the Observatoire built, and a series of triumphal arches erected at the former gates of the capital city. The royal châteaux of Fontainebleau, Vincennes, St Germain, Chambord, Compiègne and Blois all had enormous sums spent on them.

The building programme culminated in the creation of Versailles which involved, over nearly 50 years, the transformation of a simple castle into the most stupendous palace, a 'mammoth shrine to the Sun God' Apollo.[8] Louis had been portrayed as the Sun King even before his birth. In 1651 he represented the rising sun in a ballet. It subsequently became a central motif in the artistic productions of the academies and in the ceremonies, pageants and musical productions of the court. In 1663 the Academy of Inscriptions

---

[7] Much of the material for the following passage is drawn from R.M. Isherwood, *Music in the Service of the King* (Ithaca, Cornell University Press, 1973), which ranges far more widely than its title indicates and offers many splendid insights into the ideological underpinnings of absolutism.

[8] Isherwood, *Music*, p.166.

declared the sun to be Louis's official emblem. At Versailles Apollo dominates the entire east–west axis of the park, springing forth from the waters on his chariot, radiating light and warmth onto the figures of the seasons, the humours and the lesser gods who adorn him. Inside the palace Apollo is to be seen on the staircases, in the galleries and on the balconies, playing his lyre or wrestling with serpents. Versailles also provided a vast canvas on which Le Brun could record for posterity the king's triumphs. In the *salon de guerre* he depicted France receiving the homage of Spain, Holland submerged in water, and Germany kneeling blindfolded, whilst in the *salon de paix* she rides a chariot pulled by two doves from whose necks dangle the arms of Louis's allies. Between the two salons the gallery of mirrors contains 30 tableaux expanding on the theme. Louis's determination to dispense with a first minister, his independence of the papacy, his encouragement of commerce, are all extolled with an abundant use of mythology and allegorical detail; the figures of France, Justice, Victory and Fame join Mercury, Mars, Minerva and the Muses in hailing Louis the personification of France. The themes and imagery are identical to those of Lully's operas. 'How often' in these observes Isherwood, 'Louis crushed discord, received the laurel crown from glory and basked in the accolades of the Graces, Talents, Games and Muses' as he does in Le Brun's *Le Roi gouverne par lui-même*.[9] In *Proserpine* the king is represented as Jupiter whose victory over the giants is intended to parallel the former's victory over the Dutch, Spanish and the emperor.

By its very nature the culture of absolutist France was primarily a court culture and the impact of royal propaganda inevitably diminished as one moved from Paris. Nevertheless it should not be thought that the provinces were just allowed to go their own way. The French academies' authority for instance extended over provincial academies founded in five provincial centres between 1670 and 1700. The provincial élites were undoubtedly familiar with the great themes of classical literature, and occasionally, thanks to the efforts of travelling players or the amateur productions of the Jesuits, they could savour at first hand the tragedies of Corneille and Racine with their constant juxtaposition of patriotic duty and self interest. Moreover intendants, provincial governors and prelates were all instructed by the government to ensure that no chance was missed to extol the virtues of the monarchy. Every royal victory, royal birth, royal visitor was the occasion for services of thanks giving, fireworks, processions with *tableaux vivants* accompanied by cannon fire, music and the pealing of bells, as well as an excuse for feasting and dancing. *Te Deum* ceremonies in the bigger cities, although not on the scale of the Parisian ones, became spectacles in their own right and an opportunity, with the magnificently robed municipal and royal *officiers* in attendance, to reinforce the legitimacy of the established social order. Even the smallest parish held *Te Deums*, as and when instructed, and from their priest the inhabitants imbibed the same message. In 1704 the birth of a royal heir provided the opportunity for the bishop of Châlons-sur-Marne to draw up a model sermon for use by all his priests elaborating on the virtues of an assured succession.

[9] Isherwood, *Music*, p.169.

In addition to fulfilling a straightforwardly propagandist function, the royal academies also served the monarchical order through their assiduous promotion of a classical culture, which in both content and form put a premium on order and harmony. It was no accident that, although there was a baroque element in the operas and spectacles as well as in the elaborate decorations at Versailles, the baroque which was characterized by its emotional appeal, its fluidity in architecture, its exaggeration in painting, gave way to a restrained classicism with its careful appeal to the intellect. The rejection of the baroque was symbolized by the abandonment of Bernini's proposed undulating east wing for the Louvre in favour of Claude Perrault's supremely classical façade, which still survives in all its simplicity. Similarly in drama and literature rambling plots were no longer allowed to detract from overall impact; indeed since the 1630s plays had been expected to incorporate the principle of the three unities, that is, of time, place and action. Parallel developments can be seen in the order which was instilled into both ballet and opera. Ballets which at the beginning of the century had merely been a combination of poetry, dance and music linked by loosely structured plots, gradually acquired shape and precision. It was paradoxically the work of the Florentine Lully to develop a uniquely French form of opera by suppressing the disorderliness of the Italian style in which the plot sometimes had little purpose save as a background to a series of arias. Lully abandoned the distinction between recitative and aria, he forbade unnecessary vocalizing and the embellishment of individual parts, and, above all, in his own compositions he made the music correspond to the rhythm of the words. His was dramatic music bound to a recitative which was itself essential to the unfolding story. It was however in the work of the Academy of Painting that the desire to regulate the techniques of creative activity became most explicit. Le Brun's categories of invention, proportion, colour, expression and composition provided the basis for extensive discourses by writers and painters to establish rules for each. Whilst Le Brun himself endeavoured to correlate specific bodily movements with the range of human emotions, Poussin apparently felt that colour tones could be used to arouse different feelings. There was clearly a link here with the use of various balletic postures for the same purpose and with the widespread view that music could be employed to generate certain responses as appropriate, to arouse for war or to soothe and divert in times of peace.

More than anything else it was the insistence on ideological conformity in the service of a king who was elevated to the level of a demi-god that lends to the reign of Louis XIV its distinctive character. For the search for order and harmony became an end in itself, seemingly quite detached from the military, economic and financial pressures which had pushed France in an absolutist direction. Indeed the revocation of the Edict of Nantes revealed with brutal clarity that religious orthodoxy occupied an infinitely higher place in the scale of values than economic utility. Yet the process did not stop there, for the order that was projected through the classical culture of absolutist France was not just concerned with the unity of king and people in one faith. Its propagators sought in fact to bring men into closer correspondence with the harmony of the universe and to penetrate the essence of a reality which lay beyond the material world. This neo-platonic idealism was present in virtually every art form. Music, of course, had long been held to express the harmony of the cosmos and to constitute the most admirable medium for bringing order to society and instilling virtue in the soul. But painting, not held in the greatest esteem by Plato because it merely depicted immediate reality, was also used by the French classicists to make universal statements about human nature. Their stylized figures were not real people but representations of virtues, emotions and attitudes, the significance of which could be appreciated by those familiar with the principles of composition and classical mythology. Even the landscapes were not accurate depictions of reality but imitations of nature. Similarly, tragic operas and dramas explored with a brilliance that has made so many of them timeless the mainsprings of the human condition. Their characters were not just historical or contemporary figures in disguise, but vehicles through which the eternal conflicts between reason and passion, love and duty, self-interest and virtue, were utilized to make simultaneous observations about human nature and how men ought to conduct their affairs. Nothing symbolized more obviously the desire to bring human society into harmony with an idealized universal order than Louis's appropriation of Apollo. Chief of the Muses, God of Music, Ruler of the Planets, the Sun, God himself – Apollo was the quintessence of the harmony of the cosmos.

Illusion and Reality in the Absolute State

The image of the absolute monarch did not correspond to the reality. Royal power was not all-pervasive and the obedience of the people not easily obtained. Although there were no major uprisings after the Breton revolt of 1675 it should not be imagined that violence ceased. Mutinies, attacks on the soldiers, tax farmers, inspectors of cloth and grain hoarders remained features, albeit momentarily less significant, of French life. In 1689 the sailors of Hendaye on the Spanish frontier rioted against the imposition of the naval levies, declaring that they would serve in their own manner without recruitment. Troops were required to restore order. That the need for coercive measures was in a sense an indication of government weakness is suggested by Colbert's repeated admonition of those officials who used them too readily. Yet in 1680 there were no less than 162 agents making forcible tax collections in the *généralité* of Bordeaux. In addition the government had to contend with persistent and ingenious forms of non-co-operation. Some municipalities for instance impeded the operation of naval levies by abusing their rôle as suppliers of essential provisions. Lack of assistance from the inhabitants of Auxerre in the establishment of lace workshops compelled Colbert to stipulate that parents were to ensure that their daughters aged six years or more were to be sent to work in them on pain of being fined; but the refusal of the municipality to enforce the regulations, compounded by the bad pay, meant that the results of his efforts were meagre. Opposition to both monopoly companies and privileged manufacturers was also widespread; the resentment felt by the *bonnetiers* of Paris towards the silk stocking gild established in 1672 was such that they obtained a decree from the *parlement* empowering them to inspect the shops of the silk stocking workers, despite a royal council decision to the contrary. This episode also illustrates the way in which the *parlements* continued to use their legal powers to obstruct the royal will. When the *parlement* of Aix ordered an intendant of the galleys to release a convicted deserter it required direct intervention by the royal council to get the judgment withdrawn. As these examples indicate, much of the absolutist flavour of government activity was actually the consequence of its constant struggle to prevent the subversion of agreed policies. In ideological matters the failure was even clearer. Attempts to prevent the dissemination of Cartesian philosophy and physics were more or less futile. The Jansenist problem persisted despite the destruction of Port Royal. When Louis turned once more to the pope for aid the price was high; the papal bull *Unigenitus* (1713) actually included an article asserting the right of the pope to excommunicate the king and to absolve his subjects of their natural allegiance. As far as the Huguenots were concerned, a tacit acknowledgment of the failure of royal policy came in a government declaration of 1699 which, whilst upholding the principle of religious conformity, forbade the use of physical constraint to achieve it. Even the implementation of this new approach became almost impossible when, three years later, the Protestants of the Cévennes rose in a belated outburst of defiance.

A major problem for Louis, as for his predecessors, was to ensure the loyalty and co-operation of his own officials. Economic policies were hindered by gild wardens who failed to follow the manufacturing regulations or turned a blind eye to those dealing with apprenticeships. Naval plans were thwarted by *commissaires* who indulged in illicit commerce or accepted bribes from merchants who sought to avoid their obligations, as well as by authorities who disliked the power of the naval intendants; the lieutenant general of the *sénéchaussée* at St Jean de Luz obstructed the naval levies at Toulon and usurped the disciplinary powers of the *prévôts* of the ports, whilst the governor of Le Croisic retained sailors from the naval levies for use in his own ships. As far as the fiscal officers were concerned, Colbert's correspondence reveals the same sorts of complaints against them as had been current for 50 years. Apparently, despite the reduction in their power, many *élus* were still depriving the communities of the right to appoint their own tax collectors and arranging matters so that the burden of the *taille* fell on those least able to bear it. Reports of 1681 suggested that it was not uncommon for the distribution of the *taille* to be determined at meetings held in the homes of the local notables. Even in the army the problem of exacting obedience was not fully overcome, particularly as Louvois's direction of military campaigns was resented by experienced field commanders. Condé and Turenne felt that Louvois merited the title of valet rather than captain. In 1673 Marshal Bellefonds actually countermanded the instruction to retreat from the Netherlands. Although such behaviour gradually became a thing of the past, as late as 1692 Louis was obliged to reiterate the order to besiege Charleroi several times before the duc de Luxembourg complied. On this occasion it was resentment of Vauban which partly accounted for the duke's obstinacy.

Clearly the king's agents had not yet come to identify their own interests totally with his, and despite the changes which had occurred there was no bureaucratic mechanism capable of guaranteeing the implementation of instructions sent down from on high. Moreover, apart from the largely abortive investigation of seigneurial justice, no attempt was made to rationalize the labyrinthine judicial and financial administration with its multitude of competing jurisdictions. Indeed, the policy of the government appeared to be to achieve some sort of harmony and discipline by regulating the relationship between them and ensuring for each its legitimate functions. Colbert was certainly more than anxious that the intendants should not exceed their responsibilities by trespassing on the powers of established bodies. He intervened in a dispute between the intendant of Tours and the *cour des aides* in 1670 so that the king could resolve it without depriving a sovereign court of its 'natural and ordinary competence'. Three years later an intendant in Normandy was condemned for establishing an 'ordinary' jurisdiction and thus usurping the functions of the *élus* and the *cour des aides*. A general circular of 1676 instructed the intendants to leave the appropriate judges their authority in matters of taxation. The crown also encouraged the intendants to utilize the services of those who could help in the implementation of policy. After 1668 it became normal procedure to instruct the naval intendants to seek the assistance of the governors. A number of governors also assisted with the implementation of economic policies and, of course, they retained military authority. Similarly (although Colbert apparently toyed with the idea of extending the *pays d'élections*) provincial Estates had a rôle to play. In Languedoc they were instrumental in helping the textile company of Villeneuvette to survive when royal funds dried up.

The prestige and the authority of the *parlements* was very little diminished. Despite the restrictions imposed on them, they retained the right to register royal legislation, to issue remonstrances and, perhaps more importantly, their own judicial and administrative decrees. The magistrates found little difficulty in accepting the civil and criminal codes, which it should be emphasized regulated procedures only; the fundamental character of the French law with its largely customary basis did not alter. Nor did the Parisian *parlementaires* express opposition to the extraordinary commission dispatched to the Auvergne, which was not really surprising as it was composed of 20 of their number. No such commissions operated outside the jurisdiction of the *parlement* of Paris, partly because of the sensibilities of its provincial counterparts. On the other hand, some of these were called upon to assist with the aggrandizement of the monarchy in a rather different way by providing the manpower and legal expertise for the infamous *chambres de réunion* used by Louis to advance his claims to territory on France's eastern frontier. Thus a special chamber of the *parlement* of Metz was created to adjudicate on the sovereignty of Metz, Toul and Verdun, whilst the *parlement* of Besançon was employed to sustain French rights to over 80 villages in the country of Montbéliard between Franche Comté and Alsace.

If the capacity of the *parlements* for independent political action had been much reduced, the crown's own recognition of their usefulness thus ensured that it would not be entirely destroyed. This became apparent in 1713 when Louis endeavoured to pressurize both the clergy and *parlement* of Paris into accepting the bull *Unigenitus*. For the first time since 1673 there was a demand for remonstrances and when the bull was finally registered it was with a number of qualifications designed to maintain the autonomy of the French Church. Thus the *parlement* resumed its position as the prime defender of gallican liberties. The whole affair is a reminder of the fact that for much of the reign parlementary docility had been encouraged by the king's independence *vis-à-vis* the papacy. As he once again changed tack, forsaking the principles enunciated in the four articles of 1682, so too did the magistrates. Yet even the quarrels of the last months of the reign could not prevent the king acknowledging the indispensible rôle played by the *parlement*; for it was in its care that Louis placed his will and with it the fate of the regency which followed.

Royal policies reflected more than just the need to compromise with powerful institutions and the crown's dependence on them. They also show an underlying acceptance by the government of the corporate and hierarchical organization of French society and the continued existence of privileged groups and bodies within it. Despite the elevation of the state, the idea that all subjects existed in an equal relationship to it had not yet taken root in public opinion or government practice. Although Louis displayed no great reluctance to override privilege as expedient, the underlying principle was not abandoned: privilege had not yet acquired the pejorative overtones that were to come with the Enlightenment. The Estates of Artois were revived and periodically convoked, as were the lesser assemblies of Hainault, Lille and Cambrésis. The *escartons* of Dauphiné continued to have a vigorous existence alongside the assemblies of the great *pays d'états*. One of the most contradictory features of Colbert's activity was that, whilst it rested on state control and direction of the economy, this control was still exercised through the dispensation of privileges which exempted the beneficiaries from general regulations and rendered less likely the development of a uniform practice. Trading companies, gilds and specified towns all received exemptions of one sort or another. Marseille was even made a free port in 1669 and virtually relieved of all commercial duties. Rouen and Dunkirk were the only Atlantic ports allowed to trade with the Levant, whilst, for a period, the West Indian trade was restricted to four towns. Such decisions could only reinforce the marked sectionalism of the different merchant communities, impeding the development of a sense of national identity which Colbert's mercantilism otherwise required. Paradoxically, in order to enlist the co-operation of the population, Colbert had to take steps which actually sustained those features of French society which made greater centralization essential. Even sailors taking their turn to serve in the fleet were exempted from the billeting of troops, guard duty and payment of the *taille*.

In those areas where there was a commitment to structural reform the difficulties proved insuperable. Thus Colbert's desire to extend the *taille réelle* throughout the realm foundered on the intractable problem of drawing up the necessary land survey and the opposition of all those who had every reason to oppose such a step. Similarly the attempt in 1667 to bring the fiscal frontiers of the country into harmony with the geographical ones by establishing duties payable at the point of entry, foundered partly because of the division of the country into the areas which paid the *aides* and those which did not. The high level of the new duties also provoked the bitter hostility of the Dutch who finally obtained their withdrawal at the Peace of Nymwegen (1679).

Inevitably, the return of prolonged warfare, to which the tariffs themselves contributed, had a profoundly damaging effect on Colbert's plans. The budget was already beginning to get out of hand in 1670 and 10 years later the budgetary deficit reached 4.5 million *livres*, notwithstanding the anticipation of 16 millions of revenue for the following year. Payment of war debts in 1679 and 1681 amounted to 130 million *livres*. Subsequently all hope of fundamental reform faded; sale of office, extraordinary taxes and fiscal devices returned with a vengeance. In 1691 the six major Parisian gilds paid 634,000 *livres* for newly created offices. The capital could boast no less than 2,000 officers attached to the wholesale and retail markets; even the masters of the *petites écoles*, the renters of furnished rooms, tripe and lemonade sellers were formed into gilds, a privilege for which they were obliged to pay. But all the fiscal devices in the world could not prevent the decline of state subsidies to manufacturers or overcome the difficulties imposed by the interminable years of war which contributed directly to the collapse of the great trading companies. Moreover the mounting burdens on the countryside drained it of specie, thus undermining Colbert's efforts to stimulate the domestic market. Although roadways were improved, a score of waterways made navigable and the splendid Canal du Midi linking the Mediterranean and the Atlantic completed in 1681, the increase in traffic was disappointing. France's difficulties were probably compounded by the general economic malaise which affected most of Europe from the 1650s or 1660s, but given the fact that military expenditure never took less than 30 per cent of the state's revenue and in times of war rose to 70 per cent, it is impossible to escape the conclusion that war was a central cause of the distress which overtook the country in the last years of the Sun King.

Nonetheless, one should be wary of attributing the limited nature of the government's achievements solely or even largely to the exigences of war; above all care must be taken not to treat war as though it were an extraneous or accidental factor which happened to get in the way of plans for a radical reconstruction of the state. In the first place the need to compromise with vested interest, although intensified by the strains of war, was an independent factor. Not only had the government an inadequate bureaucratic apparatus at its disposition, it still depended on patronage and patrimonial mechanisms to make the system work and this inevitably limited its freedom of manouevre. Secondly, the rulers of France, despite the efforts to encourage the nobles to engage in commerce, continued to believe that birth, rank and the aristocratic values counted for more than merit, hard work and bourgeois sobriety. The drive to war itself sprang in part from a society the ethos of which reflected the still powerful influence of a class whose *raison d'être* was to bear arms.

For all these interrelated reasons there was no question of Louis using his power to effect a radical break with the past. Beneath the compromise made with the most prestigious political institutions lay a compromise with the privileged classes. Nothing perhaps shows this better than Colbert's rapid abandonment of his proclaimed intention of abolishing the *paulette* and making savage inroads on venal office-holding. Instead, in 1665, he contented himself by renewing the *paulette* for three years rather than the customary nine and by reducing the value of existing offices. At the same time minimum age requirements were imposed on members of the magistracy and this was followed in 1669 by legislation designed to prevent relatives sitting in the same court. Had even these limited reforms produced the intended results, the patrimonial interests of the office-holders would have been adversely affected. Yet, at least as far as the Parisian *parlementaires* were concerned, the consequences were negligible. The value of their offices came down only slowly, not reaching the official levels until the 1680s, whilst the other regulations were virtually ignored, leaving the magistrates in control of their own recruitment and composition. Indeed the crown frequently granted dispensation from the age requirements and in November 1673 legalized this procedure in return for a fee. Apparently the drop in the value of the offices in the *parlement* of Brittany was much more rapid, but this notwithstanding, the general impression is that in the provinces too the members of the sovereign courts consolidated their position as the most prestigious, influential and wealthy part of the local community. In most parlementary cities by 1700 the magistrates outshone both the merchants and the lesser nobility of the countryside. Instructive also was the failure of the government to carry through its declared resolve in 1664 to liquidate all the *rentes* created in the previous 25 years. Not only did the crown capitulate before the storm of protest, but in the years that followed it steadily raised the rate of interest; amongst the greatest beneficiaries of this policy were the *parlementaires*. A similar compromise with vested interest can be seen in the abandonment in 1673 of the investigation into seigneurial jurisdictions in Brittany in return for a lump sum payment. Moreover the Breton Estates managed to incorporate all but a small proportion of the agreed 2.5 million *livres* into the ordinary tax levies, thus passing the cost of the retention of noble privilege on to the populace. The barons who sat in the Estates of Languedoc were even encouraged to accept royal proposals by the payment from 1670 of regular gratuities of 2,250 *livres*. Given the burden of indirect taxation under Louis XIV and the harsh treatment of the urban communities, there is considerable justification for the view that the relative calm of the privileged classes stemmed from the willingness of the crown to compromise with them at the expense of the labouring population. In Burgundy Condé observed that only the third estate caused any real difficulty, for it was on this that the burdens fell.

For those who gained access to the court the pickings were rich indeed. It was, as Madame de Motteville observed, 'a great market' where courtiers arranged advantageous marriages, dealt in army commissions and obtained lucrative privileges. In 1693 the maréchal de Noailles was granted the right to install a new kind of machine to operate the hammers in a paper or fulling mill. Like many courtiers he also acted as broker for others, receiving in 1703 50,000 *écus* from a grateful manufacturer for whom he had secured a patent. Consortia of courtiers even came into being to wheel and deal in newly created offices although this was forbidden. The greatest families in the land did not find it at all demeaning to accept the benefits of the grubbiest forms of revenue. Of the duc de Montausier's total income of 100,000 *livres* in 1664 nearly half came from his military offices which included the governorship of Angoumois and Saintonge; but his connections with the region were reinforced by an interest in the tax farms on the river Charente which, together with revenue from taxes on paper, provided him with 14,500 *livres*, in itself a substantial income. Income from land came to less than 40,000 *livres* per annum. In general, although land accounted for the major part of the capital investment of the dukes and peers, royal offices and pensions furnished between one half and two thirds of their revenues. If Louis XIV domesticated the magnates, it was at a price.

Even more significant for the future of the regime was the success of the financiers in preserving their influence at the heart of affairs. Colbert began his term of office by creating a *chambre de justice* to investigate them, but in 1669 it was suppressed with the minister complaining of obstruction and declaring his intention to share out the profits derived from the chamber's activities. In fact all that it achieved was the transfer of profits and influence from one group of financiers to another. As on previous occasions, the collection of the fines was simply farmed out to a new consortium in whom Colbert had confidence. After all, he was himself the son of a financier and these were people with whom he had dealt closely ever since his days as Mazarin's personal intendant. Now, by choosing carefully on whom to levy fines and by exerting other pressures, Colbert was able to ease out of office those not acceptable to him. His own clients were installed as receivers in the *généralités*, in the tax farms and even as treasurers of the provincial Estates of Languedoc and Dauphiné. Moreover, the financiers played a leading rôle in funding the trading companies, cloth manufactures and projects like the Canal du Midi. One of the most notable was André Pouget who combined an office in the *cour des aides* at Montpellier with tax farming, an interest in the Canal du Midi as well as a leading rôle in the royal company of Villeneuvette. Then there was Pennautier who divided his time between similar interests, his functions as general receiver for the clergy, and the treasurership of Languedoc. Although the EIC was supposed to be under the directorship of a board dominated by active merchants, the financiers assumed the dominant rôle. After 1666 all the Parisian directors were financiers. These developments clearly perpetuated the unhealthy confusion between public office and private property, with the financiers occupying positions in the state apparatus of which they were the creditors. Thus Daliès, the principal provider of funds for the navy at Toulon, was his own paymaster as naval costs were charged to the receipts from Dauphiné of which he was the treasurer.

The central rôle played by the financiers and their close ties with Colbert have led a recent scholar to suggest that perhaps what he was directing was not so much a national enterprise as a family one.[10] Certainly, if one adds to the financiers those relatives of the minister who occupied significant positions in the political and social hierarchy, the argument has weight. One

---

[10] D. Dessert and J.L. Journet, 'Le lobby Colbert', *Annales ESC* 30 ii (1975), pp.1303–36.

brother was ambassador to England, another intendant in the army, whilst his son succeeded him as minister of the navy; a first cousin became intendant of the navy at Brouage where the naval levies were first tried, a brother-in-law intendant at Soissons. Other sons and cousins acquired bishoprics, four daughters became abbesses, whilst three married dukes. Even distant relations received the benefits of the minister's protection. In 1675 it was the abbé d'Urfé, a first cousin of his daughter-in-law, who did so; on another occasion Colbert wrote to the intendant at Tours asking him to help the duc de Luynes – the father of one of his sons-in-law – with his peasants who were causing trouble. Colbert's family epitomizes the fusion between high finance, military and clerical interests which underpinned the absolutist state. Colbert himself was the contradictory personification of the embryonic bureaucrat within a fundamentally patrimonial system.

Despite the undoubted growth of royal power the absolutism of Louis XIV did not rest on bureaucratic efficiency but on a compromise with the dominant social classes on which the government depended. In some ways 'compromise' is a misleading term because the values and attitudes of those who ruled were in tune with those of the social élite. Louis XIV hardly knew how to receive a merchant properly, and even Colbert bought himself a chateau, claimed royal ancestry (Scottish) and married his daughters off to dukes. When the government wished to urge nobles to trade it encouraged them with the prospect of heroic deeds to be accomplished in foreign lands, and when it wished to reward those families which engaged in commerce for three generations, it did so with titles of nobility. The king himself was greatly attached to 'distinctions of rank which are virtually the first motive of all human actions'; he believed profoundly in his own divinely sanctioned authority, in the need to defend his patrimonial interests, and the normality of war. This was a king who traipsed his wife and two mistresses around the battlefields of the Low Countries and ostentatiously 'took charge' of the sieges (but never visited a port until 1680); this was the man who sanctioned the devastation of those parts of Holland not occupied in 1673 and the systematic destruction of Mannheim, Heidleberg, Oppenheim, Wurms and Speir in the winter and spring of 1688–9; and this was the ruler who in the last years of the reign continued to place dynastic considerations above the miseries of his people. It was appropriate that Louis should be depicted as Mars as well as Apollo.

The savage treatment of the Palatinate seems not to have been a necessary consequence of the logic of large-scale warfare. Even the commanders in the field endeavoured to avoid executing the orders which came from Versailles. Like the deployment of violence against the Huguenots four years previously, the onslaught on the Palatinate had the quality of an outburst of anger against those who persisted in defying the royal will. The assertion of the king's military might, emanating from a system born out of warfare, assumed under Louis XIV the character of a somewhat desperate attempt to obscure reality and forestall criticism. The reality was that after a triumphal march through the Netherlands in 1672, France had got bogged down in an unexpected and seemingly interminable European conflict which quickly left her without any friends of stature. In the years that followed, the crown's aggressive pursuit of its dynastic and territorial ambitious only confirmed France's isolation, for which the people paid dearly. During the War of the League of Augsburg (1688–97) victories were few and between 1702 and 1708 the French forces did not win a single major encounter. The population was debilitated, agricultural prices collapsed, and the state bankrupt. In 1709 an exceptionally cold winter, followed by a poor harvest, suddenly sent grain prices soaring, thus engendering widespread famine. The most powerful king in Europe was now on the verge of defeat at the hands of a coalition largely sustained by the republican 'herring merchants' of Holland and the English who did not know what a 'true' monarchy was.

The years of greatness were already over when the court finally moved permanently to Versailles in 1682. Lionne, Turenne, Molière, Le Vau amongst others were dead. Colbert died in 1683, Corneille the following year, Lully in 1687 and Lebrun three years after that. There were no new reforms in the offing, no new commercial foundations, no major changes even in the army, and barely a new idea to be heard. Louis rarely visited Paris which Colbert had done so much to glorify and when he did vagabonds and beggars were kept away. At Versailles however, life carried on normally. In 1690 the official government journal noted that the *divertissements* had taken place as usual, for in Louis XIV's France art and entertainment were not halted during war. Commenting on the carnival season of 1708, it maintained that money was plentiful, industry productive and that in spite of all the military reverses the balls given by the king, the duchess of Burgundy and James of England were unusually extravagant. To reassure the populace *Te Deums* were ordered to celebrate insignificant battles, and to provide an opportunity for the clergy to expatiate on the wickedness of the king's enemies. 'Whenever the king wins a battle, takes a city or subdues a provence', wrote Pierre Jurieu in 1690, 'we light bonfires and every petty person feels elevated and associates the king's grandeur with himself; this compensates him for all his losses and consoles him in all his misery.'

Yet as this acid observation shows, the magic had gone. Jurieu was but one of a host of critics of the regime whose works, although frequently published abroad, received a wide circulation in France from the mid 1680s as the brutality and futility of the revocation of the Edict of Nantes began to dawn on the public consciousness. Most notable, in addition to Jurieu's *Soupirs de la France Esclave*, were La Bruyère's *Caractères* which went through eight editions between 1688 and 1694, Bayle's *Dictionnaire Historique et Critique* (1696–7), Boisguilbert's *Détail de la France* (1695), Vauban's *Dîme Royale* circulated in 1707, and the writings of Archbishop Fénelon whose celebrated *Télémaque* appeared in 1699. Although many critics of the regime were refugees from persecution like Bayle, a number of these authors were also distinguished and loyal servants of the crown. Until his disgrace in 1699 Fénelon was tutor to the king's grandson. Not surprisingly in view of their social standing, many of their criticisms of the regime amounted to no more than a conservative reiteration of the view that kings were established to serve the people and that there were therefore restraints on the exercise of power. Fénelon likened a monarch to an architect who needs others to help, carry and build. He wished to see the return of representative assemblies and their extension on the lines of those that existed in Languedoc. Jurieu complained that the royal authority 'had mounted so high that all distinctions disappear.' Yet conservative though such views were, their enunciation and wide dissemination reveals very clearly the failure of the crown to overawe or intimidate its critics. The further tightening up of the system of censorship was eloquent testimony to government anxiety. In 1699 a new office of overseer of books was created in the chancellory and a register of potential authors drawn up. These were required to submit their manuscripts for scrutiny with written justifications for their publications. Subsequently a census was made of those in the printing and bookselling business. Yet all this could not stem the influx of illegal works from abroad or defeat the ingenuity of those determined to evade the law or deceive the censors.

Moreover, although most of the views contained in the works of the great authors, clandestine or otherwise, were conservative in outlook, it is possible to discern some ideas of a radical nature. Bayle's forthright attack on superstition and dogma asserted, by implication at least, the pre-eminence of individual conscience in matters of religion. La Bruyère's emphasis on the duty of the king to provide security and happiness anticipated the secular utilitarianism of the Enlightenment, whilst Vauban's arguments in favour of a system of universal and progressive taxation amounted to a fundamental reversal of the principles underpinning both fiscal practice and traditional concepts of social status. Boisguilbert not only brought together in a systematic way the ever-strident objections to the state's economic practices, but also expressed the opinion that the free pursuit of individual gain was not incompatible with the general good, thus preparing the way for the proponents of *laissez-faire*. A new story was now beginning. But, as the great reforming ministers of the eighteenth century were to discover, obtaining co-operation for their enlightened ventures from those who had secured a privileged niche within the framework of the absolutist state was to prove an impossible task.

Conclusion

Viewed as a system of government and not just as personal rule, the essential institutional features of French absolutism are easily located. These were a standing army, a developed fiscal apparatus, a 'bureaucracy' of venal office-holders foremost amongst whom were members of the judiciary, specialized departments of state, and a corps of salaried intendants who were responsible directly to the royal council for the exercise of their comprehensive administrative, financial and judicial powers. Some of these features could be found in non-absolutist regimes; but in France the exceptionally inflated state apparatus drastically curtailed the rôle of representative institutions both national and regional, as well as destroying the autonomy of the municipalities. State intervention in the economy went well beyond the provision of protective legislation familiar elsewhere; government participation in, and direction of, commercial and manufacturing activity reached unprecedented heights. Moreover royal authority was sustained by theories of divine right and *raison d'état* which obscured the traditional notion that there were restraints upon its exercise and certainly precluded any right of resistance. The idea of consent to taxation – and taxation was at the heart of it all – though never completely vanquished, did not find effective expression through the medium of a national representative institution.

Yet as soon as one makes this observation the central paradox of French absolutism comes to the surface. For the absence of such an institution reflected not only the strength of the monarchy but also its weakness. Without a representative body French kings had the greatest difficulty in gathering support for their policies throughout the realm. In a sense the administrative apparatus that came slowly into being filled the vacuum which existed. But it was never a complete substitute. During the worst days of the War of Spanish Succession the government, desperate to secure the support of the people for yet more sacrifices, seriously considered summoning an Estates-General before deciding that to do so would be injurious to the royal image. The lack of an arena for the mediation of the relationship between the monarchy and its more privileged subjects left the former confronting a host of disparate institutions with powerful regional ties and separatist tendencies. It is indeed in the particularly acute contradiction between the centralizing and decentralizing elements of the body politic that the genesis of French absolutism should be located. As Frederick Engels noted well over a century ago, absolute monarchy '*had* to be absolute just because of the centrifugal character of all elements'; but precisely for this reason 'absolute' could not be understood 'in the vulgar sense'. The monarch was 'in constant struggle partly with the estates, partly with the insurgent feudal lords and cities'.

Furthermore, as royal institutions began to take root they themselves acquired a highly ambivalent character. This was most obvious in the case of the provincial *parlements* and the governorships which were at one and the same time a means of asserting royal authority and vehicles for the defence of provincial privilege. But the tension between centralizing and decentralizing pressures was present even within the *parlement* of Paris which insisted that one of its central functions was to preserve customary rights from an arbitrary exercise of royal power. Like other corporative bodies, the *parlement*'s autonomy was further strengthened by the need of the crown to sell offices.

The response of the government to this situation was to create layer upon layer of officials. In one sense the seventeenth-century intendant was merely the medieval *bailli* writ large, the ultimate manifestation of the protracted struggle to come to grips with both provincial separatism and the wayward-ness of the existing royal agents. Although distinguished by their non-venal character, it should nonetheless be remembered that the intendants had achieved their position, virtually without exception, by progressing through the ranks of the office-holding hierarchy and did not break their links with it. Nor were they used by the crown to supplant the *officiers* whose essential judicial and administrative functions remained intact. Indeed the installa-tion of the *sub-délégués* represented yet another compromise with the provin-cial élites from which they were drawn.

This is not to deny the vast increase in the political power of the monarchy. The expansion of its judicial fiscal, ideological and coercive capacities was apparent enough even during time of great danger. Both the civil wars of the sixteenth century and the conflicts of the mid seventeenth were in part struggles for a *share* of this growing royal power, for the benefits of *its* patronage and for control of *its* administrative apparatus. Even the corps of venal office-holders – over 60,000 by the reign of Louis XIV – constituted a significant extension of the royal presence. For venal office-holding created new avenues for social and political advancement in the service of the crown and a mechanism for extracting the wealth of the labouring population. On the other hand, precisely because of this, the office-holders constituted a parasitic burden on the realm; not surprisingly it was the fiscal officers who became the prime targets of the embittered peasants and artisans. At the same time, the office-holders themselves became equally resentful about the way in which they were manipulated by the crown and by the subordination of their material interests of its fiscal needs. Opposition to the financial policies of the crown became so widespread that for a moment in the mid seventeenth century it seemed that the entire fiscal edifice on which the government depended would collapse.

The net effect of the endemic unrest which culminated in the Frondes was to reinforce the ambiguities already embedded in the regime. On the one hand it provoked a further assertion of the authority of the royal council, contributed to the development of the intendancies and stimulated the repressive policies associated with Richelieu. On the other hand it became plain that the government would have to compromise with the principal corporate bodies, provincial institutions, and the members of the social élites that composed them. In fact the major compromise which rendered the privileged orders largely exempt from taxation was by this time a well-established fact; but it was cemented under Louis XIV by confirmation of the privileged position of the great office-holders and the institutionalization of the financiers. The financiers were indispensible not only because of the military needs of the state but also to sustain royal patronage on the scale required to satisfy the aspirations of the privileged classes. If the collapse of royal patronage in the sixteenth century contributed directly to the collapse of royal authority, so the restoration of both went hand in hand. Indeed it is arguable that, despite the growth of bureaucratic forms of government, royal dependence on patrimonial mechanisms was actually heightened through venality of office and the penetration of the fiscal apparatus by the private financiers. The royal bureaucracy certainly never detached itself from the complex maze of lineages, clienteles and patrimonial interests out of which it emerged. Social control, particularly in some of the most troublesome provinces, continued to depend as much on the informal operations of personal relationships as on an institutionalized chain of command.

What is also suggested by this analysis is the very large measure of continuity running through the entire period under consideration. Absolutism did not involve any dramatic break with the past. This was true not only in the sense that it operated within the constraints of a traditional social structure, but also at an ideological level. Divine-right monarchy had its roots in the spiritual powers attributed to the Capetians, and indeed to their predecessors. It was understood to operate within a divinely ordained hierarchy of which the civil order was but part; whilst the picture may have been refined, and the human rungs of the ladder even juxtaposed to cope with the intrusion of the *noblesse de robe*, its fundamental character had not changed. If anything the belief that privileges were bestowed on people according to rank and membership of corporate bodies grew stronger during the sixteenth and seventeenth centuries partly because of the action of the crown itself. Certainly the elevation of the state did not lead immediately to the conclusion that all subjects stood in an equal relationship to it. For what the crown sought was a restoration of an idealized traditional order in which each social group played its appropriate rôle, in which justice was readily available, venality restricted if not abolished, and in which monarchical authority was ensured by a greater uniformity of fiscal and judicial administration. Above all the government desired the restoration of religious unity. To these objectives France's neo-classical culture was harnessed without difficulty. For this, like the religiously based world view, assumed a perfect, harmonious cosmos, as well as placing a premium on general good order and personal discipline.

Absolutism was therefore not the projection of some radical blue-print for change. What pushed France in an absolutist direction were the tensions embedded within the existing political and social structures. To those mentioned above must be added the drive to war, which sprang from the dynastic and territorial rivalries lying at the heart of feudal society. Nothing illustrates better the self-reinforcing nature of absolutist development than the progressive extension of royal military power, which in turn demanded greater control of the realm's resources and thus a further development of the state's coercive capacity. The gradual concentration of power in fewer and fewer hands was a logical consequence of these dynastic rivalries which then resolved themselves into seemingly interminable struggles between the dominant European houses; the Habsburg-Bourbon confrontation was one of the most remarkable. Notwithstanding the emerging idea of a balance of power which heralded the arrival of modern inter-state relations, dynastic considerations played a powerful part in shaping foreign policy down to the beginning of the eighteenth century. So too, it might be suggested, did the need to channel the bellicose energies of the magnates into the service of the state. France's standing army came into being in the mid fifteenth century primarily to occupy the nobility during the interludes of peace; the failure of this policy became clear in 1559 when, on the conclusion of general peace, the French magnates simply used their military capacity to turn on one another. It took another hundred years for the state to secure an effective 'monopoly of violence' and this was achieved partly by subsuming the aggressive tendencies of the nobility in its own commitment to war.

Yet to insist on the continuities underpinning the evolution of French absolutism to the point of implying that it was no more than a linear extension of traditional monarchical rule, would be manifestly absurd. In the first place the expansion of the armed forces which occurred in the period between 1620 and 1650 was so massive that it virtually rendered the existing administrative machinery inadequate overnight. This was the period which saw the crystallization of the intendancies, the systematic subordination of the army to civilian control, the most dramatic leap in sales of offices and the entrenchment of the financiers. It was characterized by the ruthless exercise of power by Richelieu, itself justified by a developing *raison d'état*. In addition the European context in which France found herself changed rapidly with the arrival on the scene of the maritime powers of Holland and England. Alongside the traditional struggle with Spain, the French monarchy now had to meet a new kind of challenge from burgeoning capitalist economies. For this reason the early seventeenth century was the crucial period in the formulation of *dirigiste* economic policies designed to enable France to compete with her rivals. It also marked the most dynamic phase of the French counter-reformation which culminated in the crusade against La Rochelle.

The pressures on the French crown now became hopelessly contradictory. Most obvious was the contradiction between the attempt to stimulate the development of the economy and escalating military expenditure; time and time again measures taken to protect or direct economic activity degenerated into mere devices for raising cash. Sale of office not only compounded the economic difficulties by diverting resources and energy into non-productive channels, but also involved a fragmentation of royal authority at precisely the same moment that the government wished to achieve the opposite. Thus it became necessary to subordinate the treasurers and *élus* to the intendants. What the commitment to the war against Spain certainly precluded was the restoration of the idealized traditional order. Marillac, the most notable proponent of peace, retrenchment, administrative reform and the final liquidation of the Huguenot problem, ended his days in goal. Richelieu had his way; but then found himself obliged to defend France's dependence on Protestant allies for the war against Catholic Spain, as well as the brutal consequences for the people, by claiming that the actions of rulers were not to be judged by the same criteria as those of subjects. This view accorded ill with the traditions of the French monarchy and was heavy with secular overtones about the nature of political authority which the royal pamphleteers struggled manfully to reconcile with divine right. Significant sections of public opinion, either attached to established notions about the obligations of monarchs, or hostile to the war, or both, remained unconvinced.

Within this context it is possible to approach Louis XIV's personal rule in two different ways. From one perspective it does represent the culmination of a seemingly remorseless process of political centralization and bureaucratization. The administrative and coercive apparatus at his disposition was certainly remarkable. Indeed ministerial and bureaucratic forms of government had reached the point at which the need for the personal and day-to-day involvement of the king had actually begun to diminish. Yet it was just at this moment that the king was elevated to the level of a demi-god and it is this fact which more than anything suggests the need for a rather different perspective on the reign; for what made the cult of the king so vital to the regime was precisely the failure to resolve those contradictions which themselves made absolutism necessary. Louis's government did not succeed in overcoming the enormous problems created by large-scale warfare, nor in placing France on a par with the Dutch and English. Such plans as there were for major reforms were abandoned in return for a compromise with a multiplicity of vested interests. The embryonic bureaucracy was distorted by financial need and patrimonial interest. Orders dispatched at the centre disappeared in the labyrinth of competing jurisdictions or foundered in provincial inertia. And there was always the fear of renewed unrest and disaffection. The response to all this was Versailles, the cult of Apollo, the systematic projection of an idealized and harmonious universe and an obsession with hierarchy and obedience.

In part the deification of the king was an ideological illusion perpetrated by those who sensed that it was necessary for the stability of the regime. Yet it was not imposed in any crude fashion on an unwilling or hostile public. On the contrary, the educated public were themselves steeped in the classical idiom in which the propaganda was couched; many of its members benefited from royal patronage, and they certainly accepted, as did the populace at large, the religious foundations of royal authority. As we have seen, the widespread movements of resistance to the crown, from whatever quarter they came, had not generated any alternative to the ideology of divine-right absolutism. In this respect the failure of the Huguenots to produce a specifically Protestant conception of government was of profound significance; for they proved quite unable to respond to the Catholic offensive which furnished Louis XIII with the means of restoring royal authority. The

Huguenots beaten, opposition to government policies acquired a markedly conservative and sectarian character with a tendency to degenerate into no more than a competition for a place in the sun. The 'market-place' of Versailles with its elaborate ritual and pecking order was the ultimate expression of this competition; its social values were not just those of the king. Furthermore the ideological predelictions of the well-to-do had been reinforced by their experience of constant popular agitation and violence which threatened all too easily to get out of hand: the best thing to do with the poor was to provide them with gainful employment or to lock them up and keep them off the streets.

For all these reasons the upper classes were predisposed to accept the ethos of the absolute state. Yet the tensions within the system were so acute that the concensus could not last long. Louis overreached himself at home and abroad. After the revocation of the Edict of Nantes the ripples of disquiet broadened into a flood of criticism. Although it was far from strong enough to sweep away the extraordinary edifice which Louis bequeathed to his successors, the illusion was broken. Within a few hours of the king's death Versailles was all but deserted. It was clear that the forces which had brought it into being were at last played out. Slowly the reforming ministers and writers of the eighteenth century began to contemplate the merits of other forms of political organization.

Select Bibliography

The bibliography consists only of works which have been directly utilized in the development of my analysis. Many of them carry extensive bibliographies of their own. Of the works cited below those of Bonney, Hamscher, Harding, Kettering, Knecht, Major and Ranum have been particularly useful as sources of both material and ideas although these authors may well dissent from my overall perspective. Cole's now rather old-fashioned studies of mercantilism remain mines of precious information. Students wishing to explore further the central themes of this book might begin with Salmon, Mousnier (1973), Parker (1980) and Mettam. Of the items in French the article by Dessert and Journet is critical for a full understanding of Louis XIV's government.

Anderson, P., *Lineages of the Absolute State*, (London, NLB, 1974).

Asher, E.L., *Resistance to the Maritime Classes. The survival of feudalism in the France of Colbert* (Berkeley, University of California Press, 1960).

Battifol, L., 'Louis XIII et la liberté de conscience', *Revue de Paris* (1907).

Baxter, D.C., *Servants of the Sword* (Urbana, University of Illinois Press, 1976).

Beik, W.H., 'Two intendants face a popular revolt', *Journal of Canadian History* 9 (1974), pp.243–62.

Benedict, P., *Rouen During the Wars of Religion* (Cambridge, CUP, 1981).

Bercé, Y.M., *Histoire des croquants* (2 vols., Geneva, Droz, 1974).

Bercé, Y.M., *Croquants et nu-pieds* (Paris, Gallimard/Juliard, 1974).

Blet, P., *Le clergé de France et la monarchie* (Rome, Libraire éditrice de l'université gregorienne, 1959).

Blet, P., 'Le plan de Richelieu pour la réunion des protestants', *Gregorianum* 48 (1976), pp.100–29.

Bonney, R.J., 'The French civil war', *European Studies Review* 8 (1978), pp.72–100.

Bonney, R.J., *Political Change under Richelieu and Mazarin* (Oxford, OUP, 1978).

Bonney, R.J., 'Cardinal Mazarin and the great nobility during the Fronde', *English Historical Review* XCVI (1981), pp.818–33.

Bonney, R.J., *The King's Debts* (Oxford, Clarendon Press, 1982).

Briggs, R., *Early Modern France 1560–1715* (Oxford, OUP, 1977).

Church, W.F., *Richelieu and Reason of State* (Princeton, Princeton University Press, 1972).

Cole, C.W., *French Mercantilist Doctrines Before Colbert* (New York, R.R. Smith, 1931).

Cole, C.W., *Colbert and a Century of French Mercantilism* 2 vols., (Hamden, Archon Books, 1964).

Dégarne, M., 'Etudes sur les soulèvements provinciaux en France avant la Fronde; la révolte de Rouergue on 1643', *Dix-Septième Siècle* 56 (1962), pp.3–18.

Delumeau, J., *Catholicism Between Luther and Voltaire* (London, Burns and Oates, trans. 1977).

Dessert, D. and Journet, J.L., 'Le lobby Colbert', *Annales ESC* 30 ii (1975), pp.1303–36.

Dupont-Ferrier, G., 'Les institutions de la France sous le règne de Charles V', *Journal des Savants* (1932), pp.432–45.

Dupont-Ferrier, G., 'Le sens des mots "patria" et "patrie" en France au moyen âge jusqu'au début du XVII siècle', *Revue Historique* CLXXXVIII (1940), pp.89 104.

Ekberg, C.J., *The failure of Louis XIV's Dutch War* (Chapel Hill, University of North Carolina Press, 1979).

Fawtier, R., *The Capetian Kings of France* (London, Macmillan, 1960).

Ferté, J., *La vie religieuse dans les campagnes parisiennes 1622–1695* (Paris, Société d'histoire ecclésiastique de la France, 1962).

Garlan, Y. and Nières, C., *Les révoltes brétonnes de 1675* (Paris, Editions Sociales, 1975).

Goubert, P., *L'ancien régime* (2 vols., Paris, Armand Colin, 1969–73). (Trans. vol. 1 London, Weidenfeld & Nicolson, 1973).

Goubert, P., *Louis XIV and Twenty Million Frenchmen* (London, Allen Lane, 1970).

Greengrass, M., 'Dissension in the provinces under Henry III', in Highfield, J. and Jeffs, R.M., eds., *The Crown and Local Communities in England and France* (Gloucester, A J Sutton, 1981), pp.162–82.

Greengrass, M., 'Mathurin Charretier: the career of a politique during the wars of religion in France', *Proceedings of the Huguenot Society of London* 23 (1981), pp.330–40.

Guenée, B., 'L'histoire de l'état en France à la fin du moyen-âge', *Revue Historique* CCXXXII (1964), pp.331–60.

Guenée, B., 'Etat et nation en France au moyen âge', *Revue Historique* CCXXXVII (1967), pp.17–30.

Hamscher, A., *The Parlement of Paris After the Fronde* (Pittsburgh, University of Pittsburgh Press, 1976).

Harding, R.R., *Anatomy of a Power Elite. The provincial governors of early modern France* (New Haven, Yale University Press, 1978).

Hayden, J.M., *France and the Estates-General of 1614* (Cambridge, CUP, 1974).

Henneman, J.B., *Royal Taxation in the Fourteenth Century* (Philadelphia, American Philosophical Society, 1976).

Hurt, J.J., 'The parlement of Brittany and the crown', *French Historical Studies* IV (1966), pp.411–34.

Isherwood, R.M., *Music in the service of the king* (Ithaca, Cornell University Press, 1973).

Jones, C., 'The military revolution and the professionalisation of the French Army', in Duffy, M., ed., *The Military Revolution and the State* (Exeter, University of Exeter, 1980).

Judge, H.C., 'Louis XIV and the Church', in Rule, J.C., ed., *Louis XIV and the Craft of Kingship* (Columbus, Ohio State University Press, 1969), pp.240–64.

Keohane, N.O., *Philosophy and the State in France from the Renaissance to the Enlightenment* (Princeton, Princeton University Press, 1980).

Kettering, S., *Judicial Politics and Urban Revolt in Seventeenth-Century France. The parlement of Aix 1629–1659* (Princeton, Princeton University Press, 1978).

Kettering, S., 'A provincial parlement during the Fronde', *European Studies Review* XI (1981), pp.109–51.

Kierstead, R.F., *State and Society in Seventeenth-Century France* (New York, Franklin Watts, 1975).

Kitchens, J.H., 'Judicial commissions and the parlement of Paris', *French Historical*

Studies XII (1982), pp.323–50.

Klaits, J., *Printed Propaganda Under Louis XIV* (Princeton, Princeton University Press, 1976).

Knecht, R.J., 'The early reformation in England and France', *History* 189 (1972), pp.1–16.

Knecht, R.J., *The Fronde* (London, Historical Association, 1975).

Knecht, R.J., 'Francis I and Paris', *History* 216 (1981), pp.18–33).

Knecht, R.J., *Francis I* (Cambridge, CUP, 1982).

Labatut, J.P., *Les ducs et pairs de France au XVII siècle* (Paris. PUF, 1972).

Levron, J., *Daily Life at Versailles in the Seventeenth and Eighteenth Centuries* (London, Allen & Unwin, 1968).

Lewis, P.S., 'The failure of the French medieval estates', *Past and Present* 23 (1962), pp.3–17.

Lewis, P.S., *Later Medieval France* (London, Macmillan, 1968).

Lewis, P.S., *The Recovery of France in the Fifteenth Century* (New York, Macmillan, 1972).

Lis, C. and Soly, H., *Poverty and Capitalism in Pre-Industrial Europe* (Hassocks, Harvester Press, 1979).

Lot, F. and Fawtier, R., *Histoire des institutions françaises au moyen age* (2 vols., Paris, PUF, 1957–8).

Major, J.R., *Representative Institutions in Renaissance France 1421–1559 (Madison, Wisconsin 'University Press, 1960)*.

Major, J.R., *Representative Government in Early Modern France* (New Haven, Yale University Press, 1980).

Maland, d., *Culture and Society in seventeeth-Century France* (London, Batsford, 1970).

Mettam, R., *Government and Society in Louis XIV's France* (London, Macmillan, 1977).

Moote, A.L., *The Revolt of the Judges* (Princeton, Princeton University Press, 1971).

Mousnier, R., *Le conseil du roi de Louis XII à la révolution* (Paris, PUF, 1970).

Mousnier, R., *Peasant Uprisings in Seventeenth-Century France, Russia and China* (London, Allen & Unwin, 1971).

Mousnier, R., *The Assassination of Henry IV* (London, Faber & Faber, 1973).

Mousnier, R., *The Institutions of France Under the Absolute Monarchy* (Chicago, University of Chicago Press, 1979). I

Mousnier, R., *Les institutions de France sous la monarchie absolue* (Paris, PUF, 1980). II

Nichols, D., 'Social change and early protestantism in France', *European Studies Review* 10 (1980), pp.297–308.

Parker, D., 'The social foundation of French absolutism', *Past and Present* 53 (1971), pp.67–89.

Parker, D., 'Hugeonots in seventeenth-century France', in Hepburn, A.C., ed., *Minorities in History* (London, Edward Arnold, 1978), pp.11–30.

Parker, D., *La Rochelle and the French Monarchy. Order and conflict in seventeenth-century France* (London, Royal Historical Society, 1980).

Parker, D., 'Law, society and the state in the thought of Jean Bodin', *Journal of History of Political Thought* 2 (1981) pp.253–85.

Pérouas, L., *Le diocèse de la Rochelle. Sociologie et pastorale* (Paris, SEVPEN, 1964).

Petit-Dutaillis, C., *Les communes françaises* (Paris, Albin Michel, 1947).

Pillorget, R., *Les movements insurrectionels en Provence 1596–1715* (Paris, A. Pedone, 1975).

Porchnev, B., *Les soulevements populaires de 1623 à 1648* (Paris, SEVPEN, 1963).

Ranum, O., *Richelieu and the Councillors of Louis XIII* (Oxford, Clarendon Press, 1963).

Ranum, O., *Paris in the Age of Absolutism* (New York, Wiley, 1968).

Richet, D., 'Aspects socio-culturels des conflicts religieux à Paris dans le deuxième moitiè du XVI siècle', *Annales ESC* 32 ii (1977), pp.764–83.

Rothkrug, L., *Opposition to Louis XIV. The political and social origins of the French enlightenment* (Princeton, Princeton University Press, 1965).

Rule, J.C., 'Colbert de Torcy, an emergent bureaucracy and the formulation of French foreign policy 1698–1715', in Hatton, R., ed., *Louis XIV and Europe* (London, Macmillan, 1976), pp.261–88.

Salmon, J.H.M., *Society in Crisis. France in the sixteenth century* (London, Benn, 1975).

Shennan, J.H., *The Parlement of Paris* (London, Eyre & Spottiswoode, 1968).

Skinner, Q., *The Foundations of Modern Political Thought* (2 vols., Cambridge, CUP, 1978).

Sutherland, N., *Catherine de Medici and the Ancien Régime* (London, Historical Association, 1966).

Thomson, J.K.J., *Clermont de Lodève 1633–1789* (Cambridge, CUP, 1982).

Treasure, G.R.R., *Seventeenth-Century France* (London, Revington, 1967).

Westrich, S., *The Ormée* (Baltimore, Johns Hopkins University Press, 1979).

Wolf, J.B., *Louis XIV* (London, Panther Books, 1970).

Wolfe, M., *The Fiscal System of Renaissance France* (New Haven, Yale University Press, 1972).

Index